Law Touched Our Hearts

Law Touched Our Hearts

A Generation Remembers

Brown v. Board of Education

Mildred Wigfall Robinson
and Richard J. Bonnie, Editors

Vanderbilt University Press
Nashville

13 12 11 10 09   1 2 3 4 5

This book is printed on acid-free paper
made from 30% post-consumer recycled paper.
Manufactured in the United States of America

Library of Congress Cataloging-in-Publication Data
Law touched our hearts : a generation remembers *Brown v. Board of
Education* / Mildred Wigfall Robinson and Richard J. Bonnie, editors.
p. cm.
Includes bibliographical references.
ISBN 978-0-8265-1619-0 (cloth : alk. paper)
1. Segregation in education—United States—History. 2. Law
teachers—United States—Public opinion. 3. Segregation in
education—Law and legislation—United States—History. 4. Brown,
Oliver, 1918– —Trials, litigation, etc. 5. Topeka (Kan.). Board of
Education—Trials, litigation, etc. 6. Public opinion—United States.
I. Robinson, Mildred Wigfall. II. Bonnie, Richard J.
LC212.52.L39   2008
379.2'630973—dc22
2008017729

Contents

SOUTH CAROLINA

TENNESSEE

VIRGINIA

WASHINGTON, D.C.

PART III
De Facto States

Acknowledgments

We invited almost five thousand of our colleagues in law teaching to partici-pate in what we expected would be "an intriguing project that intertwines personal, professional, and written history." We would not have been able to make that initial contact without the financial and logistical support provided by Dean Robert Scott and the secretarial and mailroom staffs here at the Uni-versity of Virginia law school. Dean Scott provided the financial resources we needed to acquire mailing lists from the Association of American Law Schools and the materials for the mailings themselves. The massive job of preparing, stuffing, sorting, stamping, and mailing the first five thousand letters took four days—an eternity in the operation of a busy organization.

Two colleagues were particularly supportive during the early phases of this project. John Monahan and W. Laurens Walker were always available to com-ment on ideas and to offer suggestions. Russell R. Bruch (Law, '04), Michael Lee (Law, '05), and Michael Snow (Law, '06) helped us analyze our returns, contact potential contributors, and initiate the editing process. Dianne John-son of our secretarial staff provided indispensable support in the final phases of the project. The law school's superb reference librarians helped us track down long-forgotten details of the *Brown* era.

Obviously, we could not have brought this project to fruition had it not been for the wonderful response of our professorial cohort in the nation's law schools. We are grateful to everyone who responded to our survey, whether by telling their stories or simply wishing us well, and are especially appreciative of the patience shown by our contributors, who never lost confidence that we would bring this project to completion.

Special thanks are also in order for our editor, Michael Ames. We are deeply grateful for his enthusiastic support for this project and for his gentle and unerring editorial guidance.

Finally, we express heartfelt thanks to our families for their encouragement and for their own emotional connection to this deeply personal undertaking.

Law Touched Our Hearts

Introduction

Richard J. Bonnie and Mildred Wigfall Robinson

In February of 1954, President Dwight D. Eisenhower invited Chief Justice Earl Warren to dinner at the White House. Among the other guests were well-known opponents of school desegregation, including John W. Davis, the lawyer who had recently presented the states' argument for upholding segregated schools before the Supreme Court in *Brown v. The Board of Education of Topeka, Kansas*. In his memoirs, Warren notes that he "was the ranking guest, and as such, sat at the right of the President and within speaking distance" of Davis. During that evening, Eisenhower famously commented to Warren that "law and force cannot change a man's heart."

Later that spring, on May 17, 1954, the Supreme Court handed down its decision in *Brown*. The court unanimously held that "separate but equal is inherently unconstitutional." Its pronouncement was met with undisguised hostility in the states in which public school segregation had been legally sanctioned since the end of Reconstruction. Violence—sometimes life-threatening—was visited on children who attempted to exercise the right to attend schools of their choosing, as well as on the adults who supported them. Troops were ordered into embattled classrooms in an attempt to restore order. In displays of "massive resistance" to the Court's edict, a number of school districts suspended public education completely, while white children streamed into newly opened private schools and black children went uneducated. When schools were begrudgingly desegregated, black teachers and administrators across the South often lost their jobs. The sudden change in law did not erase the deeply entrenched attitudes and customs instantiated by racial segregation. Nor did restoration of order in classrooms lure back white children whose parents sought at every turn to frustrate the Court's holding.

But what of the children themselves? What impact did all this have on their hearts and minds? The two of us belong to the "*Brown* generation." We are among the children who were enrolled in the nation's public schools either when *Brown* was decided on May 17, 1954, or during the decade of transition thereafter. The civil rights movement and the accompanying litigation culminated in sweeping legislative changes in the 1960s—the Civil Rights Act of 1964, the Voting Rights Act of 1965, and the Fair Housing Act of 1968—all intended to bring to an end decades of racial separation, whether legally sanctioned or tacitly accepted. These events affected us profoundly, as we discovered when we met in 1984 and again recalled with the fiftieth anniversary of *Brown* twenty years later. While *Brown* did not itself propel the nation toward racial harmony, that powerfully symbolic decision seemed to us to capture the best hopes of an era.

We wondered whether others of our generation were similarly affected. In order to discover what we could about collective memory, we turned to our colleagues in the legal academy who had been in elementary or secondary school either when *Brown* was decided or during the ensuing decades. We confess that we strongly suspected that the unique moral force of the Supreme Court's pronouncement in *Brown*—that separating white children from black children by law was profoundly wrong—had propelled many of our colleagues toward careers in law, just as it had done for us. But we were less interested in their career choices than in the effect of the school experience during the 1950s and 1960s on their social development and sense of civic identity. Although we did not seek to elicit analyses of either the Court's reasoning or its holding in the case (there has been no shortage of such commentary, of course), we expected our colleagues would be particularly well situated to reflect on the meaning of the *Brown* decision—as it affected them personally and, perhaps, as it affected the history of our country. We were not disappointed.

With the assistance of the Association of American Law Schools, we identified the "*Brown* generation" of law professors—a target group of law teachers who had been born between 1936 and 1954. We then sent them short surveys, asking what they could recall as children upon hearing of the *Brown* decision, about any changes in their schooling thereafter, and about the overall impact of the decision on their educational experience. Further, as we had hoped, among the one thousand colleagues who responded to our survey (the results of which are summarized in the appendix), a number offered to write essays reflecting upon the personal meaning of the *Brown* decision. Forty of those essays are collected in this book.

Awareness of *Brown*

About a quarter of us recalled hearing of the *Brown* decision within six months after it was handed down. Reported awareness did not differ significantly among regions of the country. As one would expect, though, awareness of the decision was greater among respondents who were in secondary school at the time than among those who were in primary school. Several of the respondents in the older group heard the news at school, including one writer whose eighth-grade teacher announced in class that she would "not continue teaching if the races were mixed." Indeed, a number of our respondents reported that adults reassured them that they needn't worry, because "nothing is going to change." One respondent enrolled in a public high school outside the South reported that he did not react to the news at all because he "thought that the decision would impact only schools in the South."

The largest number of responses came from contributors who were in elementary or middle school in 1954. Many reported that they learned of the decision in their homes. As one would expect, the reactions of the adults around them strongly affected their reactions. A few reported that news of the decision ending state-mandated racial separation was favorably received in their homes. Many more recall adult expressions of outright hostility to the Supreme Court's audacity. No one expected immediate Southern compliance with the decision.

Brown's Impact in the South

In the District of Columbia and twenty-one states, almost all in the South, segregation in the public schools and other places of public accommodation was mandated by law (i.e., it was de jure). Most of our responding colleagues grew up in states with de jure segregation. The range of personal emotions they recalled when learning of the decision included approval, elation, anger, fear, defiance, and anxiety, as well as intense curiosity: "What happens next?" "What will happen to my school?" "Will I be with my friends?" "What will it be like to be in an integrated classroom?"

Some of us were caught up in the maelstrom of resistance, including politicians' decisions to close the public schools rather than desegregate them. Several of our respondents were among the relatively few children who attended newly desegregated schools in the first years after *Brown* was decided. A student in Little Rock remembered the presence of the 101st Airborne on campus—deployed to enforce the order to desegregate. A student enrolled in a seventh-grade class in Virginia desegregated by a lone black girl recalled his concern for that student's reaction to white parental hostility and press attention. And a first-grader from Delaware, then a de jure state, reported harassment from white classmates due to her friendship with her lone black classmate.

Others wrote of penalties—both direct and indirect—imposed upon families who dared to cross the color line in ways that contravened local mores. For example, one wrote of the treatment to which her family was subjected by the white community as a consequence of hiring a black registered nurse to provide care for an elderly relative. The caregiver had been the target of economic sanctions because she had the courage to send her daughter to a previously all-white school.

A few of our responding colleagues grew up in districts where desegregation had been achieved more fully and more rapidly. Several of these writers recalled important ways in which students themselves were occasionally able to identify and address inevitable—sometimes difficult—transitional challenges. In retrospect, the difficulties and tensions were deemed less important than the opportunity to learn from each other. Our respondents also reported many instances in which teachers, administrators, and parents created and maintained a positive, inclusive environment for all students. Without exception, these experiences were characterized as important lessons for life.

As it turned out, however, most of our respondents had little to report about the impact of *Brown* on their schooling. Nothing happened. Resistance to the *Brown I* mandate (a straightforward holding in 1954 that separate was unequal) was widespread in the de jure states during that first year subsequent to the Court's pronouncement. This resistance did not abate with *Brown II*, in which the Court in 1955 famously directed that segregated schools be dismantled "with all deliberate speed." The first decade after the decision, then, was marked primarily by intransigence. This intransigence denied most of us of who were then schoolchildren the integrated educational experience envisioned by the Supreme Court in *Brown*. The decisions had very little immediate impact on the educational experiences of the *Brown* generation, despite all the *Sturm und Drang* in the courts. Most of the *Brown* generation remained in segregated schools. Indeed, ten years after *Brown I*, only an estimated 2 percent of black children in formerly de jure states attended school with white children. Meaningful school desegregation did not begin to occur until after the passage of the Civil Rights Act of 1964. According to a 2004 study conducted by the Harvard Civil Rights Project, the percentage of black students in the South attending majority-white schools rose to 44 percent from 2 percent from 1964 to 1968.

Many of our respondents remember the awkwardness of that continued enforced separation. One white respondent wrote of "brown children" who sometimes used one end of her school playground even though those children were not allowed to play with the white children and "certainly did not attend class with us." Another described in detail initial resistance to the desegregation of his state's separate schools for the blind. Several wrote of youthful irritation with policies that closed local swimming pools, thus making the pools unavailable to the children on hot summer days. The pools, of course, had been closed in order to avoid integrating them. (It soon became clear that the principle underlying the *Brown* decision was not restricted to education—legally enforced segregation in every area of life was ultimately deemed unconstitutional largely as a result of the passage of the Civil Rights Act of 1964.)

Beyond the South

Segregation was no less real outside the South, even though it was not legally mandated. Respondents who were students in the public schools of New York, New Jersey, Ohio, and Michigan reported that their academic classes remained segregated de facto because of tracking—separation by perceived intellectual ability, all too often resulting in classes defined along racial lines. Others reported that their schools remained racially segregated because attendance zones were defined by neighborhoods that were themselves racially segregated as a result of discriminatory housing practices or worse. One responding colleague wrote of a black family threatened and intimidated to such an extent that the family moved away from a California town in which they had lived for only six weeks.

Importantly, several respondents wrote of the life-changing realization that discrimination was not experienced only in black and white. They recalled the misfortunes of Asian Americans in California, Latinos in Denver, Hispanic Americans in New York City, and Sicilians in New Jersey. One respondent put it this way:

> I wonder where you account for people like me who grew up in what later became the "rust belt." My town had about 75,000–80,000 residents virtually none of whom were black or brown. Ethnicity meant Polish, Hungarian, Czech, etc. We all learned how to discriminate against others—just didn't associate it with color!! Imagine the shock of confronting that mind-set.

The Essays

The voices heard in the essays assembled in this book are those of adults who were, importantly, public school students during the *Brown* era. We are men and women, black and white, hailing from all regions of the country—North and South, East and West—whose backgrounds and experiences reflect the many diverse strands of our national community. As law professors, we do not share a common expertise; we teach tax, property, torts, health law, civil procedure, and every other domain of law. But, as members of the *Brown* generation, we have this in common: We have all lived lives affected by *Brown* in some measure and we all yearn for our country to live up to its promise—equal opportunity for all Americans.

Our essays present vignettes of life in the United States before and after the *Brown* decision, providing accounts of the everyday experience of having been born into a segregated society and living in the shadow of ongoing racial tension and change. We write of our confusion, our moral struggles, and our dreams. Black children who had borne the life-thwarting burden of "difference" dared to aspire to achieve fully, dared to dream that race would become irrelevant. White children realized that they too had been victimized by segregation. They too sought to make sense of changing times, even as the chaos of progress and resistance swirled around them. Taken together, these essays look at race relations in the second half of the twentieth century from many angles, providing glimpses into the world in which we grew up and the world that we have helped to shape as adults. The essays collectively present a portrait of an entire nation—not just a region of the nation—in flux.

We present the essays in three parts. The introductory essays in Part 1 are connected thematically by the idea that racial separation—indeed race itself—is a wall that limits human flourishing. Parts 2 and 3 collect the essays by contributors who grew up in de jure states and de facto states respectively. The essays differ in focus within each part. For example, some describe the experiences of nine- to sixteen-year-olds who, for the first time, became aware of "otherness"—either their own or that of children who had previously been invisible to them. Others focus on the immediate effects of *Brown*—the actions and reactions among school boards, parents, and courts, and changes in our contributors even if schooling remained unchanged. Still others reach more widely across the lifespan, presenting glimpses into lives that unfolded in the shadow of *Brown*. Some of our contributors write of choices yet to be made.

Brown's Meaning

The vision of an integrated society for which *Brown* stands transformed our law and culture, and the moral life of the American people, in ways much deeper and more enduring than the limited impact the legal decision had on public education. Hearts changed as a result of the Court's pronouncement. The personal narratives assembled in this book say more about *Brown's* larger meaning than any synthesis we can provide. Instead of trying to speak for our generation, therefore, we will add just a few words about the continued salience of *Brown* for public education more than a half-century later.

If one looks only at the public schools, the *Brown* vision has clearly not been realized. The current pattern of resegregation in elementary and secondary education is deeply disturbing. The 2004 study conducted by the Harvard Civil Right Project to which we alluded earlier found that the proportion of blacks attending majority-white schools declined 13 percent during the 1990s, reaching its lowest level since 1968. The most segregated group of students, according to the report, is white; they attend schools where, on average, 80 percent of the students are white. By contrast, black and Latino students on average attend schools where, on average, 54 percent of the students are black or Latino, respectively.

Moreover, the nation's largest city school systems account for a shrinking share of total school enrollment and remain, almost without exception, overwhelmingly nonwhite and increasingly segregated. In the effort to obtain an education, children in these schools continue to struggle with disadvantage in many forms—unsafe or obsolescent facilities, inadequate materials, disproportionally inexperienced teachers. Many of the most rapidly resegregating school systems since the mid-1980s are suburban. The South remains the nation's most integrated region for both blacks and whites but is rapidly going backward as the courts terminate many successful desegregation orders. In short, segregated education and resegregation and the inevitably compromised educational quality are no longer a uniquely Southern phenomena; they are part of an accelerating national tragedy.

These concerns take on increased urgency in light of the Supreme Court's 2007 decision in *Parents Involved in Community Schools v. Seattle School District No. 1, et al.* In that case, the closely divided Court held that race alone cannot be taken into consideration in student school assignment. The Seattle School District, seeking to maintain racial balance in particular high schools, used race as a tiebreaker to allocate available slots. Four of the five justices in the majority said that the Constitution bans the use of race in making student assignments for all purposes. The fifth justice in the majority, Justice Kennedy, would allow the use of race in plans "narrowly tailored" to achieve a "compelling" government interest. Justice Kennedy did not, however, provide any insight into the features of such a plan. In light of continued residential segregation and the resultant segregative effect on public schools, the decision denies school districts the latitude they need to seek to achieve and maintain diverse classrooms as a "compelling" government interest per se.

Three out of ten Americans today are people of color. Demographers estimate a majority of us will be people of color by the middle of the twenty-first century. Unlike 1954, the racial divide is no longer along black and white lines. Rather, Americans increasingly range across the spectrum of human complexion and cultural experience. Genuinely multiracial classrooms might do more for achieving the *Brown* vision for all children than anything the law has been able to achieve. However, it is also possible that the nation is headed toward less, not greater, unity.

Do the lessons drawn from *Brown* remain relevant in this troubled environment? We think the answer is yes, not because *Brown* provides convincing answers to these seemingly intractable problems, but because it provides a continuing inspiration—an exhortation, really—to find effective solutions to them. *Brown* represents a dual commitment—to erase wrongs rooted in the birth of our nation, and also to achieve a more perfect union. In short, *Brown* looks both backward and forward, and so do the essays in this collection.

PART I

The Context—
Skin Color and Walls

1   Learning about Skin Color

Marina Angel

I was born in New York City in 1944 and grew up on 145th Street and River-side Drive. The block between Riverside and Broadway was predominantly white; the block between Broadway and Amsterdam Avenue was predominantly Hispanic; Harlem started at Amsterdam Avenue. In the 1940s and 1950s, this area was one of the most diverse in the world, not only economically but also racially and ethnically. I vividly remember waiting at a bus stop on 145th and Amsterdam Avenue, holding my mother's hand, and listening to a black politician on a loud speaker. She told me he was an extremely important man. Later, I learned he was Adam Clayton Powell. I learned from schoolmates, predominantly Hispanic, at a Catholic school on 140th Street and Riverside Drive, and street mates, predominantly black, on 145th Street, that skin color mattered: the lighter the better.

My father was a dentist and Sunday was our time together. We'd go to his office on Seventy-second Street between Broadway and West End Avenue. He usually worked in his lab, and I made the chairs go up and down and squirted water. We then would go to lunch—a different ethnic restaurant every time so I'd learn about different people and their cooking. I remember trying to order soup à l'oignon in a Chinese restaurant, with both my father and the waiter stifling their laughter.

We then went to the Embassy movie theater on Broadway between Seventy-second and Seventy-third Streets. (There is an Embassy apartment house on the site today.) Sundays it showed only cartoons and newsreels. The time period was actually pre- or early television, and we didn't have one. In 1954, most people got their news from newspapers and newsreels in movie theaters. Dramatic action on the big screen with equally dramatic voice-overs had an impact that TV evening news viewers can't imagine.

My father knew I was watching the newsreels, because he quizzed me about them afterward. But he probably thought I found the cartoons more interesting. I didn't.

I am now fifty-nine, old enough to understand that it takes a lot of time to put together the pieces of your life to understand who you are. A few years ago, while watching a television documentary on African American history, I realized that I'd seen the incorporated newsreel before, when I was ten at the Embassy movie theater. It was about evidence used in an important lawsuit. Only years later did I learn the name of the case, *Brown v. Board of Education*. Black girls who were my age when I saw this newsreel preferred white dolls to black dolls. A scene like that has much more impact on a child the same age who can identify with the children in the newsreel, a child who can experience empathy. I believe most adults experienced only sympathy. Empathy is a very powerful way of knowing. I was horrified by that scene and absorbed the term "racial self-hatred"—something no child should know or experience. The newsreel had a deep and lasting impact on me.

In 1954, I was in the sixth grade. The next year, one of the girls at school told me my hair was bleached blonde. She said she could tell because my eyebrows were a different color, brown. I looked in the mirror and saw that she was right. That day I went home and asked my mother if she had been bleaching my hair. She said she had been using something to help make it lighter, because it had darkened as I had gotten older. I had an extremely strong reaction. I understood from the newsreel that my mother didn't want me. My eye color was good, hazel. My skin color was good, light. But my hair was bad, brown and not blonde.

I believe this was the first time I showed what has developed into an extremely stubborn streak. I would not let my mother near me when I washed my hair. As a result, my hair was predominantly bleached blonde but brown at the roots. I remember asking her to give me money to have my hair dyed all brown. She wouldn't, probably thinking that I would get sufficiently embarrassed to break down and let her bleach my hair again. I didn't. Instead, I found a very cheap colored hair spray and tried to use it to color the blonde hair brown. Unfortunately, the spray didn't stick very well. It came off on my pillows and clothes. It also changed color quickly to an obnoxious shade of red orange. It took over a year for my hair to grow out enough so that the bleached blonde could be cut off.

Let me add at this point that I am Greek American. My mother was Greek from Constantinople, now Istanbul, and my father came from the southern part of Greece. They met in New York City. Greeks also believe "the lighter the better." They don't understand the element of ethnic self-hatred involved in this. If you've ever seen an Olympic Airline ad, you know that all the stewardesses and stewards are blonde—an extremely unusual circumstance for Greeks. Up to her death in 1990, my mother told people that my hair was blonde when I was born and stayed that way while I was a child but that it changed color. The reason she gave was totally bizarre—I washed it too often. My mother never understood my strong reaction to her insistence that I was blonde—no matter how often or how carefully I explained it.

On the streets of my neighborhood, I learned about both race and gender.

One vivid recollection is sleigh riding on Riverside Drive. There was a hill and I had a very fast sleigh that I was very good at maneuvering. One day all the white boys decided to gang up on me and block me. I simply stopped, got off, and went back up to the top of the hill and started over. After a while, they got tired of my failure to react and left me alone. The next day three black girls showed up with a sleigh. It was clear they had not done much sledding. There was an unstated but clear agreement between the white boys and the black boys. The black boys harassed the black girls until they left the hill. It became obvious to me at that point that the hill was reserved for males. If a girl trespassed on that male domain, she would be harassed until she left, or, if she insisted on staying, she was ignored and excluded from the game.

When I was in the eighth grade, my father suffered a massive diabetic stroke and was hospitalized until he died three years later. My mother went to the hospital every single day. I'd been mugged a few times too many and learned how to make a zip gun, so my mother stopped allowing me to go out to play after school. She understood, however, that it was not a good idea to leave me alone in an apartment by myself all day.

For three summers, from the eighth grade when my father was hospitalized until my junior year of high school when he died, I was shipped off to cousins in Warren, Pennsylvania. Warren is a town in northwestern Pennsylvania that seemed to me to be surrounded on all sides by fifty miles of Allegheny National Forest. There were no blacks or Hispanics. The elite of the town—those who belonged to the country club—clearly thought Greeks, Italians, and Jews were blacks, a feeling shared by the Ku Klux Klan. Clearly, there was a massive disconnect involved in moving between the ethnically, racially, and economically diverse "way upper West Side" of Manhattan and Warren, Pennsylvania.

One summer, I was taken to visit some cousins in nearby Salamanca, New York. The town was built by white people on land leased for ninety-nine years from the Seneca Indian tribe of the Iroquois Nation. I remember walking down the main street of the town with my cousin and seeing a sign in a restaurant window saying "No dogs or Indians allowed." I was stunned, thinking, "This is New York State in the twentieth century, not the Wild West in the nineteenth century."

When I was in high school in 1962, there was a controversy over the building of the Kinzua Dam in Warren County, Pennsylvania. The area was subject to severe flooding. The U.S. government had no qualms about breaking a 1794 treaty signed by George Washington to build the dam on Seneca land. I remember one of the inhabitants of Warren commenting that the government had even supplied the Indians with brand-new houses but they weren't keeping them up properly. If "they" couldn't adjust to "our" lifestyle, that was their problem.

While driving across the state of Pennsylvania to get to Warren, a nine- or ten-hour ride from New York, I remember hearing a radio broadcast sponsored by a local chapter of the Ku Klux Klan. This was announced in the same manner and tone as every other sponsorship.

I remember being told that there was only one black in Warren, an elderly chauffeur who was not allowed to marry so that there wouldn't be any other blacks in the town. I don't know if that story was true, but I've never forgotten it. When the Kinzua Dam was being built in 1964, there was a black construction worker who temporarily moved his family to Warren. I remember a comment about how cute this little black girl was and how she wasn't a problem at all.

Growing up on the way upper West Side of Manhattan, seeing the newsreel on the evidence in *Brown v. Board of Education*, and then experiencing Warren, Pennsylvania, were major factors shaping my career decisions. I went to law school to do civil rights work. I did extraordinarily well my first year at Columbia and was pushed by the prevalent status system to make two choices: to work as a research assistant for one of the teachers and to accept a three-week offer from Cravath, Swaine and Moore to work on a case involving the bankruptcy of a company owning a ship, the SS *Westhampton*. By the end of the summer I realized I was not very happy with the solitary experience of living in a library with little human contact or working at a Wall Street law firm on a case I cared nothing about.

At the beginning of the second year, I began to question the route I had taken. I dropped out for a year, working for the NAACP Legal Defense Fund, Inc. (the Inc Fund), on their Death Sentence Survey. (This is where I got the idea, which I've used in much of my research, that you survey to find patterns, intentional and "unintentional," of discrimination.) I traveled alone in Florida and Virginia in 1966 and 1967, driving to computer-selected counties and gathering information on all sex-related cases where the death penalty could have been given, whether it was or not. When I was growing up in a sheltered Greek American family as an only child, sex was never discussed. I had no idea that American society had such massive hang-ups on the subject of interracial sex, or that, de facto, only black men were subject to the death sentence for being convicted of raping white women. No white man was ever executed for rape in either Florida or Virginia.

During the summer between my second and third years, I worked on criminal cases at the main office of the Inc Fund. The work I did was meaningful and important, and the legal experience and training I gained that summer were first-class and invaluable. I very much wanted to work for the Inc Fund after I finished law school. I had a series of difficult conversations with myself regarding whether it would be appropriate for a white woman to take a job with the premier black legal organization in the United States when that would be one of the few opportunities available to a promising black student.

At the time, there were very few good legal jobs available to women of any race. It would have been self-defeating for me to refrain from applying for every job attractive to minority candidates, but the Inc Fund was unique. I decided not to apply.

Over the past twenty-five years, my teaching and practice have focused on those traditionally discriminated against by individuals and by public and private organizations, including law schools. I spent two years of an LLM program in criminal law and litigation working with the predominantly minority clientele of the Philadelphia Voluntary Defenders Office. When I started teaching at Hofstra law school, I taught criminal law, criminal procedure, prisoners' rights, and juvenile rights. When I took a two-year leave to work with a labor and employment firm, I represented unions and handled antidiscrimination cases. When I returned to teaching, I picked up a labor and employment teaching load, retaining only an advanced course on violence against women from my former criminal law package. When I walk into a room, I immediately notice the racial and gender composition of the group and its hierarchical ordering. Virtually all my writings have been on discrimination, particularly how organizational structures change to the disadvantage of all women and men of color. I constantly survey.

I doubt that my life would have taken this road if I had not watched that newsreel in the Embassy Theater in 1954.

Marina Angel was born in July 1944 in New York City and attended elementary and secondary schools there from 1952 to 1961. She is now professor of law at Temple University's School of Law in Philadelphia.

2 Segregated Proms in 2003

Alfred Dennis Mathewson

Racially segregated high school proms are in the news. The coverage superficially depicts these incidents as vestiges of racism in rural Southern school districts. I moved away from the South over thirty years ago and I know there is far more to the story. There was no media scrutiny of the proms in 1971 when I graduated from Bertie Senior High School in Windsor, North Carolina. No one cared about them except the students who had gone to school for nearly twelve years and were looking forward to this rite of passage. You cannot appreciate what the proms meant in the South then without some idea of that nearly twelve-year journey. My own journey occurred in at least three schools, beginning at W. A. Patillo High School, a K–12 school in Tarboro, North Carolina.

When I entered first grade in 1959 five years after *Brown v. Board of Education* was decided, the schools were segregated, and they stayed that way until strange things started happening during my junior high school years. Then we heard of something called freedom-of-choice plans, under which children could attend any public school of their parents' choice. Of course, this meant that black children could choose to attend the much better financed white schools. I believe we were the third black family to go to the white schools in Tarboro when my mother chose to send my younger brothers to Bridgers Elementary in the spring of 1967. They have stories to tell. It was my turn to go when I entered ninth grade, but we moved to Ahoskie and I attended the white school there, where integration had advanced beyond that in Tarboro. There, many black students opted for Ahoskie High School over the all-black R. L. Vann High School.

My family moved twice more so that I wound up finishing at Bertie, where freedom-of-choice plans had progressed to consolidation. In 1963, Bertie County built two identical high schools—one white and one black. By the time we moved there in 1969, the white high school had become the county high school for all students and the black high school had been designated the junior high school for all students. It was majority black.

Back then there was no prom, black or white, in Bertie County. The school board had eliminated the homecoming dance and the prom upon consolidation, along with virtually every other social event at which white girls might socialize with black boys. Integration created problems even with the cheerleading squads. When no black girl made the squad during my freshman year at Ahoskie High, black football players organized a boycott of classes by black students. There had been a competition, but none of the black cheerleaders who had left R. L. Vann had been deemed good enough to make the squad. Faced with the decimation of a state championship contender, the school reconsidered and a black cheerleader was added.

The wave of separate proms today has been defended on the grounds that this is the way things have always been. Lost in these apologias are the stories of the black and white students who tried to make integration work, students who tried to do things a different way. The prom, or rather the absence of the prom, was a unifying event for my senior class. My classmates in the class of 1971 believed that a prom was a fundamental right. Several of us, black and white, girls and boys, got together and decided we did not need the permission of the school board, superintendent, or principal to have a prom. If they would not give us one, we would give ourselves a prom. We arranged to have it at the National Guard Armory. When the authorities learned of our plans, they capitulated. If there was going to be a prom, it was going to be held somewhere they could monitor the situation. It was held in the gymnasium instead.

We had a wonderful time. The last thing on our minds as we danced the penguin was that the prom was integrated. We were teenagers—juniors and seniors having a dance. I did not take my girlfriend home until 3:00 AM, ruining my reputation with her parents as a nice young man. After the prom, we went to a segregated club, not because it was segregated but because it was where we could go. I presume my white friends did the same.

Our bringing the prom back was not an act of courage. We were merely obstreperous teenagers. The most courageous stand I saw occurred in my sophomore year while I was attending Selma (North Carolina) High School. There were a handful of black students in the senior class—freedom of choice was still in effect. The seniors cast a black girl and a white girl as sisters in the senior class play. The principal and the school board said, "No way," but the class refused to back down. The school board played hardball. The students were given an ultimatum: Either they would recast the play or there would be no play. The seniors, the overwhelming majority of whom were white, chose to have no play. That was not merely an act of courage; it was an act of personal sacrifice recognizing that they were all just students.

I left the South a long time ago. I have heard of the separate proms, and separate reunions. I attended one two years ago but not for my high school. My friends at W. A. Patillo were forcibly removed from there to Tarboro High School through consolidation in their senior year. One year of Tarboro High could not break the bonds formed and the nurturing received through eleven grades. The commemorative T-shirts said Tarboro High School but it was really a reunion of the W. A. Patillo High School class of 1971. They invited me back because I had been with them for eight years. I went back not because they were black. I went back because they were the people who taught me how to hit a baseball, play basketball, and dance. These were the friends who comforted me when my father died, who came to my twelfth birthday party even though we did not have indoor plumbing. It was not about race, it was about the bonds of friendship.

When I heard the story about the separate proms in Taylor, Georgia, I thought about this point. My class at Bertie held an integrated prom, but it was virtually our only social event together. I never visited a white friend's home while in high school, and no white friend ever visited mine. In fact, to the best of my knowledge no white person, other than an insurance salesman, ever set foot in my mother's house. You cannot expect students to hold integrated proms or reunions if they do not or will not forge social bonds outside school. The classes of 2002 and 2003 in Taylor both held integrated proms. The difference this year was that many white students also held a whites-only prom. If those white students had gone through trials and triumphs outside school with their black classmates, I suspect the white kids would have been far less likely to exclude them.

By the time students reach the senior year, too few interracial bonds have been formed. There are forces at work to prevent such bonds from forming. My youngest brother vividly remembers an experience from his year at Bridgers Elementary. He had made friends with the nephew of a very prominent politician. The friend invited him home after school a few times. One day the friend's mother permanently revoked the invitation and ordered him off the property. He was six years old at the time. When I turned eighteen, I vowed to vote against the politician. I do not recall if I did or not. White parents erected barriers to prevent the forming of interracial bonds.

Many people think that those days are gone. I remember nearly crying when my eldest daughter was invited to a birthday party when she was in kindergarten. The invitation that had been stripped from my brother had been re-extended. But any comfort I may have drawn that things had changed was removed when she was in elementary school. A parent of one of the kids in her class called me one day to ask if I was aware of what had happened. One of her classmates had a birthday party and brought invitations to school to everyone except my daughter. The birthday girl had told the class that she could not invite any blacks to the party. The informing parent became aware of the incident because the other kids refused to come without my daughter. There was good news in that her classmates felt some bond with her, but nevertheless, there was still that parental barrier. The birthday girl's parents invited us over through the other parents, perhaps as a result of pressure by the other parents, and we eventually acceded. It remains our only contact with them. No bonds were formed.

It is easy to gravitate toward the view that the barriers to interracial bonds are a Southern phenomenon, but clearly they are not. My daughter's incident happened here in New Mexico, the multicultural Land of Enchantment. For whatever reason, the barriers to interracial bonds appear to be well entrenched by high school. As my daughter's experience demonstrates, some bonds do form. Her best friends—not merely her friends—continue to include people from an assortment of races. There are not, however, enough such bonds. Not all barriers are erected by the parents. Fellow students construct some barriers. On more than one occasion, I observed Anglo friends of my children sub-jected to ridicule for playing with them. I have been called by Anglo parents to commiserate about the harassment their children are receiving for associat-ing with mine. It thus comes as no surprise that many white students in Taylor abandoned the interracial pioneer spirit that their upper classmates adopted the previous year.

It is no wonder then that too many students of all colors at the colle-giate level reject interracial social bonds or find them undesirable, even pain-ful, experiences. Those students who seek them and try to encourage them find themselves ostracized. The result is reflected in many of the problems oc-curring in integrated educational institutions today, as students from different backgrounds go to the same classes, attend the same events, and live in the same dormitories amidst institutional cultures that impede the formation of such bonds. Consequently, hate speech, hostile environments, and nonopti-mum academic performances abound. These students then graduate and join gender- and race-based private clubs so that people of color and women seek-ing interracial and intergender social and business bonds are forced to obtain them with legal bayonets.

Perhaps they find too few role models in the generation of their parents. I have often commented that the civil rights warriors knew how to knock doors down, but they had no way of preparing the beneficiaries for what awaited them on the other side. It is equally true that white parents had no blueprint for dealing with the integration that followed. Parents on both sides of the door grew up in an era in which racial diversity was proscribed by law. In fact, the refusal to engage in racial diversity was legally permitted. The very essence of the Jim Crow laws was to prevent voluntary actions on the part of individu-als and institutions to form such bonds. The efforts of individuals and institu-tions have met with mixed results ever since. Several years ago, my wife and I decided to take one small step to work toward making integration successful. We consciously broadened our social circle and sought experiences that led to interracial bonds. We have enjoyed interactions with colleagues, socialized with the parents of the friends of our children, and participated in a variety of organizations. It is true that we belong to organizations that address issues of concern and provide support to professionals of color, and we will continue to do so. However, we do not belong to any organization that limits membership on the basis of race. Our social circle is not merely black and white; we have discovered a rich multicolored racial mosaic in America.

I did not march in the streets or stage a sit-in at a lunch counter during integration. I never met Bull Connor and my knowledge of the Freedom Riders is limited to what I have read. Somehow though, I do not believe that Martin Luther King saw segregated schools, neighborhoods, and workplaces in his dream. The unfinished business of the civil rights movement is to make its successes meaningful. If we are ever to achieve one America, then the generation of beneficiaries of all colors must rise to the task to engage in affirmative action to reach out and bond with others. The most logical starting places are educational institutions. The students are there, brought by their parents who attend school events. The interactions are there. Now, we just need to create bonds that last outside the school grounds and campuses.

Alfred Dennis Mathewson was born in May 1953 in Tarboro, North Carolina, and attended elementary and secondary schools in Tarboro and Ahoskie, North Carolina. He is now a professor of law at the University of New Mexico School of Law in Albuquerque.

3   The Wall

Kate Nace Day

It was 1957. I was eight years old. My father had just joined the faculty of a Canadian university. He was a professor of anatomy and physiology and a research scientist. He had a wonderful lab at the university, graduate students from around the world, and funding for summer research as well. We spent our first summer in Woods Hole, Massachusetts, where he would conduct his research for the remaining summers of my childhood.

That first summer, my father bought an old wooden outboard motorboat. He often took us out with him, teaching the lessons of the sea, how to read the tides, winds, currents, and back eddies of the small string of islands that flow off Woods Hole. As we cruised down along the islands one afternoon, my father pointed out a line of stone walls. He loved to teach and I was used to listening. He told me that all the Elizabeth Islands were criss-crossed with these wonderful, elegant stone walls that carved the islands from rocky shore to smooth beaches, through sheep grazing fields and across scrub pine and oak. There are no paved roads on any of these islands even today; then, there were sheepherders and there were horses, but very few houses and buildings.

My father pointed out these wonderful rocky walls and asked whether I noticed something different about them—different than what I noticed about the rest of the island. I said no, I didn't. They were grey and they were beautiful and the island was green and grey and beautiful. My father told me they were man-made; he said nature had not placed them there. And then he told me that it remains a mystery today why the stone walls are there. The white settlers who took over the islands had no written history of why the islands are carved with walls. These stone walls remain the markings of some unknown human purpose. My father thought it odd that I didn't know the difference between that which he saw as natural and that which is man-made.

That fall, when we were in Canada, my father would go off to his lab. In the evenings, he would come home with his students. They filled our very small house that was already filled with four children, a mother, a grandmother, and a dog—students from England, from Scotland and Poland, from Czechoslovakia; there were students from Hong Kong and there were students from Africa. I did not yet know that man had made walls between the races.

But that winter, we watched the television images of what has come to be called "massive Southern resistance." I am ashamed to say that I don't remember the faces of the black children walking up the schoolhouse steps, or stepping down off buses. I remember the angry white faces, the ugly face of white racism. I remember what my father said to me: "Race science made the color line and the color line is man-made. There is no moral significance to the color of one's skin."

Thirty years later, when I started law teaching, I was intrigued by how something of no moral significance had come to dominate our lives and control our destinies. My father had shown me that walls carved the islands and taught me that there were sources you can turn to that will illuminate the mystery. I turned to Zora Neale Hurston and John Hope Franklin, Toni Morrison and W. E. B. DuBois, Judge Julia Cooper Mack and Justice Thurgood Marshall—all the voices of men and women of color who illuminate the lies and myths and images that went into the construction of the color line. I taught Race and the Constitution; I wrote about white shame; I tried to keep *Brown* alive, not an empty symbol of some sentimental hope. I tried never to forget the ugly face of white racism. I tried.

Life is short. Voices, perhaps, live on. My father retired and lived again in Woods Hole. Early one fall, he and I headed out down along the islands. It was a still afternoon and a light fog hung over the water. We rode in silence. Before we headed in, he pulled into one of those island coves and slowed the engine. "Beautiful," he said and smiled. As we headed in, he turned, took a long look back, and smiled again. His eyes scanned the scene. "I guess I will never know why," he added, and I looked back and saw the stone walls and knew that my father was dying.

NOTE

A portion of this essay was previously published in Kate Nace Day, "Judicial Voice: Judge Julia Cooper Mack and Images of the Child," *Howard Law Journal* 40 (1997): 331. Reprinted by permission.

Kate Nace Day was born in August 1948 and attended elementary and secondary schools in Brooklyn, New York; Woods Hole, Massachusetts; and Hamilton, Ontario, Canada. She is now a professor of law at Suffolk University Law School in Boston.

4 And the Walls Came Tumblin' Down

Harvey A. Feldman

When *Brown* was decided, I was a fourth-grade student at Girard College, the free boarding school in center city Philadelphia for "poor, white, male orphans" that became a legal battleground in the integration movement over the fourteen years following *Brown*. Although persistent litigation ultimately integrated Girard with respect to both race and sex, I spent eleven years behind the ten-foot walls that separated the school's residents from the surrounding, predominantly African American neighborhood, and I graduated on June 14, 1962.

Shortly after *Brown* was decided, Raymond Pace Alexander and Sadie Alexander began the fight to integrate Girard. I remember crowds of pickets with bullhorns outside the front gate as the Alexanders articulated the position that because Girard, a private school, was administered by a public body, the Board of City Trusts, it was bound by *Brown* and required to integrate. The pickets returned from time to time throughout my tenure, but, as a consequence of various Girard stratagems, the litigation did not conclude until 1968, when I was a second-year law student. Cecil Moore, another prominent Philadelphia lawyer, had picked up the cudgel from the Alexanders and pushed the litigation to its successful conclusion.

The following year, when the school was finally integrated, I returned to Girard for an alumni reunion. In a conversation with several of my classmates, I related that I had just finished law school. One of them said that it was too bad that I hadn't finished a couple of years earlier so that I could have helped defend the school. I replied that I would have been on the other side. He turned and walked away; we have not had a conversation since.

Regrettably, I was a sixteen-year-old senior in high school before I was able to appreciate that my upbringing was corrupted at its core by Girard's chosen isolation. A classmate and I were playing tennis on the court behind the senior dormitory just inside the campus's north wall. An African American boy perhaps ten or eleven years old climbed the wall from the outside and sat atop it to watch us play. He said nothing. Without provocation my classmate angrily began to direct epithets at the boy and threatened him until he jumped down. I did not join my classmate, but neither did I challenge or chastise him. I simply froze with the sudden realization that something was fundamentally wrong with the way I had been raised. And I do not excuse my lack of courage at the moment with the fact that I was the smallest and weakest member of my class.

At Girard's Founder's Day in 1987, I had the honor of representing my class as our twenty-fifth reunion speaker at a traditional afternoon chapel ceremony. I worried over how to state my support for the dramatic changes in the school without generating heat from my classmates and the older alumni who had resisted the school's integration. I tried in the speech to link change and continuity and to use some of the school's own traditions and the dramatic events of the intervening twenty-five years to encourage everyone in the audience to embrace the school as it continues to fill an important void for children from homes that lack at least one parent.

The graduating class traditionally sang a song during the graduation ceremony that includes the line: "We have run our marathon from childhood to growing man." In my speech, I said: "Some of us have children who are, as we were twenty-five years ago, completing the marathon from childhood to growing person." At one point I noted: "We were traumatized by the senseless assassinations of two Kennedys, a King, and a Beatle. We were moved by courageous advocates of racial and sexual equality to adopt an array of laws intended to guarantee voting rights, fair housing and educational opportunity, and nonbiased employment policies. We've seen men on the moon and a black and a woman on the Supreme Court. . . . Girard, too, has changed. Gone are West End, Banker Hall, and Lafayette [all dormitories]. Allen Hall [the dormitory for seniors] is beautifully refurbished. No longer is the school all white and all male."

Near the end of my speech, I said: "There were two other shortcomings in my own Girard upbringing that, happily, present and future Hummers [the nickname for the school's students] will not experience. It wasn't until my college years that I began to appreciate the wonderful broadening of knowledge and deepening of character that come from the cross-fertilization of ideas and perspectives from diverse cultures. And I was already in law school before I was comfortable with sharing the special bonds of friendship—as opposed to romance—with a woman." I am happy to say that I received a vigorous standing ovation. One member of the Board of City Trustees asked for a copy of the speech to circulate to the other members. For months afterward, I received thank-you notes. It was a very proud moment.

There's an ironic postscript. In 1969–1970 I was a law clerk for Judge Joseph L. McGlynn, who was then serving on the Court of Common Pleas of Philadelphia County. During the year, the court administrator undertook to reduce the backlog of criminal cases belonging to several very busy criminal defense lawyers by assigning each of those lawyers to a single judge. Cecil Moore was assigned to Judge McGlynn. Moore and I talked at length about the Girard experience and the litigation. He was a fine man as well as a skilled lawyer. My relationship with him made me feel that I had been able to overcome the prejudices with which I had been raised.

Harvey A. Feldman was born in Philadelphia in 1945 and attended elementary and secondary school at Girard College in that city. He is now professor of law at the Pennsylvania State University, Dickinson School of Law, Carlisle, Pennsylvania.

5 The Commutative Property of Arithmetic

Robert Laurence

I recall the question precisely: "You mean you disagree with the opinion in *Brown versus The Board of Education of Topeka?*" And the questioner: my father, who was a scientist, not a lawyer, and would have spoken out the full name of the case, "*Brown versus The Board of Education of Topeka.*" Not the lawyers' familiar *Brown*, or *Brown vee Board*. The full name.

And I recall the person questioned: me, the middle of his three sons. And the occasion: dinner. Precisely, dessert after dinner, my mother's chocolate cake having just been served.

The date is harder to pin down. We were in the dining room, and we didn't move into the house with the dining room until 1958. And I had not graduated from high school, I know that. So: the fall of 1958 at the earliest; the spring of 1963 at the latest. I would have been between thirteen and seventeen.

I have no memory of my answer, though I suspect it was along the lines of "(mumble mumble mumble) May I be excused?"

Nor do I recall what I had said to provoke the question; *Brown* was several years old by then and it would have not been news. But it's easy enough to reconstruct. You see, my father was a physicist with the Space Agency. Well, it wasn't really the Space Agency back then, but you know what I mean. NASA, then, was NACA. No S. The National Advisory Committee on Aeronautics. NASA was formally created in October of 1958, roughly a year after *Sputnik*, but we still pretty much thought of it as NACA until men started flying in the 1960s.

Anyway, my father was a physicist and the Laurence boys were brought up to be scientists. In two instances, it took; my brothers are an industrial hygienist and a plant pathologist. And I was on my way to becoming a mathematician, until, some years later, I hit the wall, math-wise, became a schoolteacher for a while, then stumbled my way into law school and discovered a profession that dealt in words, not numbers. It was a great relief. I gave mathematics a shot, I really did, but, in the end, family expectations were not met and I became a lawyer. But, you see, at the time of the dinner and the cake and the question, I still fancied myself a young mathematician, on my way toward a career doing whatever it is mathematicians do, about which I could not exactly have said.

My mother did not go to college, a result of the social milieu in which she grew up and her family's poverty. A well-to-do uncle promised college tuition for her brother, Todd, but when Todd died as a child, the money was put to a different purpose and the girl child never saw the inside of a college. Sure, she could have gone to college after we kids were at school, but what can one say? Such things seemed different then. So, she became a scientist by osmosis from my father, was terribly proud of his career, and admired until her dying day his scientific ways of thinking. But her sensibilities, I think, lay elsewhere than in science, sensibilities that I, in the end, perhaps have carried on.

Where was I? Yes. I fancied myself a young mathematician. And I must have suggested in dinner table conversation, just prior to my father's question, some application of the concept of mathematical equality to political or civil rights matters. Something like this: "What's wrong with separate but equal? Equal is equal, right?"

I should say something about what was going on then. The house with the dining room was, and is, located in a Cleveland suburb, a small college town with a small African American community plus a few black students— African and African American—at the college. We would have said "Negro" then, and my parents would have insisted on the capital N. This was in the late 1950s or early 1960s, before the Latin phrases *de facto* and *de jure* came into common use, and before the northern suburbs got their comeuppance and lost their smugness. Well, some of them. My high school was integrated, but our church was not. My Boy Scout troop was all white, but my Little League team was not. The era now called "the Sixties" did not arrive in such places until mid-decade, and the complacency of the Fifties lasted well into the next numerical decade in Berea, Ohio.

Instead, at dinner, years after *Brown* had been decided and the Board of Education of Topeka was told to get with it—not *right now*, you understand, but "with all deliberate speed"—I said something at the dinner table, over the chocolate cake, about how equality was a simple enough concept to understand, and was unmodifiable. Equal means *equal*, and if two things are equal then what does separateness have to do with it? And was rebuked. And life went on.

★ ★ ★

The commutative property of arithmetic is that the order in which an operation works on two numbers does not matter. A plus b equals b plus a. Simple enough.

Not really. Readers will have learned long ago that it doesn't matter in which order you add or multiply, but it does matter in which order you subtract or divide. A plus b equals b plus a, but a minus b does not equal b minus a, not usually, anyway. They will have learned this so long ago and at such an early stage of their educations that it will now seem to go without saying. It will seem inherently true. Necessarily true. Built into their understanding of the manipulation of numbers. Sometimes the commutative property holds and sometimes it doesn't. Order matters in subtraction and division but not in addition or multiplication. The concept seems so basic that it is not worthy of study. To call it an application of "the commutative property," or not, seems an unnecessary complication, the misuse of the very notion of a "concept" or a "property."

The theoretical foundations of elementary arithmetic turn out to be very, very difficult, well beyond, let me assure you, that wall of theoretical mathematics that I hit long ago at Ohio State. I cannot explain *why* the commutative property does not apply to subtraction, nor can I understand the proof when it is set before me. It just doesn't. The best I can do is to give you about a million examples where it doesn't, but that's no proof. One of the difficulties in constructing a sensible mathematics curriculum for schoolchildren is that the theoretical underpinnings of calculus, which comes late in the students' lives, are simpler to explain and understand than those of arithmetic, which comes early on.

And the theoretical meaning of "equality" is even more basic than the commutative property of addition. What does it *mean*, after all, *really* mean, to say that "a plus b" equals "b plus a"? This is what mathematicians do, and I don't do it anymore. I never did it very well.

★ ★ ★

Back to dinner. I was a teenager, trying to apply a mathematical concept so fundamental that I thought it went without saying to a real-world problem. My father, I suspect, was result oriented, for remember that he was a scientist, too, training me to become one. "How can you think," I can imagine—but do not recall—his saying, "how can you think that the chemistry lab at a Negro school in Atlanta is equal to the one at a white school across the city?" "But, then," I can imagine—but do not recall—my replying, "they aren't *equal*. If they were equal, then . . . well, they'd be *equal*. Right?"

I did not intend—I do not believe I intended (Am I sounding a little defensive here?)—a racially motivated statement, in this statement that preceded my father's question, at least the statement that I think preceded my father's question. I honestly believe it was a *mathematically* motivated statement, and therein lies its relevance to my education. My father's question that evening was merely one part of a central quandary of my early, and not-so-early, education: how to fit my book learning into the real world. Stated that way, it is surely a central quandary of every person's education. Because of the science-related expectations of my family, the quandary for me took the shape of trying to relate the precision and logic of mathematics to an imprecise, illogical world. For others, I suppose, the quandary presents itself in different ways, but we all have it presented.

I am reminded of one of my own students, a seventh-grader, many years later, and many years ago now. The class was studying the prescribed science curriculum at the same time we were keeping an eye on the approach of a comet that was supposed to be spectacular. (It, in fact, turned out to be a dud.) An excited girl came to class one morning and announced that she and her uncle had seen the comet the night before.

"Uh oh, look at our sky map. See where the comet is? It's still in the *morning* sky. Remember, it won't be in the evening sky until it passes behind the sun later in the year."

She was crestfallen. "But maybe God wants it to get there early."

Maybe, indeed. How could I tell her that she was wrong? She would have to work out for herself the tension that she had just found between the science she was learning and the religion that was so important to her. I trust that she did, eventually; most of us do.

The role that *Brown* played in the statement, if not the resolution, of my educational quandary was partly happenstance. The tension between theoretical analysis and real-world problems could have, and did, present itself in many other ways as I grew up. But partly the role that *Brown* played in this part of my education was not coincidence. The case was about racial justice, about which my parents felt strongly and which was an important element of the at-home part of my education. Perhaps the tension between theory and practice always arises most memorably when the clash occurs over the dominant precepts of one's life. As it presented itself regarding religion to my young student, it would have sensibly presented itself regarding race in my family, for my parents had educated us carefully in that regard, as they saw the issues and as best they were able.

And maybe this memory of *Brown* foretold my eventual interest in the law, or, more likely, my eventual interest in the law managed to resurrect the memory of the dinner-table question. I have written of the intersection of science and legal theory, and to the extent there's a theme there, it is that one must apply the science only carefully to the law, for the analogies are imprecise and the unwary can be trapped. For example, in the article just mentioned, I looked for applications of the concept of symmetry from modern physics to a field I study and found that asymmetry, its more flexible but more complex sibling, was the better tool.

It wasn't until many years later, in law school, that I actually read *Brown*.

And discovered this: "Separate educational facilities are inherently unequal," surely one of the most thoughtful sentences the Supreme Court has ever written. Inherent inequality was the idea that my young, mathematically inclined brain was rejecting at the dinner table that evening. Thinking back, it now seems to me that *Brown* could have been explained mathematically: "Look. The Supreme Court is just defining the initial conditions under which the problem must be solved. 'Suppose x is a number greater than 0. Then find the solutions for $1/x \sin x = 0$.' We do that all the time. The Supreme Court is defining what the word 'equal' means."

But definitions of equality are probably too much for young mathematicians to tackle—for *this* young mathematician to have tackled, at any rate. Besides, it was probably more important, at that stage of my life, for me to struggle with the quandary than to have it resolved. For the quandary itself was elemental to my education. In the end, I would have to learn how to apply the mathematical concepts I was studying to the world in which I was living, even after I quit studying them.

★ ★ ★

What I have tried to set out here is the way in which *Brown* affected my education at a most profound level, not in its holding but in its essential meaning: the ways in which the theoretical, the rational, the precise, relate to the actual, clumsy, imprecise world that I live in. A world in which terms like "equality" are as complex as they are in that advanced theoretical world that inhabits the space beyond the mathematical wall that I can't climb over. A world in which "separate educational facilities are inherently unequal."

In the end, perhaps, the personal importance of *Brown* to me is that it has provided me with a glimpse beyond that wall. I may not be able to understand why addition has the commutative property but subtraction does not. The theoretical mathematical underpinnings of the concept of equality may remain too complicated for me to understand. But, by removing the "equal" of the Equal Protection Clause from the realm of mathematics, *Brown* showed to me that those same kinds of ideas inhabit the world on this side of that wall, where the concept of equality is a sophisticated one, difficult to get one's brain around, not susceptible to tidy, mathematical description.

Robert Laurence was born in Newport News, Virginia, in September 1945 and attended elementary and secondary school in Berea, Ohio, from 1952 to 1963. He has retired from the law at the University of Arkansas in Fayetteville, where he was the Robert A. Leflar Distinguished Professor of Law, and now raises equally retired horses near Hindsville, Arkansas.

PART II

De Jure States
and the District of Columbia

6 Training in Alabama

Paulette J. Delk

In May 1954 I was seven years old, and I had just completed the third grade at the all-black, de jure segregated Baldwin County Training School in Daphne, Alabama. The all-white high schools in rural counties all over the South were named for their counties, for example, Baldwin County High School. The all-black schools were distinguished by the replacement of the word "high" with the word "training." Many people gave many different reasons why the word "training" was used, but not one of those reasons was positive. My school was a first- through twelfth-grade school, and it served as the high school for students who lived as far away as forty miles. In rural Alabama, as much of Baldwin County was then, segregation of the schools was achieved though busing. Many of these students passed by several white schools, which were much closer to their homes and which they were legally prohibited from attending, in order to obtain a high school education.

These students endured the long drive twice each day, the targets of taunts from their classmates like: "The kids from Foley, Alabama, have never seen Foley during the day; it's dark when they leave in the morning, and it's dark when they get back home." They endured all of this so that they could get a high school education at a school that had no gym, no foreign language lab, no lab equipment in the science lab, a meager library, and hand-me-down books, desks, and chairs from the white high schools that they passed each morning and evening.

Although I was an avid reader and an avid eavesdropper on my schoolteacher parents' conversations, I recall little fanfare over the landmark *Brown* decision. With the obvious disparity in treatment between the white and black schools by the Board of Education, one would expect that the Supreme Court's decision in *Brown* would have been a hot topic of discussion among the many African American schoolteachers and students with whom I lived. Actually, the Court's decision went virtually unnoticed among African Americans in the rural communities of Alabama, even among those whose lives would be most affected by it—schoolteachers and schoolchildren. (I was concerned that my recollection of the immediate impact of the *Brown* decision on my community might have been affected by my youth, so I talked with three persons who were schoolteachers in those rural communities at the time of the decision. Each of them agreed that the Supreme Court's decision received little to no attention in their communities in 1954. One person recalled that she was aware that the Supreme Court had held that "school segregation was unconstitutional," but that nothing was said openly about it, partly out of concern for their jobs.) It was not until 1971 that the public schools in Baldwin County were integrated—a full seventeen years post-*Brown*. As a result, all of my school years were spent in the de jure segregated Baldwin County Training School.

What did receive a great deal of attention among most people, including me, all over Alabama in the period around 1954 was the Montgomery bus boycott. My parents and their friends knew many people in Montgomery, and the weekly updates on the boycott were much awaited and discussed. I think that I paid such close attention because it represented for me the first time that large numbers of people were publicly stating their dissatisfaction with the current system and its unfairness. I recall feeling suffocated by the entire Jim Crow system, yet feeling completely helpless. The fact that there were good public libraries nearby that I was prohibited from using was a tough reality for a bright little girl with a gift and passion for reading.

In the early 1960s, national television, the big-city newspapers, and my family and friends began to talk more about *Brown* as it became inevitable that the segregated schools would have to integrate in the near future. As one family member who was a teacher in a rural Alabama county told me, the white superintendent of education, in an open meeting, said that integration was a "bitter pill to swallow, but swallow it we must." It was at this point that *Brown* began to have some meaning for me. It was not clear when the schools would integrate, so each year we wondered if that year would be the last that our classmates of many years would continue to be our only classmates.

In 1963, my senior year of high school, my principal called me into his office. He was there along with the guidance counselor, and together they told me that with my grades of all A's, I would definitely be the class valedictorian, and, in addition, my standardized test scores were the highest in the county for any student—African American or white. This, they reported, qualified me to receive a four-year scholarship to the University of Alabama. Apparently a written policy, or maybe just tradition, held that the student with both the highest grade point average and the highest standardized test score in the county would receive a four-year scholarship to the flagship state school. (In the years since then, I have not been able to obtain any written policy regarding this scholarship.) The principal and guidance counselor thought that this year, unlike earlier years when the student with those statistics happened to be African American, I might actually receive the scholarship to the University of Alabama rather than a scholarship to one of the other state-supported colleges. Although I was not sure that the experience would be a good one, I was willing to attempt to attend the University of Alabama.

On May 15, 1963, almost exactly nine years after *Brown*, at the commencement exercises for my high school graduation from the segregated Baldwin County Training School, I listened angrily as my high school principal announced to the crowd that I was valedictorian, had received the highest standardized test scores in the county, but had not been awarded a four-year scholarship to the University of Alabama. Instead, I had been awarded a scholarship to a school that had recently lost its accreditation. Although this was 1963, nine years post-*Brown*, my educational prospects were little different than they would have been pre-*Brown*.

This turn of events, along with the many civil rights events of this time, led me to select Fisk University as my college of choice. Fisk students were at the forefront of the civil rights movement, and I desperately wanted to be among people who were actively involved in helping to bring about the changes that were sure to come, and quickly.

Although *Brown* did not have a direct impact on my life during my school years, it has given me an opportunity to educate my law students, today, about the realities of life pre-*Brown*. *Brown* is included in the structural injunction section of most remedies casebooks, and I have used it as a springboard for many discussions in my remedies classes. My students have told me how much my story added to their understanding and knowledge of the conditions that led to the Court's decision. My objective in sharing my story with my students is to help them to come to know the story behind the story of *Brown* and similar cases during that era. The lives of real people had been adversely affected by segregated schools, and the lives of real people were positively affected by the *Brown* decision. Although the teachers at Baldwin County Training School were bright and dedicated people who worked miracles with the meager resources that they were given, the quality of the overall educational experience under the de jure segregated system was clearly inferior. It was inferior in part because of the inequitable distribution of resources, including the number of teachers and facilities, but in large part it was inferior because of its single-dimensional focus. Just as I believe that my students can benefit from hearing my story and my perspective, I believe that my educational experience could have been significantly enriched through interaction with different-minded students. I, and the white students at Baldwin County High School, missed out on the intellectual growth that often takes place through grappling with differences and unpleasant topics. As I reflect on my school days in Alabama, which I remember quite fondly, I believe that the Supreme Court got it right in *Brown*: "Separate educational facilities are inherently unequal."

Paulette J. Delk was born in Mobile, Alabama, in February 1947. She attended elementary and secondary schools in Daphne from 1952 to 1963. She was formerly an associate professor of law at the University of Memphis, Cecil C. Humphreys School of Law in Memphis, Tennessee. She is now a U.S. bankruptcy judge and since July 2006 has sat on the bench of the U.S. Bankruptcy Court for the Western District of Tennessee.

7   Loss of Innocence

Angela Mae Kupenda

I don't wanna go to school with those mean white kids,
cause they don't want me there. I wanna go back to a school
where people liked me.

>   —Me to my mother in 1966

You might as well forget about making A's. You won't be
making those anymore. Next year you'll be in school mostly
with white kids. And you'll see that Negro kids are not as
smart as white kids. I'm not trying to hurt your feelings, just
prepare you.

>   —A black teacher to me in 1971. (I responded,
>   "Yes, ma'am." But I said to myself, We'll see.)

Yes, the white students and teachers are wrong. . . . They are
ignorant, not racist. . . . I know it hurts. But I'm sorry, . . .
I have no power here, . . . I can't help you. You're on your
own.

>   —Typical comment from numerous sympathetic
>   and unhelpful white teachers to me from 1971 to
>   the present

As you read the dates on the epigraphs, you may think my history is off. It is not. *Brown v. Board of Education* was decided in 1954. Although I was born after *Brown* in Jackson, Mississippi, in 1956, I did not attend student-integrated schools until the 1970–1971 academic year, when a mini-busload of about twenty white children began to attend our otherwise black elementary and junior high school. I was in the ninth grade.

Although I remain firm in my conviction that *Brown* was necessary, I know that everything necessary is not necessarily easy or pleasant. *Brown* and the entire civil rights struggle opened new opportunities for me and many others, bringing many positive changes.

Still, the more things change, the more they stay the same. Therefore the purpose of this essay is, first, to examine some of the voices from my past during that turbulent time and, second, to reflect on how these voices continue to echo in my present.

"I don't wanna go to school with those mean white kids, cause they don't want me there. I wanna go back to a school where people liked me." I can remember crying those words to my mother as if I had said them yesterday. But it was in 1966. I was almost ten years old and preparing to enter the fifth grade in the fall. For years, I knew something was going on in Mississippi. Although we lived in colored neighborhoods and shopped mainly in stores with colored people, I had learned from television and from riding in the car that paler colored people lived in big houses in our city. Whenever colored faces—other than the colored people on the *Amos & Andy Show* and colored people the police were looking for—came on television, the station would suddenly have trouble and the screen would black out. I had heard the whispered adult conversations at my grandparents' house in Port Gibson, something about a NAACP and boycotts. At times I worried about the whispers, but mainly I concentrated on playing with my white dolls with the long pretty hair and my one colored doll that my uncle in the military had sent me from overseas, and studying ants. I nagged my mother to buy all the hair products the pink girls on television used to remove all the tangles from their hair. And I watched the way the ants in the yard of our shotgun house worked hard to rebuild their homes whenever their mounds were accidentally knocked down by rain or my own feet.

All of this started to change in 1965 when I was told that all the schools were being redistricted. I was attending my favorite elementary school, Walton Elementary School, which was a short walk from my house. My mother explained I would have about an hour walk to attend my new school, Morrison Elementary School (she wanted us to walk around the street and not cut through the alleys). She explained the student reassignment had to do with a law requiring white and colored kids to go to school together. I was naively excited and wondered aloud if there would be white kids at my school. She laughed and said no, explaining the city was redrawing district lines but maintaining mostly separate schools. Even my small eight-year-old brain realized that did not make any sense if they really wanted to have integrated schools. My mother shook her head and laughed some more, murmuring that maybe the white folks really don't want equality. I was not satisfied with her answer and started to watch white people even more intensely whenever I came across them. Even more interesting to me was the way colored people acted all prim and proper around white people.

The next year I walked the long walk to Morrison Elementary School. Walking on the other side of the street were the colored students who had to walk the long opposite way to my old school, Walton. Those colored kids were mad and would holler nasty things across the street to those of us going to their old school, Morrison. My mother explained to me that they were angry and hurt and looking for someone to blame. So she made my older brother walk with me for a few weeks, but eventually I was on my own again and along the way trying to make new friends. I made it through that year. Even though I never really fit in, I made good grades.

Before school turned out, the school sent home a deceptively lovely letter explaining that now all the Negro and Caucasian children could pick the school they wanted to attend. The list included all the Negro and Caucasian schools in the city. I was so excited. I wanted to return to Walton. But my mother had promised some lady that she would try to encourage me to attend the white school, which was just a little farther than the school I loved. I didn't want to hear it. All I could think about was going back to Walton, where people liked me and where my only worry walking to school was always needlessly wondering if the big machine washing the streets would wet up my clothes or if the man driving the machine would cut off the water as the machine approached me. So we checked the box for Walton and I helped mail the form in.

I busied myself that summer watering my plants and studying white people on television and wherever I saw them. We also visited my grandparents, where I hid around the corners to hear the adult talk about voting, boycotts, and the NAACP. When the school registration information on the freedom-of-choice program came back in the mail, I saw that I had been assigned to the white school, not Walton. And I cried, "I don't wanna go to school with those mean white kids, cause they don't want me there. I wanna go back to a school where people liked me." I had seen the white people on television saying they did not want the integrated schools. They did not want their children in school with Negroes (but they never said the word "Negro" quite right). They had looked so mean and hateful and had said many nasty things about Negro people. I cried and cried (and am almost moved to tears right now remembering all of this). My mother told me that I was as smart and smarter than those white kids. She said they wanted some smart Negro kids to go to the white school. But when she saw how upset and scared I was, she promised to straighten it all out. By the time she did, we ended up moving out to the county, in the "country." Good grief—I didn't want to go to the white school, but I didn't want to move way out in the woods either. My father had made that decision without discussing it with any of us. We had liked living in the city, taking the buses, walking to the stores. But we had no choice. So we moved to the county.

There I attended an all-black school from the fifth through the eighth grades. White neighborhoods were right next to Negro neighborhoods, but blockades separated the ends of the streets, and there were separate schools.

I attended West Side Elementary and Junior High School. For a while, my family members were "big shots" because we were from the city, made good grades, and lived in a brand-new three-bedroom, two-bath home. My father was making almost a hundred dollars a week and my mother was selling Avon, so others thought we were rich. But we weren't. And we were in chaos at home, as my mother was realizing she was going to have to leave my father, who was becoming more and more abusive and controlling and staying out later and later at night.

At West Side, I made very good grades. But the world was changing. We became "black" people, and we were proud. Good people like Dr. King were murdered. Adults whispered more and more. In my seventh and eighth grades we got some white teachers and lost some of the favorite black teachers. I watched the white teachers closely. Some kids were mean to them. And some kids gushed all over them, asking to touch their hair and stuff. I did neither. I did my work and studied them. If they were nice and helpful white teachers, I took up for them when my classmates said mean things about, or to, them. In the ninth grade, a few white kids came to our school. It seemed to me that the more white people came to our school, the more things we got. When the white teachers came, we got a library and better books. Then we got a science lab. A few years later, we actually got equipment for our science lab. But we students worried because didn't know what would happen to us after the ninth grade; West Side only went to the ninth grade.

We were finally told. The kids at my school were going to have to be bused. There was no high school near our neighborhood. We were given a choice of being bused about thirty minutes to a predominantly white school, or about one and a half hours to a predominantly black school. Most of us chose Forest Hill High School, the predominantly white school. Some black kids had already attended there under the freedom-of-choice program. So we had heard about the very hard time they had there with the white students and teachers.

At the end of the ninth grade I graduated as valedictorian of my class, almost straight A's. The other kids in the top four had parents who were college educated, teachers, lawyers, et cetera. By my ninth grade, my parents were separated and my mother was working two jobs to support us and carrying a baby. Six of us were living in a one-bedroom shotgun house. With everything going on, I was surprised and proud that I was valedictorian.

Maybe I was looking too proud. One of my black teachers approached me and said, "You might as well forget about making A's. You won't be making those anymore. Next year you'll be in school mostly with white kids. And you'll see that Negro kids are not as smart as white kids. I'm not trying to hurt your feelings, just prepare you." "I responded, "Yes, ma'am." But I said to myself, We'll see.

When the black teacher said that to me, I became scared and angry. I had watched the white kids on television and the ones who came to my school. They did not seem like they were that "bad." (You see, "bad" meant "good," when blacks talked in hip slang.) But they did seem to carry a certain power with them and seemed to think they could have whatever they wanted. I told my mother what the teacher had said. My mother laughed and told me, "You will still make A's. Because you are a smart girl. Doesn't that Negro teacher know that most black folks are smarter than white folks?" Well, I went to the white school. I did not expect good treatment from the white students. But I thought the sympathetic (former hippie-type) white teachers would be more helpful.

I learned, though, that the hip and sympathetic white teachers were actually scared of the white students and other white folks! For example, when we could not get a black cheerleader elected or could not get black officers elected, or when no black was allowed to read the prayer on the intercom during the schoolwide Christian devotion each morning, or when the black athletes were punished for refusing to stand at attention as the Confederate flag was waved while the band played "I wish I were in Dixie" during the pep rallies, and on and on, some of the sympathetic white teachers would say things like, "Yes, the white students and teachers are wrong, . . . They are ignorant, not racist. . . . I know it hurts. But I'm sorry, . . . I have no power here, . . . I can't help you. You're on your own." Although I was a good and disciplined student, I did not consider myself a leader. Still, those sympathetic teachers would always seek me out especially to say that to me. At first I would try to explain to them what they could do to help. But eventually I realized that my reasoning with them was useless, and I would just look at those teachers without speaking and walk away.

A few times, though, one would seem to almost understand. I was taking speech and was in a play. By then, I was so disgusted with the racism in my school that I really did not want to participate. But my eleventh-grade white speech teacher had persuaded me to give it a try. I played the role of a schoolteacher in the play. And at one point in the script I was to have a conflict with the students and was to push some of them to the side. I was not supposed to really push them—the speech teacher had told them to spread apart when I reached my hands out toward them. Well, one of the white girls was quite competitive with me and had been harassing me all year (she had a twin sister, though, who was very pleasant). But I refused to argue or fight with her. Before the scene, I saw her whispering with the other white students in the play. She encouraged the other white kids not to spread out when I reached out my hands and to face me off. In the rehearsal when I, according to script, yelled for them to step back and reached out my hands, they would not move. The mob of reddened white faces just sneered at me with the meanest and most evil looks. The one girl spat out, "Make us!" And that was not in the script. I was almost in tears. The white teacher jumped up, after a while, and screamed for me to knock the "hell" out of them if they wouldn't move. And I then sure tried to. After that, I quit the play and stayed out of school for a few days. The teacher, I was told, gave the white students a hard lecture that made a number of them cry. She made some of them formally apologize to me. Then she told me, "Yes, the white students are wrong. Some of the teachers are wrong. They are ignorant, and some are racist. I know it hurts. But I'm sorry. I hope you return to the play for yourself, not for them. I will help you all I can, but I have little power here." I did return to the play and the performance went off without a hitch.

I did graduate as the first black valedictorian of Forest Hill High School in 1974, but only after several white teachers tried to take the honor from me to bestow on a white girl whose grade average was slightly lower than mine. Their justification was that I had attended a black school for the ninth grade, and those grades should have been discounted. The night of the graduation we could not afford to pay the official photographer for a picture. My older brother was determined to get a picture of me doing my valedictory speech. (He was one of those athletes who had been punished for not saluting the Confederate flag.) He climbed over the railings onto the football field with his camera and took a lovely picture of me wearing all my green eye shadow and saying my speech. Before he snapped the picture, someone yelled, "Nigger, get off the field." I just kept saying my speech. But I wonder now if they were yelling to him or me.

So in a sense, I won and *Brown* made it possible. I proved to myself that I am at least as smart as white people, in spite of the racism and financial struggles I experience. If it were not for *Brown*, I don't know what my inner and outer life circumstances would be. I can't imagine living in a society today where I would be working hard and paying taxes for fancy public schools that the law mandates little black children cannot attend because of the color of their skin. I have a hard enough time dealing with white flight and all of the covert and overt racism I still face.

Moreover, I am not persuaded at all that over the past fifty years white folks' hearts would have changed so that all of the past lawful discrimination and state-sanctioned oppression would have ended because they all finally found Jesus and love. Even with *Brown*, we still face a racist society. White teachers make more money than I do for doing the same, or less, work. We still have hate crimes, racial profiling, conscious and unconscious racism, et cetera.

Although in many ways I won with the help of *Brown*, along the way I lost a lot. I lost my racial innocence. The voices from my past keep showing up in the present. Even today I face many sympathetic white people who are still afraid, or unwilling, to challenge racist white people and systems. They are afraid to face the racism even in their own hearts. Dr. King called these fearful and unhelpful ones the "white moderates" and said they are as much a problem as the active white racists.

I also lost my innocence about my own people. Just like the black teacher in 1971, some of us black people really think that white people are smarter. Not only do we pollute our own minds with those lies, we pollute each other and hold each other back.

And perhaps the greatest loss was I realized I will probably never feel at home again in most predominantly white settings and in many places in the United States. I keep looking for a job or school where I am accepted and given an equal opportunity. In my fifty-two years, I've had only a few work experiences like that.

The voices from the past continue to echo in my present. But as time goes on and those of us who are scared find courage to be just and brave, perhaps the echo will become fainter and fainter. And one day, maybe our country will not only celebrate audibly the victory of *Brown*; one day, hopefully, the message of equality from *Brown* will also resonate in our hearts and deeds.

Angela Mae Kupenda was born in Jackson, Mississippi, in September 1956 and attended public elementary and secondary schools in Mississippi from 1962 to 1974. She is now professor of law at the Mississippi College School of Law, Jackson.

8   Toto, I Have a Feeling
We Are Still in Kansas

Sharon E. Rush

Brown v. Board of Education shapes the lives of everyone in this country, even though most people are not aware of the details of the decision. In fact, the lay understanding of *Brown* probably is limited to knowing that it ended de jure segregation in public schools. While the importance of this cannot be overstated, white society's enduring attachment to *Brown* is not so much its holding as what the case has come to symbolize: the end of racism in the United States.

I suggest this because most whites today believe in racial equality and think racism is an extreme form of behavior practiced by individuals. In its grossest form, of course, racism is slavery. When we abolished slavery, however, we entered into the period of de jure segregation, which today's whites also recognize as racism. Today's whites probably also agree that the de facto segregation that persisted as some states resisted integration also was racist. But many whites think all those racist practices were years ago. Today's racists, then, are KKK members or whites who use racial epithets. They are *not* white people of goodwill, most of whom sincerely think that racism all but ended with *Brown*.

Three aspects of my life give me insights into *Brown* that cause me to disagree with most white folks about its meaning. My family roots are in Lomax, Alabama, where my extended family still is clustered around what was once my grandparents' home just off the main two-lane highway between Montgomery and Birmingham. The seeds for fighting racism were planted at an early age. More influential, however, are the facts that I am the white mother of a black daughter and a professor of constitutional law specializing in racial equality issues. My background, my love for my daughter, and my research on race enable me to understand racism in ways I otherwise would not. Because my deeper understanding of racism comes from my experiences straddling the color line, perhaps my insights can help other whites gain a deeper understanding of their own limited views of racism.

My Earliest Memories about Race

When I attended first grade in Birmingham, Alabama, in 1958, I had no idea that segregation was unlawful. But I knew all too well that segregation was white society's preferred social system. By the age of six, I had been taught that blacks and whites should stay far away from each other, because blacks were not really human beings. I do not remember being told this in so many words, but I got the message just about everywhere I went. White/Colored signs still hung over drinking fountains; I was not allowed to play with black children across the railroad tracks; some of my relatives would openly deride blacks; I was not allowed to pet a dog if its owner was black.

By second grade, my family had moved to upstate New York. I cannot remember what the so-called racial climate was in Ithaca then, and certainly the South did not have exclusive claims to racism, but my summer visits to Alabama brought mixed emotions. I liked going on vacation, but I dreaded the atmosphere of racism that I knew would sweep over me as we pulled into my grandmother's driveway. Children made up games to describe blacks in dehumanizing ways. It made me ashamed and I hid under the front porch to avoid participating. Like the rural poverty and Alabama summer heat, racism had its own oppressive heaviness that weighed me down.

My parents played a huge role in teaching me that racism is wrong. What I did not understand as a little girl is why other whites did not know that. Over the years, of course, I have learned that whites have always known racism is wrong, but, to this day, white society is unwilling to assume responsibility for the havoc it has wreaked on the souls of blacks, as W. E. B. DuBois described it. The older *Brown* gets, the more unwilling white society is to explore our history and its connection to modern racism and inequality. *Brown* has become the turning point for racial equality and provides proof that white society no longer regards blacks as less than human. "The human race is the only race" is a common mantra in white society.

My Research on *Brown* and the Color Line

Notwithstanding the rhetoric, however, deep inside their minds and hearts, most whites continue to believe they are superior to blacks and people of color, generally. They will never admit this and, in fact, probably most whites do not even realize they believe it. As Charles Lawrence explains, most whites' racism is "unconscious."[1] Most whites remain unaware that racism is only partially about discrimination; it also is about white privilege. Whites are privileged in the United States because we do not have to overcome the consequences of slavery, de jure segregation, de facto segregation, the negative stereotypes about people of color, and all the concomitant inequality that accompanies our history. In fact, unlike people of color, whites can mediate everyday activities without thinking about their race because most whites are unaware they even have a race. In this way, whites think *Brown* means that people of color can stop thinking about race too. Just like the yellow-brick road led Dorothy to Oz, the *Brown*-beaten path has taken America to color blindness. If people of color would just accept color blindness, then all this talk about race would go away.

Ironically, rather than erasing the inequality color line in the United States, *Brown* razored it deeper into the white mind. Rather than taking us to color blindness and nationwide equality, *Brown*'s path has taken us right back to what Topeka, Kansas, looked like before *Brown*: segregated and unequal. America's journey to equality has been a dream, not like the one Martin Luther King envisioned, but more like Dorothy's nightmare.

This entrenchment of racial inequality stems from two core assumptions made by the Court: that black and white schools were equal with respect to "tangibles," and that de jure segregation sent a message of black inferiority that hurt only black children. These assumptions reinforced white society's belief in the validity of the race myth—the myth of white superiority and black inferiority.

Let me focus on the first assumption, that black and white schools were economically equal. Everyone knew, of course, that black and white schools were not equal *by any stretch of the imagination* with respect to "tangibles." The *Brown* Court made this assumption so that it could focus on de jure segregation and rule it unconstitutional. Ignoring economics to focus on race seemed like a good idea—as if the history of slavery and de jure segregation had nothing to do with the extant economic inequality. Yet future Courts would use this utterly false assumption to justify the enduring racial inequality that we see today.

All it took to unravel *Brown* was a case involving racial minority children attending a racially identifiable school where the "tangibles" were woefully unequal. Enter *Rodriguez*, decided only one generation after *Brown*. The Mexican American plaintiffs in *Rodriguez* argued that their schools were not economically equal to the schools attended primarily by white children. Whereas the *Brown* Court ignored economics to focus on race, the *Rodriguez* Court ignored race to focus on economics. Unable to acknowledge the connection between the historical and the enduring racial inequality in America, the *Rodriguez* Court held that economic discrimination in public school funding is constitutional. *Rodriguez* ensured the persistence of racial inequality in our public schools because neighborhood schools remain racially identifiable and their funding is based on property taxes. Like de jure segregation, *Rodriguez* is premised on the inferiority of minority children, because it sends a resounding message across the United States and the world that children of color are unworthy of receiving an education of equal quality to that of white children.

There is another hidden message in both *Brown* and *Rodriguez,* which brings me to the second faulty assumption made by the *Brown* Court. No one questions that de jure segregation hurt black children, but the Court was wrong to assume that it hurt *only* black children. The myth of black inferiority exists against the backdrop of white superiority, but the Court never mentions this latter component of racial inequality. De jure segregation was not just about keeping blacks in their place as less than human, it also literally was about preserving the best public places for whites. The *Brown* Court's silence about the assumption that the race myth hurts all children, including white children, essentially rendered whiteness invisible to discussions of race discrimination *except* when the allegedly injured person is white.

In the context of public schools, *Brown*'s silent assumption that whites are superior to other races plays out in affirmative action, beginning with the seminal case of *Bakke.* An extremely important point about *Bakke* is missing from the debate, which I think highlights how shallow America's commitment is to racial equality in education, notwithstanding *Brown.* Most applicants to medical school are about twenty-two to twenty-three years old, yet Allan Bakke was denied admission to Davis in 1973 and 1974—only nineteen to twenty years after *Brown.* The minority applicants in Davis, like Allan Bakke, were born during de jure segregation. Moreover, some states fiercely resisted *Brown* and obstructed integration efforts well into the late 1960s. It was impossible to think for a minute that the minority applicants applying to Davis presented educational backgrounds equal to those of Bakke and other white applicants. Not enough time had elapsed between *Brown* and *Bakke* for the minority applicants to be old enough to have escaped the inequality visited upon them *by de jure segregation itself.* If any applicants to a state university deserved to be considered under an affirmative action policy, surely it was the minorities who applied to Davis.

Yet Bakke won his suit under a theory of "reverse discrimination." The silent voice of white superiority in *Brown* came roaring out of its den in *Bakke.* Ironically, the *Bakke* Court was not concerned with the *absence* of racial minorities at Davis sending a message of inferiority. Rather, the *Bakke* Court said that the minorities' *presence* at Davis under the set-aside plan sent a message of their inferiority by stigmatizing them. Within one generation of *Brown,* a white person essentially was able to shut down the theory of affirmative action—a very modest policy in the struggle for racial equality.

Thus, *Brown*'s core assumptions explain both why our schools remain segregated and unequal, and why white society is unmotivated to do anything about it. Ruling de jure segregation unconstitutional was the right holding, but

Brown nevertheless sanctioned the myth of white superiority and black inferiority as seen in cases like *Rodriguez* and *Bakke*. It is impossible to underestimate the silent effect *Brown* has had on the lives of both people of color and whites in this country. Let me share a bit about how it has affected my personal life as a mother of a black daughter.

Brown and Its Impact on Personal Lives

As a mother, I am particularly concerned with equality in education, the heart of *Brown*, and the role teachers in public schools play in promoting equality. For at least thirty years, over 90 percent of public schools teachers in the United States have been white and over 80 percent have been white women.[2] Reluctantly and sadly, but consistent with the theory of unconscious racism, I have concluded that most white teachers are teaching the validity of the myth of white superiority and black inferiority. This lesson hurts *all* children because it is quite destructive of both democratic and human ideals.

One example illustrates how the limits of *Brown* are lived in the modern classroom. The example stems from my daughter being assigned *Huckleberry Finn* in middle school. Although her school was private, this is a good example because the inclusion of *Huck* in our children's mandatory public school curricula is an issue that affects thousands of students nationwide every year.[3] Only Shakespeare is assigned more frequently than *Huck*.[4] My daughter's personal reaction to it inspired me to reread it so that I could better understand the impact it had on her. My experience with *Huck* gives me insights into the nature of the debate that I think most whites fail to understand or they would not continue to revere and teach the book as an antiracist classic.

By the second page of *Huck*, my daughter was bewildered and asked me, "Why would my teacher have me read this?" She was offended by Twain's use of the racial epithet that appears 213 times in the novel, and could not understand why her teacher, I'll call him Mr. Smith, would ask her to read a book that portrays blacks as less than human. Moreover, Mr. Smith did not even give her (or me) a heads-up warning or talk with her about the book before assigning it. She clearly felt betrayed by him, a man she truly loves and admires. In her final assignment, she summed up her sentiments: "I think Mark Twain was racist because he made even Huck call himself the N-word. To me, this meant Twain was saying blacks have no heart, no dignity, no soul."

When I asked Mr. Smith if he would assign a book that was as demeaning of any other racial group as *Huck* is to blacks, he replied, "I might if it were a classic." Silence followed as we both tried to think of what *that* book might be. I concluded his point was rhetorical, because he broke the silence by extolling the virtues of *Huck* and justified his decision by reminding me that blacks were called by the epithet in Twain's times. In other words, *Huck* was historically accurate, and how can anyone be upset when teachers teach history? he wanted to know.

Mr. Smith, like most white people of goodwill, would never intentionally promote racial inequality among his students. In reality, though, Mr. Smith's choice to assign *Huck* segregated my daughter, the only black child in the class, from her classmates. The segregation was not physical; in this way her class was integrated, consistent with *Brown's* principle that segregation in public schools is unconstitutional. Rather, the segregation she experienced was emotional, but it functioned as if she had been physically sent to her own space in the room—space away from her white classmates. My daughter was the only one in the class whose racial identity was connected to Jim, the runaway slave. She was the only one who could have been called the racial epithet in a hurtful way. She was the only one whose literary imagination had no "fun" place to go as white students ventured along with Huck, the rebellious teenager.

Educators know that undermining students' self-esteem is wrong, but black society relates that this is what happens to many black students who are required to read *Huck*. Unless one consciously or unconsciously believes in the validity of the race myth, one respectfully accepts blacks' evaluation that the book should not be part of mandatory curricula. Certainly, *Huck* is a poor curriculum choice, because it is unhealthy to ask black students to identify with a character like Jim who is portrayed as less than human, notwithstanding any positive characteristics Twain gives him. Most white teachers justify teaching *Huck* because they use it to denounce slavery and racism, goals consistent with a democratic education. Surely these lessons can be taught in ways that enable whites to learn about racism without exploiting the emotions of blacks.

In an effort to transcend the limits of *Brown*, it is also imperative for whites to acknowledge and confront the white privilege that lurks both in the novel itself and in the decision to teach the novel. Encouraging and expecting white students to identify with a character like Huck, who intentionally mistreats Jim *even after* Huck decides he would rather lose his soul than return Jim to slavery, is a lesson in the validity of the race myth, particularly white superiority. Why? Because in the end, most white readers are taught to believe that Huck's decision turns on the fact that he comes to love Jim. In what relationship, other than an interracial one, do we teach our children that love can be abusive? Disrespectful? Premised on the superiority of one partner and inferiority of the other? Indeed, when Jim reveals himself in the end to help Tom Sawyer out of trouble, Jim is unaware that he has been freed by Miss Watson and believes he will be returned to slavery. Jim's willingness to sacrifice his freedom for Tom's welfare causes Huck to exclaim, "I knowed he was white inside."[5] Huck's affection for Jim may be greater in the end than it was in the beginning of the novel, but it *never* gets beyond a fundamental belief in the race myth. The only way Huck can "see" Jim's humanity is to turn him into a white person. If Huck does not love Jim's blackness, he does not love Jim.

Finally, *Huck* is used to portray Huck's moral development from a supporter of slavery to an abolitionist. A close reading of the novel reveals that this conclusion is overstated, but even if one accepts it, it is immersed in white privilege. Huck's dilemma—whether to return Jim to slavery or help him escape—was not a *real* moral dilemma, and to present it that way privileges whiteness because it suggests that the question of the immorality of slavery was a close call. This allows whites a way out of confronting just how blatantly evil slavery was. Certainly, whites have always known that slavery is immoral, and inviting children to struggle along with Huck sanctions the validity of the race myth. All students must wonder why it is appropriate for their teacher to hurt blacks *sometimes*. This lesson is legitimized because it is has the imprimatur of the state whenever a public schools teacher imposes *Huck* on her students. All students carry this message and concomitant corollaries into their adult worlds, and the cycle perpetuates itself with each new generation.

NOTES
1. Charles R. Lawrence, "The Id, the Ego, and Equal Protection: Reckoning with Unconscious Racism," *Stanford Law Review* 39 (1987), 317.
2. "Men in Teaching Fall to a 40-Year Low, Survey Finds," *New York Times*, August 28, 2003 (citing a 2000–2001 survey by the National Education Association).
3. I expound on these ideas in more detail in *Huck Finn's "Hidden Lessons": Teaching and Learning across the Color Line* (Lanham, Md.: Rowman and Littlefield, 2006).
4. Elaine Mensh and Harry Mensh, *Black, White, and Huckleberry Finn: Re-Imagining the American Dream* (Tuscaloosa: University of Alabama Press, 2000), 13.
5. Mark Twain, *The Adventures of Huckleberry Finn* (New York: Tom Doherty Associates, 1989), Chapter 16.

Sharon E. Rush was born in Jasper, Indiana, in December 1951. She attended first grade in Birmingham, Alabama, and secondary school in Ithaca, New York. She is now the Irving Cypen Professor of Law at the University of Florida in Gainesville.

9   Becoming a Legal Troublemaker

Michael Allan Wolf

I grew up in a society stained by lawlessness. My hometown, Lakeland, Florida, dubbed "Citrus Capital of the World" by local promoters, is situated near the center of Interstate 4, the highway that runs across the midsection of the Sunshine State. As I was born in December 1952, I have no recollection of the *Brown I* and *II* decisions when the Warren Court announced them during my toddlerhood. What I do recall—and quite vividly—is the yawning gap between the law in the books and the law in practice that had a strong impact on my life and worldview even after I left my hometown for college in the fall of 1970.

Throughout the 1950s and well into the 1960s, the signs and shackles of American apartheid defined the landscape of Central Florida. The 1960 U.S. Census reports that the population of the county in which Lakeland sits was about 18 percent African American. Whites and African Americans were educated at separate schools, ate at separate restaurants, attended separate movie theatres, and sipped from separate water fountains. Sometimes the label "Colored" appeared on a bathroom door; most of the time even small children needed no sign to know which public services were set aside for those with darker skin. The white and African American parts of town were literally divided by railroad tracks, and my family and our friends rarely had reason to visit that part of Lakeland that lacked essential and decent public amenities.

By their words and actions, my parents—both born and raised in the North—taught my siblings and me that racial segregation was a shameful practice. Still, almost our only social interaction with nonwhites was between our extended family and the adults and children of the extended African American family that worked as our housekeepers and landscapers. As Jews in a small Southern city, we were keenly aware of the resentment and even hatred that many of our neighbors felt for religious and racial outliers. Despite the significant social and economic gaps that separated our two family circles, we had in common the majority's prejudice and distrust.

I wrote "*almost* our only social interaction" because my brother and I still remember that, for some curious reason, children of both races were permitted to swim together in the city-owned pool in the late 1950s. These African

American children would not join me and other whites in public school in meaningful numbers until officials closed the doors of all-black Rochelle High School in 1969. The presence of a very few token children of color who appeared in the white schools before that time only accentuated the hypocrisy of the situation.

For a decade and a half, from 1954 to 1969, Lakeland's children and adults, white and nonwhite, knew that the law in the books said that the city's separate and unequal public school system was illegal. But the law in practice said otherwise. Local and state legislators, school officials, judges, police officers, and prosecutors defied the law, and there was no loud outcry from the media, business leaders, local college professors, or, perhaps most disappointingly, the bar.

As I made my way through elementary and high school, the failure of public officials to heed *Brown* helped bring into focus other lawless aspects of my community. The Supreme Court's decisions invalidating official prayers and Bible reading in public schools appeared in the summers preceding my fifth and sixth grades (1962 and 1963), which *should* have meant the end of these and other examples of church-state commingling that in large part defined our public school day. For example, before *Schempp* and *Engel* introduced expanded boundaries for the Establishment Clause, at Cleveland Court Elementary School classroom recitation of the Lord's Prayer was commonplace, my classmates and I were rewarded with star-shaped stickers for memorizing the King James version of the Twenty-third Psalm, and membership in the Glee Club meant proclaiming to the world that "Christ the Savior is born." Nevertheless, by the time I reached high school, the overtly Christian and Jewish religious readings that had disappeared a few years before were creeping back, read by students over the loudspeaker as meditations for the beginning of the school day.

In what I look back now on as my first experience as a legal troublemaker, I confronted the school administration over this issue, pointing out that the courts had clearly ruled such practices unconstitutional. And they backed down. Would I have had the temerity to speak up in this manner had my community not been tainted by its lawless reaction to *Brown*? I earnestly do not believe that I would have.

Always a politically active family, our hopes for real change in the racial arena seemed shattered by the murder of John Kennedy. Little did we know that JFK's successor, a Southern Democrat, would so powerfully and effectively wield the tools in the federal legal arsenal to bring the hitherto-ignored substance and spirit of *Brown* to life for millions of African Americans. I can still remember watching the large, awkward figure of Lyndon Baines Johnson on the television screen. The majesty of his phrases soared over the airwaves, despite their often uninspiring medium—a thick Southwestern drawl. The activist judges that LBJ (like his predecessor) appointed to the federal bench demonstrated their strong disfavor for recalcitrant and defiant officials who failed to heed the early Warren Court's mandates in *Brown*. For many Americans, LBJ's legacy has suffered a steep declension from the grandiose dreams of a Great Society to the Vietnam nightmare. To this day, because he was the first political figure to instill hope that an active central government could effect positive social change, particularly in the area of racial equality, my admiration for LBJ has withstood the attacks of revisionists and second-guessers from all segments of the political mainstream.

My postsecondary education and career were also influenced by the negative reception *Brown* received from governmental actors before the Johnson administration. As a history and English major at Emory University in the early 1970s, I felt the gravitational pull of those professors and courses that explored in a critical way the crucial intersections between law and society. My constitutional history instructor, Jack Rabun, helped open my eyes to the many ways in which American partisan politics and law were inextricably (and often regrettably) intertwined. Bell Wiley, Emory's Civil War and Southern-history professor—a giant in his field as teacher and scholar—invited a leading African American civil rights activist to participate in a fascinating give-and-take with our class. I became optimistic that closing the post-*Brown* gap between the law in the books and the law in action might be possible should talented individuals such as our guest (who was later elected to high public office) be given the opportunity to shape the nation's statutes and legal opinions.

In my American literature classes, I had a great advantage over my classmates from suburban New York, Philadelphia, and Washington, D.C., the well-educated sons and daughters of professionals and businesspeople who had only read about the places, jobs, and social obligations that were assigned solely to African Americans. William Faulkner and Mark Twain especially were much more alive to those of us who were raised in a society scarred by deep dividing lines that stubbornly resisted the Supreme Court's stirring attempts at erasure.

When my law studies began in the nation's capital the same month that Richard Nixon left the presidency in shame, black letter law and traditional doctrines lost the battle for my attention to the political and social forces that shaped the contours of our evolving legal system. If I not been raised in a society tainted by lawlessness, perhaps this proto–legal realism would still have emerged, but it is equally likely that, like most of my classmates and professors, I would have answered the siren's call of formalism and legal autonomy. Ultimately, this frustration with the law business led me down a much different road than my classmates in the Georgetown Law class of 1977.

That road was Interstate 95 North, and the destination was Cambridge, specifically Harvard's PhD program in the history of American civilization. For the next few years, as a student and instructor in American history (social and legal) and literature, I was challenged by leading scholars in several fields to explore the ways in which law effected, and was affected by, societal and political change.

By the time of my arrival in the Bay State, the ugliness of discrimination and racial violence had besmirched the legacy of egalitarianism that Boston had cherished since the days of abolitionism. In fact, four months after my arrival, a group of African American schoolchildren from a town near Philadelphia was attacked by white youths wielding hockey sticks and a golf club as the students were waiting for a public bus after visiting the Bunker Hill Monument in Charlestown. When, a few years later, one of my African American students explained to me that her mother had warned her to stay out of certain neighborhoods and suburbs, it was clear that Boston's minorities confronted a different and perhaps more virulent brand of racial hatred than did their counterparts in my hometown.

The late 1970s and early 1980s saw the Harvard Law faculty's initial flirtations with critical legal studies. Yet, despite my deep and abiding belief in law as politics (and the positive model of provocative teacher and innovative scholar that Morton Horwitz provided), I was never attracted by that magnetic movement. Looking back on those exciting years, I believe that I can identify as the chief reason for my resistance the great disdain that many radical "crits" harbored for American liberals. To join or follow these scholars on their creative journey would have meant abandoning personal heroes such as LBJ and William O. Douglas, and this was a step I was not ready to take.

I was quite fortunate during my years at Harvard to work closely with Charles Haar, the architect of key Great Society economic development and beautification programs who in the late 1960s had provided an uncannily accurate prediction of the dangers posed to society should Washington fail to follow up initial federal forays into the inner city with more ambitious funding and investment programs. My first assignment as his research associate was to do legal historical research for a book on the common-law duty to provide equal municipal services on both sides of the tracks. This study was inspired in part by the Supreme Court's refusal in the late 1970s to adopt an effects test for racial and other invidious forms of discrimination under the Fourteenth Amendment, a move that Court critics saw as a betrayal of the message of *Brown*. It was just the beginning of our long collaboration and friendship.

When, in 1982, I left Massachusetts for my first law-teaching job in Oklahoma City, I found myself in the peculiar situation of teaching, and testing students on their knowledge of, the law in the books. Despite this obligation, not surprisingly, I also tried to instill in my students some concern that society did not always heed the most well-intentioned legal mandates.

My scholarship, almost from the beginning, overtly attempted to bridge the gap that had informed my perceptions as a child of the post-*Brown* South.

Along with legal history, the other major focus of my early research and writing was urban redevelopment, chiefly state and eventually federal enterprise zones (EZs). The idea behind EZs was to package tax, regulatory, and financial incentives in order to stimulate increased capital investment and employment in the nation's pockets of poverty and despair. By the mid-1980s, I was working closely with state and federal officials in disseminating and producing information regarding legislative, regulatory, and judicial developments throughout the nation, and in crafting, redesigning, and implementing EZ programs. This was most definitely law and social policy in action, as I explored the latest effort to improve the lives of those who lived on the other side of the tracks in too many U.S. cities and towns.

As I left Oklahoma City University in 1987, Charles and I were putting the finishing touches on the new edition of a land-use-planning casebook, a large segment of which addressed the ways in which zoning and other land-use regulatory devices exclude the poor and minorities. This was a prominent example of how I was beginning to explore a phenomenon that now falls under the heading "environmental justice." And yes, I perceive shades of *Brown* in this aspect of my scholarly life as well.

For the next sixteen years, I taught at the University of Richmond. The capital of the Old Dominion holds a special place in the American mind not only as the political and ideological center of the Confederacy but, more importantly, as the embodiment of resistance to the law's command to end racial segregation. In reality, the modern Richmond region comprises a complex and textured tableau that includes, along with vestiges of separation and stubborn (and often false) pride in the Old South, a rich history of African American achievement in many realms and important instances of interracial cooperation and mutual respect. This was certainly a fitting setting for this son of the South to continue an intellectual and professional journey that was informed by another community's rejection of *Brown*.

At UR, my childhood milieu helped determine some of my curricular and professional choices. In 1997, for example, my students (from the law school and college) and I marked the one hundredth anniversary of Faulkner's birth by participating in a seminar titled "Faulkner and the Law." A major theme of the course was the way in which this important writer served as a legal commentator for a lawless society steeped in racism and segregation, a theme that resonated in my personal experience. I also carved out a very strong pro-diversity position in the area of faculty appointments and student recruitment, a stance that was influenced by the dearth of African American politicians, judges, and bar leaders to provide effective representation for minority citizens, causes, and concerns in Central Florida during my childhood.

My Richmond years opened a new and fascinating door as well. For several years, I spent countless hours in the offices, hallways, and committee hearing rooms of the state capitol when the General Assembly was in session, serving as an advocate for local, state, and national Jewish organizations. The chief targets of our advocacy efforts were bills that attempted, in our view, to reinstate the (un)holy alliance of church and state through practices such as posting the Ten Commandments in public school classrooms; mandating a minute of silence for prayer, meditation, or reflection for all public schoolchildren; using public monies for social programs run by religious institutions; and posting signs reading "In God We Trust" in government buildings, courtrooms, and public schools throughout the state. By the early years of the new century, Virginia was a crucial battlefield in a national effort to undo the Warren Court's establishment clause mandates. We also worked with other religious and civil liberties organizations in an effort to bolster the state's protection of the free exercise of religion following the Rehnquist Court's evisceration in *Employment Division v. Smith* of the demanding balancing test.

I believe that my childhood in Lakeland in the 1950s and 1960s helped to prepare me for these battles. To me, the dangers posed by public officials who defied the spirit and letter of the Constitution were the stuff of life, not just stories in history books and newspaper articles. I had witnessed the harms that such a strategy, if left unchallenged by those with the ability to voice their concerns and organize resistance, posed to many members of society—white and nonwhite, affluent and low income, religious believer and nonbeliever alike. More importantly, as an advocate before the Virginia legislature, I discovered important allies in this struggle from the African American community, men and women lawyers, ministers, business leaders, and lawmakers who had suffered many more personal and community offenses in the post-*Brown* years than their Jewish colleague from Florida.

In the late summer of 2003, I returned to Florida, accepting a chair at my home state's flagship law school, located a little more than two hours north of my hometown. The odors and plant life in Gainesville are familiar, as are the accents of many local residents, students, and colleagues. My return home has reminded me of George Eliot's observation, in *The Mill on the Floss*, that "such things as these are the mother tongue of our imagination, the language that is laden with all the subtle inextricable associations the fleeting hours of our childhood left behind them." Although the Sunshine State and its public institutions certainly do not have the most unblemished recent record when it comes to racial sensitivity and inclusiveness, I see a much different and better place than the one I left in 1970. Many of those improvements, and our ability to perceive and, let us hope, to augment them, are attributable to the profound words of *Brown v. Board of Education* and, more importantly, to our appreciation of the gap between the word of law and the rule of law, between law and lawlessness, that *Brown* imbued in wide segments of U.S. society.

I am thankful that my wife, who was also born and raised in the South, and I had the opportunity to send our children to racially and ethnically diverse public schools; to meet African American leaders such as state and federal lawmakers, judges, and professors; and to form relationships with others based on mutual respect rather than shared prejudices and suspicions of "the other." These things would not have been possible without the revolution in attitudes and jurisprudence that was provoked by *Brown* and by the perception of many Americans in the years following the announcement of the decision that the law in practice needed to catch up with the aspirations and obligations contained in that masterful opinion.

Michael Allan Wolf was born in December 1952 in Lakeland, Florida, where he attended elementary and secondary schools. He is now the Richard E. Nelson Chair in Local Government Law at the Levin College of Law, University of Florida, Gainesville.

10 Color-Blind in Georgia

Otis H. Stephens

The decision in *Brown v. Board of Education*, on May 17, 1954, was announced near the end of my freshman year at the University of Georgia. I can well remember the widespread publicity accompanying the decision and its generally favorable reception on the all-white Athens, Georgia, campus. Some vocal students, of course, expressed immediate opposition; but in general most of my friends, including students and professors, agreed with my view that the decision was morally right and long overdue. I can remember one professor of Spanish, Dr. Karl E. Shedd, a New Englander with a Yale PhD, who suggested on the day after the *Brown* decision was announced that the Southern states should begin immediately to desegregate the public schools one grade at a time, beginning with the first grade the following September. I do not remember anyone disagreeing with Dr. Shedd on this approach. But, of course, this did not happen.

During the summer of 1954—in the months immediately following the first *Brown* decision—Georgia politics heated up noticeably. Several prominent Democrats were actively seeking the gubernatorial nomination, which, at that time, was tantamount to election. My interest in politics can be traced to my father's long-term active participation in local government in my hometown of East Point, Georgia, a suburb of Atlanta. In 1947, two years after leaving a full-time position in city government, my father ran successfully for an unexpired term on city council. He was still on the council in 1954 and was active in the gubernatorial campaign. In those days, Georgia politics was dominated by the Talmadge machine—first Eugene (Gene) Talmadge, a notorious race baiter, and later his son Herman, who started out as an arch-segregationist but eventually (after passage of the Voting Rights Act of 1965) "moderated" his political stance. My father worked hard in support of the anti-Talmadge faction throughout the 1950s. He and I supported a moderate candidate, Melvin E. Thompson, who initially seemed to have the lead in the 1954 gubernatorial race. That summer, for the first time, I had an opportunity to attend political rallies and to observe campaigning firsthand. All major candidates endorsed school segregation, but Thompson, as I thought then and still believe, would have complied with the *Brown* ruling and would not have been an obstructionist with regard to school desegregation.

As the summer wore on, negative reaction to *Brown* hardened, and a militant segregationist, Marvin Griffin of Bainbridge, Georgia, rapidly gained popularity among white voters. With the exception of those living in the Atlanta metropolitan area, most African Americans were effectively disenfranchised in Georgia. Because of the exclusion of African Americans and the existence of Georgia's notorious county unit system, Griffin emerged as the winner. The county unit system provided for the nomination of candidates by counties, rather than by direct popular vote. A candidate receiving a plurality of popular votes in a county was awarded all the county's "unit" votes. In this respect, the county unit system resembled the winner-take-all feature of the Electoral College system still in effect in U.S. presidential elections. The county unit votes, in the Georgia Democratic primary, were heavily weighted in favor of farm and rural interests. Each of the 8 most populous counties was awarded six unit votes; the next 30 largest were each allotted four votes; and each of the remaining 121 counties was given two votes. As a result of this lopsided arrangement, rural Echols County with a population of under 2,000 (almost half of whom were disenfranchised African Americans) had two unit votes. By contrast, Fulton County, with a population of nearly 550,000, including most of the Atlanta area where many African Americans had gained the franchise, had six votes.

Stressing his commitment to preserve racial segregation in the public schools, Griffin successfully forestalled progress toward integration. In fact, with the help of the Supreme Court's 1955 "all deliberate speed" formula in *Brown II*, Georgia schools did not begin to desegregate until the mid 1960s.

In the following paragraphs, I focus on one little-known result of the *Brown* revolution—the integration of the Georgia Academy for the Blind in Macon, Georgia. In early February 1949, I enrolled as a seventh-grade student at the Academy along with my sister Anne, a fifth-grader. Prior to that time, we had attended a specialized graded program for blind students in the Atlanta public schools. We had received excellent instruction from a remarkable teacher, James J. Childs, who taught all academic subjects, and from his wife, Emily Childs, who taught piano. When James Childs became ill and was hospitalized in late November 1948, my sister and I, along with the four other students then enrolled in the "Braille class," were temporarily transferred into the regular public school classes at Faith Elementary School (named for the donor of the land and having no religious connotation).

Mainstreaming had not yet emerged as a major force in special education; as a result, the teachers into whose classes we were dumped had no idea what to do with us. We listened to other students recite their lessons and tried to pick up information from the teacher's coverage of assignments, but since our textbooks were not the same as those used by the sighted students and since much information was communicated visually via the blackboard and printed handouts, we missed out on a great deal of the day-to-day learning process. Our parents soon became frustrated with this situation and enrolled us in the Georgia Academy for the Blind just after the middle of the academic year. At that time, most residential schools for the blind throughout the United States maintained high academic standards, equal to or exceeding those found in most public schools. The Georgia Academy for the Blind clearly fit this description. My sister and I thrived in this new setting and in due course graduated from high school at the Academy—I in 1953, and my sister in 1955.

Like all other public schools in Georgia, the Academy for the Blind was racially segregated. The white Academy was chartered by the Georgia legislature in 1852. In 1882, in the immediate aftermath of the Reconstruction era, the colored Academy was established. Both schools were located within the city limits of Macon, Georgia, and until 1906 were only about a mile apart. In 1906, the white Academy moved from downtown Macon to a suburban location on Vineville Avenue, while the black Academy remained near the center of the city. The white and black divisions of the Academy were operated under the supervision of a single white administrator who resided on the Vineville campus. Each division had its own principal, faculty, and students. Budgetary allocations for both divisions were modest, especially prior to the mid 1950s. As was true of the public schools generally, the black division was funded at a significantly lower level than the white division.

Students at the two divisions of the Academy during the years when I was in attendance had little if any contact with each other. Some limited faculty interaction did occur when teachers from the white Academy provided occasional special "largely vocational" instruction to students at the black Academy. In the early 1950s, anticipating legal challenges to the "separate but equal" regime of *Plessy v. Ferguson*, Georgia, along with most other Southern states, began to pour money into the construction of new facilities for black students. This belated attempt to preserve school segregation had a direct impact on the Georgia Academy for the Blind, resulting in 1952 in the construction of a modern $500,000 facility for black students. The new black campus, located on Shurling Avenue some distance from the central city, was far better equipped than the former black Academy and, in some ways, was superior to the white Academy. Nevertheless, the range of course offerings remained greater at the white Academy.

With the passage of the Civil Rights Act of 1964 and, perhaps of more direct significance, the Elementary and Secondary Education Act of 1965, the Georgia Academy for the Blind came under mounting pressure to integrate. It should come as no surprise that the presence or absence of eyesight has little or nothing to do with racial prejudice. Some students at the Academy and some faculty and alumni—both black and white—were initially opposed to integration. Others were skeptical, but many supported the change from the outset. The problem was made more complex because the change involved the integration not only of academic programs but also of living facilities at the Academy. The latter element produced some opposition among parents as well as students. A few isolated instances of racial conflict among students were reported during the first year or two of integration. Opposition and resistance, so strong at the outset, however, soon faded away.

Through extensive consultation and adroit leadership on the part of administrators and faculty in both divisions, the full integration of the Academy was achieved over a period of several years beginning in the mid-1960s. The academic programs were integrated first, while the residential facilities briefly remained segregated. By 1966, all programs, residential facilities, faculty, staff, and students were fully integrated. The approximately 60 students in the former black division joined the approximately 100 to 120 white students already residing at the formerly all-white campus on Vineville Avenue. Students in grades one to twelve occupied fully integrated residential cottages, divided by age and (except for the youngest) by gender. Prior to the advent of mainstreaming in the 1970s, the Academy reached an enrollment of approximately 200 pupils. Since that time, the enrollment has declined and in 2008 numbers approximately 125.

The role of the Academy has changed enormously since the mid-1960s. Through mainstreaming, students whose only disability is blindness or visual impairment have, for the most part, been enrolled in regular public school classes. Students who have disabilities in addition to blindness or visual loss now comprise the majority of those enrolled at the Georgia Academy for the Blind. The Academy offers a somewhat reduced, but still viable, program of academic study leading to high school graduation. In addition, it provides vocational and other nonacademic learning opportunities for students with more specialized needs. Through all this change, the racial integration of the Academy has remained constant.

It is interesting to reflect on the gradual disappearance of the race-related assumptions held by students of my generation fifty years ago. I did not become acquainted with graduates of the black Academy until long after my student days at the white Academy. Only after the passage of many years did students of both divisions begin to share their experiences at the Academy. It is remarkable how similar those separate school experiences turned out to be. Through a recent conversation, for example, I learned that a graduate of the black Academy used the same English book that I had used previously and in which I had written my name in Braille. The book was somewhat out of date when I used it in the 1950s. It was obviously older and in worse shape when it reached the black Academy a few years later. This is a good example of how "separate but equal" actually worked in the Deep South. From other conversations with graduates of the black Academy, I discovered that we shared the same complaints about food in the dining room and about what we then regarded as unnecessary rules greatly restricting our freedom, even as high school students, to go off campus after school hours. We agreed, however, that we received a solid educational foundation at the Academy and that we benefited greatly from not being singled out as "special" or "different" from other students. As a result, we enjoyed a full peer-group experience, an opportunity denied to most blind students who are mainstreamed today.

We recently compiled a history of the Georgia Academy for the Blind based on official records as well as the taped and written recollections of graduates of both divisions. The book covers the first 150 years of the school's history and relates in considerable detail the successful story of the integration of the Georgia Academy for the Blind. The history is tentatively scheduled for publication in 2008.

Otis H. Stephens was born in East Point, Georgia, in September 1936 and attended elementary and secondary school at the Georgia Academy for the Blind in Macon, Georgia, from 1949 to 1953. He is now Alumni Distinguished Service Professor of Political Science and Resident Scholar of Constitutional Law at the University of Tennessee College of Law in Knoxville.

11 Taking a Stand

Alex J. Hurder

I finished high school in Atlanta, Georgia, without ever experiencing a day of integrated education, but the case of *Brown v. Board of Education* had a profound impact on my life. I am a clinical law professor at Vanderbilt Law School. My students and I are often cocounsel in cases seeking rights for children with disabilities under the federal Individuals with Disabilities Education Act, rights that would be inconceivable without the *Brown* case. I also teach a course in public education law that has *Brown* as its centerpiece.

I have a clear recollection of sitting at the kitchen table in the summer of 1955 and asking my father what "integration" is. He told me about the *Brown* decision. In May 1954, my father, William Paul Hurder, left a job as a professor of psychology at Louisiana State University in Baton Rouge to become superintendent of the State Colony and Training School in Pineville, Louisiana, a residential institution for persons with mental retardation, now named the Pinecrest State School. The time was charged with emotion for my parents. Both my parents, who were white, favored integration.

In the summer of 1954 my father, himself a recent medical school graduate, assembled a team of psychologists, physicians, nurses, and social workers to coordinate services for the residents of the State Colony. By the summer of 1955 the new team had ended patronage hiring, completed individualized assessments of all the residents of the institution, and initiated individualized case conferences for each resident. The case conferences resulted in assigning residents to programs and services that were appropriate to their level of development. The changes began to break down the racial segregation that had existed at the institution.

Opponents of the reforms focused their attacks on the changes in relations between the races. They complained that an African American psychologist who worked for the institution had told white residents to call him "Mister" rather than by his first name. They complained that white residents had been transferred into rooms formerly occupied by black residents. They claimed that the institution was allowing sexual relationships between white and black residents.

I remember my father meeting with the psychologist at our house. Afterward, my father explained to me that it was customary under segregation for white people to call black adults by their first names and never by a courtesy title. He supported the psychologist, who wanted the signs of respect due anyone else in his position. This example of the cruelty and irrationality of segregation made a permanent impression on me. Segregation caused many injuries, but it was the personal humiliations that I felt most strongly.

A political battle raged statewide from 1954 to 1957 over the direction of the State Colony and Training School. The Louisiana State Board of Institutions held hearings in Pineville in the summer of 1956 to hear the complaints against the institution, including the ones I've mentioned. The hearing panel concluded the investigation with a strong endorsement of the reforms. A series of investigations by the Rapides Parish Grand Jury also failed to reverse the changes that had taken place. In spite of the attacks, the program at the institution gained a national reputation. In 1963 the President's Panel on Mental Retardation, appointed by President Kennedy, cited the individualized case conferences pioneered at the Louisiana institution as a model for the coordination of individualized services for persons with mental retardation.[1]

My family moved to Atlanta in 1957, and my father began working for the Southern Regional Education Board. School desegregation did not begin in Atlanta until after I graduated from high school in 1963, but the civil rights movement and the progress of integration were constant subjects of conversation among students. The fact that I was for integration was a central feature of how I saw myself. Although the civil rights movement existed long before *Brown v. Board of Education* and will continue for long afterward, the *Brown* case made me a part of that movement and invited me to take a stand. I remain convinced that racial equality is the key to progress in every aspect of human welfare in the United States.

NOTE

1.   See the President's Panel on Mental Retardation, *Report of the Task Force on Coordination* (August 1963).

Alex J. Hurder was born in May 1945 and attended elementary schools in Baton Rouge, Louisiana, from 1951 to 1954; Pineville, Louisiana, from 1954 to 1957; and Atlanta, Georgia, from 1957 to 1958; and secondary school in Atlanta from 1958 to 1963. He is now a clinical professor of law at Vanderbilt University Law School in Nashville, Tennessee.

12 Seeing the Hollow

Robert A. Burt

In May 1954, I was in tenth grade at Montgomery Blair High School in Silver Spring, Maryland, a suburb of Washington, D.C. There were no blacks among the two thousand students in that school. Insofar as I noticed this fact—and I did, though only fleetingly—I ascribed it to the complete absence of blacks living in my neighborhood of middle-class, single-family homes. I knew that there were prosperous black families nearby. I saw their imposing homes when I took the bus or drove with my father into the District of Columbia down Sixteenth Street, the so-called Gold Coast thoroughfare that led from our suburbs and ended at 1600 Pennsylvania Avenue. And I knew, too, that there were poor black families elsewhere in the District of Columbia—living in neighborhoods that I never saw, though they were only a few blocks from the route that regularly took me downtown.

I considered myself a politically aware liberal. Just before the 1952 presidential election, my ninth-grade social studies instructor took a class poll, and I was proud that mine was one of only two votes for Adlai Stevenson. His eloquence and evident intelligence made him my hero, and it was only years later when I read through a volume of his collected campaign speeches that I noticed the complete absence of any mention of black Americans.[1] It was not that Stevenson opposed black civil rights. He didn't acknowledge the issue and I didn't notice the omission at the time.

Then came *Brown v. Board of Education*. I remember seeing the headline in the *Washington Post* sitting on our front doorstep and though I was pleased, it didn't occur to me that the ruling would have any relevance to my personal life. But *Brown* turned out to touch me directly in a way that I had not imagined.

At the beginning of my eleventh-grade school year, in the fall of 1954, about thirty black students suddenly appeared in my high school. Set down among the two thousand white students in the school, this was a small number—but even so, it was a surprising number. Where did these black students come from?

I later learned that they all lived in an enclave about a half mile from the junior high school I had previously attended. Their homes in fact were closer to that school than mine was, but theirs were located down an unpaved road behind the school. If you hadn't known that this dirt road existed, you would not have seen it from the school or its surrounding network of tidy suburban homes. But now, with my newly gained driver's license, I drove down this road and found myself, amazed, in what looked like an entirely foreign setting—a setting I had seen only in photographs of the remote rural Southern states. Just a few minutes' drive from my old junior high, I saw a cluster of small wooden buildings—shacks, really—on each side of the rutted dirt road, what looked like small outhouses behind several of the homes, and refrigerators on the porches of several homes visibly connected to the electric wires that ran overhead alongside the road. The black children playing outside stared at me as I drove slowly through and I self-consciously both looked at them and tried to avoid their gaze.

I also learned that this enclave, colloquially known as the Hollow, had been deeded to a group of freed slaves during the Civil War—perhaps even by the direct mandate of Abraham Lincoln. At that time, the property was remote from downtown Washington; in the succeeding years, suburban Silver Spring had sprawled around it, but the authorities of the surrounding county stopped all municipal services at the edge of the Hollow. There were no sewers, no water, no road paving, no trash collection—and no access to the nearby public schools. The residents of the Hollow were entirely separated from and effectively ignored by the carefully groomed suburban community that had grown up around them. Separate but unequal.

Brown broke this pattern. Maryland state law authorized racial segregation of its public schools and gave control to county school boards to implement that policy; immediately after the Supreme Court decision, the Montgomery County School Board formally abolished its segregation policy—which led to the enrollment in the 1955–1956 academic year of the small group of black students in my formerly segregated high school.

I was stunned at their arrival. I had known that my school class had been all white. Or, more precisely, I was vaguely aware of this fact but thought nothing much about it, since I assumed that the explanation was benign—black families simply had not chosen to live in my neighborhood, even though some (such as the Gold Coast residents on Sixteenth Street, in homes more imposing than mine) could financially afford to do so. It had not occurred to me that the children of even well-to-do black families who might consider moving into my neighborhood would be barred from access to my schools. I had thought that the political complexion of my home county was liberal, since the electorate appeared mostly, like my family, to be transplanted Northerners and committed Democrats who worked for or around the federal government. It had not occurred me that my comfortably liberal home county maintained an explicit, official policy refusing welcome to black people (except, of course, for the groups of black domestic servants who arrived every weekday morning at my neighborhood in the municipal buses coming from who knew where across the border of the District of Columbia).

This, then, was my first and most surprising lesson from *Brown v. Board of Education*: that I was a student in a racially segregated school system and that I had not noticed this fact. I thought I knew all I had to know about race segregation—that it was an unjust policy officially maintained by unreconstructed Southern white bigots who lived far away from me. But I did not know what I needed to know about my community and my own participation in this unjust system.

The new black students in Montgomery Blair High School seemed, so far as I could tell, to keep to themselves. Occasionally one of these students and I enrolled in the same class section; but I had a social relationship, and a limited one at that, with only one student, who was chosen in our senior year as drum major for the school band and strutted with grand style at the head of the band formations for our football games. The presence of this small number of black classmates did lead to one significant event in which I participated. At the end of each school year, the elected student council at the school sponsored a Saturday beach party for graduating seniors at a Chesapeake Bay beach club, located about a two-hour school bus ride away. I was a member of the student council and I recall that when we began plans for the event, someone—perhaps it was the faculty advisor to the council—mentioned that the beach club had a policy of excluding blacks, that indeed there was a sign posted at the entrance to the club that explicitly read, "No Negroes." It would have been an easy course for us if we could simply find another beach club on the Bay with a nondiscriminatory policy; but the Chesapeake Bay was on the so-called Eastern Shore of Maryland—"redneck" territory, as we all knew—and all the beaches in the area were racially exclusionary. Our student councils may have known this in the past, but it would have seemed to have no significance for our all-white senior classes; this year was, however, visibly different.

The senior class beach party was one of the highlights of the graduates' year, and a few members of the student council were reluctant to give it up. Perhaps, they suggested, a delegation from the council could approach the black seniors—there were only ten or so of them, after all, among a graduating class of some seven hundred—and ask if they would mind that the beach party go on as it always had in the past, though obviously and regretfully without their participation. But this suggestion was quickly abandoned, even by its original proponents. The only alternative that any of us could ultimately support was to cancel the beach party because all of our classmates were not welcome to attend.

But how, we then discussed at length, should this decision be presented to the entire student body? If we announced that the party was canceled because of the beach club's racial policy, we were concerned that the black students would feel some blame and discomfort for depriving the whites of their entitlement to a farewell bash, and that some white students would resentfully see themselves as carrying an excessive burden on behalf of the blacks. Our resolution: We announced the cancellation of the party on the ground that the beach club had raised its prices and imposed other (carefully unspecified) conditions that we could not afford to meet; and at the same time, we asked our faculty advisor to write to the beach club that we were canceling the party because of the club's racially discriminatory policy and would not return our business there until they had ended this policy.

In retrospect this seems a mild and even evasive resolution. We should have protested openly; we should have taken school buses down to the beach club on the traditional party day and remained outside picketing, whites and blacks together. But we were most concerned with avoiding hurt feelings among our black classmates—which meant, so far as we could then see, that we would act on their behalf rather than directly asking them what should be done.

Our deliberations seem to me, in retrospect, to have elements in common with the subsequent national debate over university affirmative action admissions policy. Some whites understand the imperative to end racial exclusions as an unjust deprivation imposed on them to remedy injustices for which they were not responsible, and understood by some blacks as a burden more than an advantage—which leads educational administrators to adopt a resolution favoring blacks while, perhaps disingenuously, somewhat disguising this motivation. This affirmative action debate began a decade after our student council addressed the beach party issue and, almost a half-century later, it was resolved in these same terms, and barely so by a five-to-four vote of the Supreme Court in *Grutter v. Bollinger* in 2003.

But whatever the merits of our high school student council's resolution of the beach party issue, it was an unambiguously good thing that we were directly grappling with the central problem in our country's historical promise of equal justice before the law and that we understood—we could not avoid acknowledging—our personal responsibility to address this issue. *Brown v. Board of Education* forced me and my classmates to this acknowledgment.

For myself, *Brown* demonstrated how easy it was to deny any personal involvement in or responsibility for social practices that, once forced to my attention, I knew were unjust and dishonorable. And, I am sorry to say, 1954 was not the last time that this lesson was forced on me. When I entered the Yale Law School class of 1964, I was aware of and regretted the small number of black classmates; but it did not occur to me that I should be similarly concerned about the absence of women classmates. There were only five women in my entering class at Yale, and of them, only two graduated; as I recall, the numbers of black students entering and graduating were about the same. But the absence of women students seemed to me at the time, and to most of my male classmates, as an expression of women's voluntary choice—the scrappy world of law and public governance was not suited for most women, so far as we could see. I did not see the social constraints that produced these apparently voluntary self-exclusions or my personal responsibility in maintaining and benefiting from them.

Just a few years after I graduated from law school, when women began to speak openly about the constraints under which they lived, I recognized the pattern that *Brown* had previously forced into my attention—the pattern of blindness to obvious facts of injustice which, once clearly acknowledged, demand personal and social reparative response. Only a few years after the mid-1960s explosion of attention to the status of women in U.S. society, gays and lesbians began to step forward with similar accounts of unjust exclusions and humiliations. And again I could see the pattern that *Brown* had brought home to me.

I wish I could say that I learned my lesson from *Brown* and have practiced it faithfully since 1954—that my experience around that Supreme Court ruling shattered my moral complacency and stripped away my self-protective blindness to other social and personal injustices in which I participated and from which I benefited. I have found instead, in the half-century since *Brown* was decided, that I have been forced to acknowledge again and again that I have not yet adequately absorbed this lesson. But I am still trying. And I consider it moral progress that I once was more complacent than I now am, that I once was very blind and now see more than before. That has been one of the great educational gifts from *Brown v. Board of Education*.

NOTE

1.   See Adlai E. Stevenson, *Major Campaign Speeches, 1952* (New York: Random House, 1953).

Robert A. Burt was born in Philadelphia, Pennsylvania, in February 1939 and attended elementary school in Upper Darby, Pennsylvania, and secondary school from 1952 to 1956 in Silver Spring, Maryland. He is now Alexander M. Bickel Professor of Law at Yale University in New Haven, Connecticut.

13 A Glen Echo Passage

Robert B. Keiter

I understood, but only vaguely, that I would be attending a new elementary school next year to make room for the colored children from Seven Locks Road at my present school. The year was 1955, and I was just finishing the third grade in Cabin John, Maryland.

My teacher mother, I remember, had been pleased—even downright gleeful—upon learning that the Supreme Court had ordered public schools desegregated. To its credit, the Montgomery County School Board responded almost immediately, opening its previously segregated school system to the county's black children, most of whom lived in scattered pockets around the area. The monumental significance of the Court's ruling mostly escaped me. As a white child raised in a middle-class white community, all I knew for sure was that I would be moving to a new school.

Home was Glen Echo, a small town perched above the Potomac River a couple of miles west of the nation's capital. Glen Echo was a pretty typical middle-class community in those days. The town's eighty or so homes were modest, though comfortable. The residents were decidedly middle class—a baker, a plumber, a butcher, and a taxi driver, a couple carpenters, some civil servants, salespeople, and quite a few housewives. The town was incorporated, with its own mayor and town council system, bringing local government close to everyone.

Glen Echo, however, was anything but enlightened when it came to matters of race in the mid-1950s. More than once I can recall adults in town, upset over a town council decision or some other perceived slight, threatening to "sell out to niggers." Whether serious or not, the threat always seemed to alarm those listening. But my parents, refugees from the Pennsylvania coal fields who'd relocated to the Washington, D.C., area after the war, had been clear with me for as long as I could remember: Everyone was equal, regardless of the color of their skin.

The town was divided by Glen Echo Amusement Park, a longtime D.C.-area landmark situated at the end of the streetcar line. The park offered an assortment of rides, ranging from roller coasters to a merry-go-round. It had the Spanish ballroom, a shooting gallery, and cotton candy too. And it had a swimming pool, which local kids used from Memorial Day through Labor Day, a welcome respite from the summer heat and humidity. But there were no black people at the park; it was segregated and would remain that way for more than a decade. (The park was privately owned, I learned from my father, which meant it was not bound by the *Brown* ruling or any other law then on the books.)

For me, besides relocating to another nearby school, not much changed in the immediate aftermath of the county's decision to desegregate its schools. A few black children joined me at my new school, but they were in other grades, and I really didn't get to know them. I don't recall much local resistance or protest either, perhaps because there wasn't a very large black population in the county and the dislocations were minimal.

Then one day in the early summer of 1957, a friend and I ventured across the bridge to the Cabin John Recreation Center looking for a baseball game. Cabin John was another primarily white working-class community. In no time, Corky and I were on the baseball diamond trying out for the team. Beside us were other boys our own age, both black and white, each intent on proving his prowess as a fielder and batter. The coach, I soon learned, was Harold, a soft-spoken young black man who was working his way through college and who took a genuine interest in each of us.

Despite the strange surroundings, I was in heaven. Here was a real baseball team with a real baseball diamond, a coach, and a schedule of games against other Montgomery County teams. There couldn't be a better way to spend a summer than playing ball.

I met Dwight that day, little knowing that we would become friends all the way through high school. In response to Harold's query about what position I played, I said either second or third base. After I'd fielded a few ground balls, a lanky black boy sauntered by and let me know that if I wanted to play third base, I'd have to take it from him "in the ring" because it was his position. Taken aback at the time, I subsequently realized that Dwight was expressing not only his fierce athletic competitiveness but his own sense of pride. Already the team's third baseman, he wasn't about to relinquish that role without a fight. I played second base.

Over the next couple of weeks, I became acquainted with the rest of the team too. The nucleus was five black players—Dwight, Ernie, Rodney, Reggie, and Tim—and four white ones—Toogie, Bollo, Corky, and me. We didn't have uniforms or even matching ball caps, and we each supplied our own baseball mitt. But Rodney, I learned, didn't own a baseball glove; his family couldn't afford to buy him one. That's why he was the catcher, because the rec center supplied each team with a catcher's mitt.

My new black teammates were the unknown children who had displaced me from my elementary school a couple of years earlier, and we were now friends. One day, I walked with Dwight the mile or so to his home for lunch. As we entered the black Seven Locks enclave, I noticed that the streets were no longer paved, and that the houses were much smaller, almost shanty-like— a much different neighborhood than my own or the one surrounding it.

A bit later, Dwight accompanied me home for lunch. As we walked down Glen Echo's main street, I couldn't help but notice a couple of front doors being shut and window shades being lowered. Black people evidently still weren't welcome in my town, though no one confronted us. Even at age eleven, I was well aware that I'd rarely seen a black face in Glen Echo. Dwight and I spent some time discussing our racial differences and experiences. I was surprised to learn about his former two-room school, the multigrade classes, and shared textbooks—all foreign to my own experience.

On the baseball field, we were the only integrated team in the summer recreation league. Most of our opponents fielded all-white teams, kids from one of the affluent suburbs that were growing up around D.C. Many of us would soon attend junior and senior high school together, where we would be teammates on the school sports teams. But for that summer we were rivals, and our games were intense. In the end, our team from Cabin John won the league championship. For an eleven-year-old, it was heady stuff, and an eye-opening adventure into a new world.

After elementary school, my social circle shifted away from Glen Echo and Cabin John as I made new friends who lived in the upscale suburbs. But Dwight and I were reunited through sports once again. The high school that we both attended was located quite far from our homes, and we were the only local kids playing football, so our families took turns picking us up after practice. And when they couldn't make it, we hitchhiked home together.

I can clearly remember the day in August 1963, when the football coach excused Dwight from our grueling two-a-day summer practices. Even though Dwight was one of our toughest and most reliable players, this was quite unusual; practice was mandatory in the name of team loyalty and discipline. But Dwight was headed downtown for the epic March on Washington, and even the coach realized the importance of the event in his young life. I still regret that none of the rest of us had the presence of mind to join Dwight on the Mall that historic summer day.

By then, the Glen Echo Amusement Park had become a focal point for local civil rights demonstrators, who mounted picket lines near the park's entrance to protest the owner's steadfast discriminatory policies. No blacks were allowed, period. Most of the boys I grew up with had little sympathy for the protesters, judging by the profanities and racial slurs they launched toward the demonstrators whenever they passed near the picket lines. Eventually the park was forced to relent: Black customers would be admitted to the rides and the midway, but they would not be allowed to enter the swimming pool. Old prejudices die hard; the idea of black and white bodies sharing the same water was still just too much for some white people. Within a few years, after several riotous confrontations, that policy too was finally repealed.

College was another adventure in the latent racism of the day. I attended Washington University in Saint Louis and joined a fraternity, the principal source of social life on campus. During the rush period, to my amazement, one fraternity on campus still proudly displayed the Confederate flag, explaining that it was an important symbol for them. Their pledge class was quite small that year, and the fraternity soon closed its doors.

But my bigger surprise came a couple of years later when, during rush period, a gregarious black freshman athlete expressed interest in our fraternity. (It was still unusual for any black students to participate in rush, let alone join a fraternity.) As we discussed making him an offer, several fraternity brothers announced that they would blackball him. A heated and prolonged argument ensued, all to no avail. I still remember with chills the proffered clinching argument, though: "There are *niggers* and there are niggers, and he's a *nigger!*" I soon drifted away from the fraternity, left to question the worldview of several of my ostensible "brothers," most of whom went on to successful professional careers.

College over, it was on to law school at Northwestern University in Chicago, a remarkable place to study the law during the early 1970s. My entering class contained a sizeable black contingent, hailing from Chicago and elsewhere. We engaged in vigorous debates over the merits of the Chicago Seven trial as well as the nation's struggle with the Vietnam quagmire, racial unrest, and related social problems. None of us will forget the day that Fred Hampton from the local Black Panther party spoke at the law school, or his strident attack on the Chicago political establishment and the city police department's overt racism. Nor will we forget, a few months later, when the evening news announced that Hampton was dead, killed in a hail of police bullets during a clandestine drug raid. He was shot while in bed, reportedly reaching for a gun.

Law school provided me an opportunity to begin exploring how the law might be used to help others and to promote social change. Much of my education on that front came at the Cook County Juvenile Court, where I spent two years assisting in the Public Defender's Office. The daily lives of our clients, many of whom came from the city's notorious South Side, bore little resemblance to anything I had witnessed before. Gang pressures, drug activity, and grinding poverty all conspired to leave many of these youngsters with few choices but the street crime scene. And though the juvenile court may have originated in Chicago as a rehabilitative rather than a penal institution, the system I encountered offered few meaningful options to young offenders teetering on the brink of lifelong criminality.

After law school, I was off to West Virginia as a Reginald Heber Smith Fellow in the Office of Economic Opportunity Legal Services program, committed to using my legal skills to promote social justice. Not only was the "Reggie" program affiliated with Howard University, but it was administered by an imposing black lawyer, both conditions quite appropriate since Smith himself had been an early legal pioneer in the struggle for equal justice. Joining me in West Virginia was Jim Parker, a recent black Illinois law graduate seeking to help the state's underserved minority citizens. Within days of meeting, we found ourselves joined together as plaintiffs in a constitutional challenge to the West Virginia bar residency requirement that had been invoked to prevent "outsiders" like us from taking the state bar examination. We took the exam under a federal court injunction, passed it, and were sworn in together once the court invalidated the residency requirement.

My own legal work focused on improving the plight of the state's mentally handicapped populace, particularly those confined to the state hospitals, the largest of which dated from the Civil War era. Employing the same test-case litigation strategies that had precipitated the *Brown* ruling, we succeeded in overturning the state's antiquated civil commitment laws. The state supreme court, appalled by the lack of due process and treatment options, issued an unprecedented blanket habeas corpus writ, ordering the release (or recommitment) of over two thousand patients. By then, spurred by *Brown*'s substantive and remedial legacy, the courts were becoming true engines for equal justice and social change, even at the state level.

By 1976, I decided to pursue an academic career, soon landing at the University of Wyoming, where I could also indulge my passion for the mountains and outdoor activities. Constitutional law was my principal teaching responsibility. I recall working hard to bring the *Brown* decision and subsequent school desegregation rulings alive to students who had few personal experiences with overt racial discrimination, save some lingering stereotypes too readily attached to the state's Native Americans. When, however, the focus of discussion shifted to the issue of affirmative action, student views and passions were more pronounced; often-heated class discussions addressed the justice or injustice of treating individuals differently based on their race and on historical patterns of discrimination. Although the law school attracted a smattering of minority students, it had never hired a minority faculty member. Perhaps this is not surprising given Laramie's racial composition and rural location, but the *Brown* ruling was verging on its fortieth anniversary.

Lured by professional opportunity, I joined the University of Utah's law faculty in 1993. The law school's student body, to my surprise, was strikingly diverse for a state that doesn't have a large minority population. But the Utah law faculty, like Wyoming's, was devoid of any African American colleagues, though other minorities were represented in our ranks. As time passed, the *Bakke* affirmative action principles were increasingly being called into question by the courts, while the university's medical school was engaged in defending its diversity admission policies from a sharp political attack. Our own faculty diversity efforts, meanwhile, had not yielded any tangible results.

Reflecting back on my personal odyssey through post-*Brown* America, much has changed in the Maryland environs of my youth. Glen Echo has been transformed into an upscale bedroom community for D.C., where a few black and other minority citizens now live alongside the town's white residents. The amusement park closed its gates in 1968, the victim of its own obdurate segregationist policies and changing public tastes in entertainment; it is now part of the national park system, with no evidence of its past role in the local civil rights struggles. The streets in Seven Locks have long since been paved. Half its residents are now white. Some of the original homes remain, dwarfed by new upscale dwellings that occupy what has become valuable real estate. Dwight went on first to become a D.C. policeman, and then to a federal law enforcement career.

Elsewhere change has come too. Washington University now boasts a much more racially and ethnically diverse student body. In Chicago, Northwestern University now operates an extensive legal assistance clinic with a primary emphasis on the city's juvenile justice system. The Reggie program, along with the legal services office where I worked, are long gone, victims of a conservative political backlash. West Virginia permanently closed its largest state hospital in 1994; the building is now a national historical landmark. In 2002, the University of Wyoming law school hired its first African American faculty member. A year later, the Utah law faculty did the same.

Robert B. Keiter was born in the Bethesda Naval Hospital, Bethesda, Maryland, and attended elementary and secondary schools in Montgomery County, Maryland, from 1952 to 1964. He is now the Wallace Stegner Professor of Law and director of the Wallace Stegner Center for Land, Resources, and the Environment at the University of Utah, S. J. Quinney College of Law, in Salt Lake City.

14 I Can't Play with You No More

Edward C. Brewer III

I was born in Clarksdale, in the Mississippi Delta, in early 1953 and lived in nearby Lyon until I was almost fifteen. My father was a lawyer with clients, mostly paying but otherwise from all walks of life. Although I am told he believed in segregation of the races, I am not aware that he worked for such ends, but since he died in 1963 I have to content myself with hoping that he did not. My cousin tells me that my father and another lawyer successfully defended a black man accused of murdering a white woman in an Atticus Finch–like case, although the story I like better involves a friend's father who walked halfway across town in the dark so his car would not be seen to tell another black man that a mob was planning to come after him so he had better get out of town for a while. My grandmother has been referred to by name in the civil rights literature as a "rabid conservative," which fits even my loving recollection of her. My mother, who came from the hills of south Mississippi and had little use for Delta ways, reflected interesting contradictions: She regarded Aaron Henry, then president of the Mississippi NAACP, as a "troublemaker," but when serving as a voting clerk she once dressed down a federal poll watcher for being there, because she wasn't about to deny anyone their right to vote, regardless of their race. I remember visiting that polling place during the 1960 and 1964 elections, but I remember having no sense of those larger issues.

We five children were raised by my mother with the help of a cook, Mary B.; a nurse, Daisy; and a yardman, Fred—all black—whom we loved as well as we did one another. I was a tough nut as a small child, and Mary B. could crack me as well as my mother could. I still remember one day coming over to talk with Fred in the side yard, seeing that he was crying, and asking him what the matter was. He said that he never was going to amount to anything and nobody cared about him, and all seven years old of me hugged him and told him that I cared about him, to which he replied, "Thanks, honey." Until I was about ten I played in the neighborhoods and cotton fields with black children as well as white. That stopped, pretty much, one day when I saw a black friend I had not seen for some time and asked him where he'd been. He said,

"I can't play with you no more." I asked, "Why not?" and he replied, "'Cause you white." I said, "That's not any reason not to play with each other." But that's the way it was. One of my deepest fears is of having these relationships and experiences postmodernly derided as insignificant compared to the corresponding experiences of black people, and I could not very well take exception to such a comparison. Nor could I defend the moral order that I grew up in. What I can say is that some forty years later, I know that those relationships were real and loving (and in the case of Mary B., our cook and caregiver, that is still true), and were not a product of my childlike sense of the world back then. This is intrinsically important to me, although its broader significance may well be that given relationships like those, what happened in Clarksdale after *Brown* perhaps did not have to happen.

The *Brown* decision hit Clarksdale in about 1964, or perhaps it would be more correct to say that the response to *Brown* did. The machinations involving the Clarksdale and Coahoma County Schools have been described in published sources such as Curtis Wilkie's *Dixie* (2001). When I read that book last year, even having an adult's familiarity with Mississippi politics specifically and some Southern politics more generally, I was shocked to know the depth of perfidy to which persons whom I knew—who were my parents' friends and whose children I had grown up with—sank in their efforts to maintain a segregated school system. At the time, from my perspective as a junior high school student in 1965, what I knew was that beginning in 1965–1966, our first-place junior high band ("straight 1s at State with only one 1- in one subcategory") was split between the new city system and the new county system, and that the city and the county would have two separate grade-seven-through-twelve high schools with separate bands. My entry into that system was delayed for one year because I was sent off to boarding school. I spent only one year, the ninth grade from 1966 to 1967, at Coahoma County High School, and from that experience can say that things were never the same for the band after that. My involvement in that system then was cut short after the next year when my family moved to east Tennessee, where there were very few black people at all.

My next exposure to that school system was on a visit during the late spring of 1970, after we had been in east Tennessee for two years. I was riding a motorcycle past the Coahoma County High School, saw a large group of black students standing out near the road on the sidewalk, and stopped to ask what was going on. The moment I stopped and took my helmet off, I was surrounded by angry students, one of whom was glaring at me and tapping on my handlebars with a two-foot-long piece of three-quarter-inch pipe, asking me what the hell I wanted. I said that I had gone to school here and stopped to see what was going on, which produced a harder rap on my handlebars. Another of the students said that I should be let go and get the hell out of there, which I was, and which I did. It was apparent that I had narrowly escaped being seriously injured.

The broader significance of this incident was not clear to me until much later. Completing law school in 1979 and serving as a law clerk to Judge Virgil Pittman in the Southern District of Alabama during the retrials of two voting-rights cases after *Bolden v. City of Mobile*, I decided that I would not go back to Mississippi unless I went back as a plaintiff's civil rights lawyer, and I have to say that I did not have the stomach for a life that full of conflict. In the late 1980s, living in Atlanta, Georgia, I went to a photo exhibit on the civil rights movement at the Martin Luther King Jr. Center. I was startled to see a picture of a crowd of fist-waving white segregationists marching past the Woolworth's store in Clarksdale. Clearly, people had been pretty angry in the early 1970s, and my experience with the students at CCHS must have been one of many.

Looking back at those times, I am struck by the confines of my relationships with black people growing up, my lack of awareness of the changes that were coming in race relations, my ignorance of why our school and band were being split up, the profound ugliness in the actions of the persons of power in our town, my naiveté in stopping in the middle of a crowd of black students, and the strange epiphany of seeing the photograph at the MLK Center. What strikes me is that when I was a child, I was kept from any deeper awareness of my (and our) situation by my parents and larger family, whose responsibility it was to shape my view of the world. My ex-wife grew up in Selma, Alabama, and was age eleven when the Freedom March crossed the Edmund Pettus Bridge in 1965. She similarly describes a time of knowing that something was going on, but really having no sense of what it was or how dangerous things were at the time. The white children of the community, or at least those relatively privileged as we were, were sheltered and kept in the dark about these important events and changes. Perhaps those persons a half-generation behind me were more aware of what was going on, and it may simply have been our age that led our parents to keep us sheltered from the problems of our society. But I think that we lost a valuable opportunity to learn and grow in ways that would make us perhaps more competent, and certainly more confident, today in our dealings with persons of other races.

All of that leaves me wondering whether things might have been different in Clarksdale—what it would have taken for that to happen, and how things would have been different had our elders behaved differently and had we children been better aware of what was going on around us. Or if not the latter, then at least the former. If "all deliberate speed" under *Brown* ever had any hope of moral legitimacy, it was in building on the natural human affections and affinities that grew up among Mary B., Daisy, Fred, my young black friends, and me, and that rested in my mother's hill-country sense of kinship with all people. If it ever had any hope of success, at least prior to Justice O'Connor's most recent projection of 2028 in *Grutter v. Bollinger*, it was in proceeding there and then, not ten years after the decision and not in the face of every impediment that could be devised, to live together. We did not do that then, and there are many reasons to question whether we are doing it now.

During my first year as a judicial law clerk, Judge Pittman's senior law clerk was a black man, a fact that is important not in the sense that race is too often used as a primary identifier in some Deep South discussions, but in the context in which a particular discussion arose between the two of us. We were walking to lunch one day when I observed to my colleague that there was a heavy load of sadness that I experienced in thinking about relations between black and white people. His response, immediate and alacritous, was that "it isn't anything to be sad about. Just do something about it!" My colleague was very matter-of-fact about most things, racial and otherwise, and I have always thought that his advice was very good. I have never managed to implement his advice to get past the sadness, however, even in doing what I can to "do something about it."

My final thought about the *Brown* decision is that we seem to be entering a time in which we speak less openly and candidly with one another about matters of race and (although not germane to *Brown*) sex in our communities. This occurs sometimes in an entire lack of discussions about existing problems of race and sex, clandestine rather than open discussions about race and sex, talking past one another when we do talk about race and sex, and the seemingly innumerable trips and falls of language in which people discussing problems of race and sex catch one another out for either rhetorical or political ends. Perhaps my experience is not universal, and certainly I hope it is not. But it makes me just as sad as I was the day my little friend told me that he couldn't play with me any more. The fact is that we don't play very well with one another any more, and I hope we find a way to play with one another. Our differences seem to be multiplying, and the resulting sadness seems to be deepening. As in the days when Clarksdale was beginning the desegregation process, I think that it doesn't have to be this way, and that we have the ability to do something about that in the way that the contestants of 1964 did not.

Edward C. Brewer was born in Clarksdale, Mississippi, in January 1953 and attended elementary and secondary schools in Clarksdale from 1959 to 1965. He is now a professor of law at Northern Kentucky University, Salmon P. Chase College of Law, in Highland Heights, Kentucky.

15 A White Boy from Mississippi

W. Lewis Burke

Like most of the families who lived in the Beacon Street housing project, my family ate its meals around a bright-colored, chrome-edged Formica kitchen table. On Mondays we often ate biscuits with tomato gravy, butter beans, rice, and Sunday's leftover fried chicken. That probably was the menu on the day that many whites called "Black Monday," when our local newspaper, the Laurel Leader Call, ran the headline "Segregation Ended by Highest Court." To a young boy who had just turned six and was going to start school the next fall, my father's rantings at the supper table were more heated than usual. He usually cursed Eisenhower, but now it was the communists on the Supreme Court. From May 17, 1954, until today, I have often reflected on that day and the impact of *Brown v. Board* on my life.

My father worked in a mill. His family had roots in Clarendon County, South Carolina, but instead of returning to South Carolina after World War II, he moved to Mississippi, where he had met my mother during army training. She was from Clarke County, just south of Meridian. He was a high school dropout, and she was her family's first high school graduate. He was the son of a sometime employed carpenter and staunch Democrat. She was the daughter of a backwoods Southern Baptist minister who idolized both Bob Jones and FDR. During the depression, both my parents ate vegetables and chickens raised by their mothers. My mother was religious and credited FDR with saving the nation and the world. My father was not religious, and his politics were those of his fellow South Carolinian Strom Thurmond.

My mother taught me at a very early age that "nigger" was a bad word. I had heard her debate my grandfather on the biblical basis of segregation and also question our family minister about the morality of segregation. She was no liberal, but she was too intelligent and compassionate not to believe that Jim Crow was wrong. Although I had few interactions with black people in any case, my mother's admonitions and concerns caused me to question the mores of Mississippi.

When I started first grade, integration was as much on everyone's mind as polio, nuclear bombs, and television. Integration was not a daily worry, but it hung in the air like the humidity of an August day. The local newspaper had said it might be months or perhaps years away. A city bus carried me past my neighborhood school, through the mill village, to the modern Prentiss Elementary on the north side of town. But uncertainty also rode with me to school each day, and even we first-graders wondered when "it" was coming.

Soon "it" became more than *Brown*. Civil rights was the news that never left the supper table. In the summer of 1955, Emmett Till was lynched. The bus boycott in Montgomery was big news. After second grade, the fear of integration directly affected my daily life. In order to avoid providing busing to black school children, the Laurel bus system quit transporting any children to school. So in third grade, I was transferred to Beacon Street Elementary School. It was a short walk, but the school was crowded beyond belief. On the first day, we were all crammed into the auditorium, because the school was not ready for all the new students. After some renovations, we were moved to overcrowded classrooms. My father blamed the change on "the niggers."

The third grade was further interrupted when my father got a full-time job working with the Mississippi National Guard. *Brown* and civil rights moved right along with my family and the Formica supper table a hundred miles south to Gulfport. Fourth grade began with the desegregation of Central High in Little Rock. We watched it on television. As the fifth grade ended in May of 1959, Charles Mack Parker was lynched in Poplarville, less than sixty miles from our home. One Sunday afternoon soon thereafter, my father loaded my mother, my brother, and me into the old Buick and drove to the bridge outside Poplarville so we could see the place where it happened. Our insensitive voyeurism still haunts me.

In the sixth grade I followed world and national news closely. My mother subscribed to *Time*, *Life*, and *Look* magazines, so I was exposed to the views of people from outside Mississippi. I watched every broadcast of Huntley-Brinkley and all of NBC's specials on civil rights. In November of 1959, Ruby Bridges desegregated a New Orleans school under a court order. Watching the nightly news, I saw and heard the hatred spewing from the mouths of those white mothers. The federal judges in New Orleans were heroes to me. The civil rights movement was creating a revolution in America, and lawyers were playing a major role. So in the sixth grade I decided to become a lawyer.

My views were being shaped by the horrors exposed by the media, but my father's views were not. He was still talking about *Brown*. "When is integration coming?" remained the question. Although the politicians said it would never happen, my father saw the inevitable and announced that we would go to private school. I remember telling one of my best friends, John Hartley, about my father's private school idea. John's parents were rumored to be the neighborhood liberals. His mother was an "artist"! John's parents said that he and his sister would attend the "integrated" schools. The Hartleys were the first white people I knew, other than my mother, who thought segregation was wrong. In retrospect, my father was probably just ranting and the Hartleys were probably just being pragmatic. Both our families were working class and did not have any money to pay private school tuition. Moreover, the only private school in town was Catholic. In 1960, my parents had supported a Republican for president for the first time in their lives because John Kennedy was a Catholic. The idea of nuns teaching us was as foreign to them as was our going to school with black children.

Throughout junior high school we waited, but "it" still did not come. Two friends and I, in one Friday study hall, cooked up the plan of transferring to 33rd Avenue School, the black school. I was a liberal and thought it was time for integration. My two friends were probably motivated by the idea of making the news and upsetting their parents. Our plan was to tell our parents that weekend and then ask to be transferred and call the New Orleans television stations. As it happened, however, none of us was brave enough to broach the subject at home. On Monday my friends laughed it off. Before long, they had stopped talking to me.

While I was still in junior high, integration caused me to lose a job. For several years, my father had employed me as a janitor at the National Guard Armory for Friday night wrestling. It was a great job. I had free admission, ate all the "parched" peanuts I wanted, and met all the wrestlers, including Gorgeous George. But the National Guard had to stop sponsoring segregated events. So the Dixie Division guardsmen closed the wrestling matches, and I needed a new job.

I got a newspaper route across town. My first customers on the route were the residents of a boarding house, as well as the landlady and her cook. Everyone was white except the cook. The cook was very nice and always paid me on time. The landlady was always hard to find on Friday afternoons when I came to collect. But one Friday after I had delivered the paper to some boarders and to the cook, the landlady told me I must always deliver her newspaper before the cook's. I answered that I saw the "other lady" first. The landlady grew irate with me and responded that the cook "is a nigger, not a lady." I handed her the paper and retreated, forgetting to collect any money. Such rigid, racist codes of conduct were stupid to me.

My last year of junior high was 1962–1963. In the fall of 1962, James Meredith was admitted to Ole Miss. President Kennedy "federalized" the National Guard to preempt Governor Ross Barnett from using the Guard against the desegregation. My father was now a U.S. Army sergeant. Although his armory flew the Confederate flag, his unit was despised because they were working for President Kennedy. My father was a good soldier. He followed orders and counseled his young troops to remain calm and not refuse to serve. Probably for the first time in his life, he was treated like a pariah. The local whites would ride by the armory and yell obscenities. When my father and two other guardsmen went to the bank to deposit their checks, they were cursed and spat upon.

I began high school in the fall of 1963, still waiting for integration. Like most teenagers I was in turmoil and very insecure. But life in Mississippi was in turmoil and very insecure. Medgar Evers had been gunned down in the summer of 1963. The March on Washington seemed glorious to me that August. Being a Southern Baptist I knew good preaching when I heard it, and Dr. King's speech was powerful. My father and I had words over King, concluding with my father's threat to disown me. That turbulent year ended with President Kennedy's assassination. I was shocked by it, but the hatred of Kennedy was so strong in Mississippi that only my Catholic friends wept.

In 1964, I was intensely interested in the presidential election. That November a civic club recruited me to report county voting returns to the television networks. The circuit clerk, who was also the voter registrar, was quite gracious to me on election evening and happy to relate the returns of a Goldwater sweep of our county for my phone call to NBC. But the more fascinating lesson that evening was hearing the clerk explain how the poll tax and voter registration worked. He explained that he and the other local political leaders paid the two-dollar poll tax for all white voters they considered friends. Naturally, they never paid the tax for a black voter. Then the clerk gave me the literacy test he administered to potential black voters. He asked me to interpret some incomprehensible section of the Mississippi Constitution. I failed. He laughed and then gave me the white test, which he announced I had passed because I was the "right color."

As high school continued, I grew more and more dismayed with the South. The accumulated effects of the lynchings in Picayune and Greenwood, the demonstrations in Jackson, the Birmingham church bombing, the synagogue bombing in Meridian, Medgar Evers's murder, the beating at the William Pettus Bridge in Selma, the murder of Viola Liuzzo, the beatings of the Freedom Riders, Vernon Dahmer's murder not far from home, and especially the gruesome Neshoba County murders of James Chaney, Andrew Goodman, and Michael Schwerner had caused me to become, in my junior year, the "commie" of my high school.

As a senior, I really wanted to go out of state to college, but I knew we could not afford it. I picked Mississippi State for two reasons. They had had a successful basketball program and had been willing to play in the NCAA against a team with black ball players. Moreover, the school had desegregated without incident. However, neither reason meant that State was a liberal institution.

When I arrived in the fall of 1966, there were fewer than a dozen African Americans among the ten thousand students. But for the first time in my life I was in school with black students. Life at State was tough for me. My mother was dying of cancer. My roommate dropped out and so I lived alone. My first real romance had come to a traumatic end. I sought solace in religion by joining the Baptist Student Union, which may have been the only integrated student organization on campus. One black student was the most popular member because he brought life to our weekly programs and a remarkable tenor voice to our choir. Then came the rub. The local First Baptist Church, which had always welcomed the BSU choir, rescinded its invitation for them to sing at a special service. The black choir member made the choir unacceptable. I quit the Southern Baptist church and never returned.

At State, I took my first course ever in Afro American history and discovered Sojourner Truth, Frederick Douglass, Marcus Garvey, and other heroes to African Americans. I heard and met Fannie Lou Hamer. But when Dr. Martin Luther King was assassinated, many white students celebrated. Some of these students bragged about what they had done to blacks in their hometowns. I was a student who had been verbally abused all through high school and college for not standing when "Dixie" was played at sporting events, so I hid in my room in fear and horror.

In my senior year, I took the law boards and was notified by Ole Miss that my acceptance would be automatic upon application. My childhood dream of becoming an Ole Miss law student was virtually in hand. But Mississippi was not in my future. Instead, I decided to join VISTA. The application required written recommendations. The only one that I remember soliciting was the one I was most proud of being able to seek. It came from my mother's first cousin Mayjewel and her husband, Roy. I used them as references because of their bravery in their own school desegregation struggle. Roy was a lineman for Mississippi Power. Their four children attended Beacon Street Elementary, the same crowded school that I had attended in third grade. While I was in college, it was announced that Beacon Street would be desegregated. As she took her children to school on the first day, Mayjewel was threatened by the Klan. That evening she told Roy about the incident. The next day Roy took the children to school. After he escorted them inside, he returned to the street and confronted the Klan. His physical presence was imposing, but it was his bearing, his moral outrage, and his courage which really intimidated them. After that, the Klan left Beacon Street Elementary alone. Whether Roy and Mayjewel's recommendation helped me be accepted into VISTA I will never know. But their inspiration gave me the gumption to join VISTA.

While VISTA was intended as one of the federal government's antipoverty programs, it was a scary challenge to a white boy from Mississippi. My friends thought I was becoming a "civil rights" worker and that I was crazy. I was assigned to South Carolina, where *Brown* was finally being implemented. It was the summer of 1970, and the dual school system was being closed. The Republican candidate for governor was running on an antibusing platform; in fact, school buses were overturned by a mob at the urging of his aides. Klan posters littered every telephone poll. I was placed with the Horry and Georgetown counties community action agency, whose director was black, as were most of its employees. I was working in my first full-time job and black men and women were my bosses.

South Carolina was a powder keg, and Horry and Georgetown counties were as heated as anywhere in the state. Horry had a very large and open Klan. Georgetown's Klan was smaller and more underground, but we were soon all too aware of their presence.

One Sunday I attended a white church where the minister preached about how their community did not need outside agitators. As I sat there, I did not at first realize that he was preaching about me. Soon afterward, one of the VISTA volunteers in that community began receiving threatening messages from the Klan. He asked my roommate and me to spend the night and offer moral support. Being a Mississippi boy, I knew the kind of moral support we needed, and I borrowed a shotgun from the husband of one of my co-workers. He was reluctant to loan the gun, but I told him our friend's house had a snake and I had offered to kill it. That night, for the first time in my life I slept with a gun. My two friends from the North seemed happy for me to have the gun. There were no threats that night or the next, and we soon ended our armed defense. However, over the next two years we did receive intermittent threats. One volunteer was assaulted by a gang. I was chased one night, and in broad daylight I was threatened with a gun and told to get out of town.

We were so inept as "outside agitators" that we actually organized the first march in Andrews, South Carolina, by accident. It was really just a group of about thirty black teenagers who came to a meeting we held downtown in the community center on Main Street. After we broke up, the teenagers had to walk down Main Street to their homes. Someone must have reported the "protest march," but by the time the police responded everyone was home. All we ever organized on purpose for the kids was a dance. Later, we engaged in some direct community action that resulted in mass meetings and protests over the treatment of food stamp recipients.

After two years in VISTA, I applied to Ole Miss law school, but my best friends were now in South Carolina. I did not feel that my work was done. A fellow VISTA let me know he was coming to law school at the University of South Carolina, so I applied and was admitted. I tried to remain active in politics while in law school. My closest friends were more radical than anyone I had ever met. We participated in political campaigns, labor union organizing, and fighting utility rate increases. After law school was over, I applied for only two jobs. One was working with Indians in Neshoba County, Mississippi, and the other was with the local legal services office. I did not want to return to Mississippi and feared moving to the place where Chaney, Goodman and Schwerner were murdered, so I was glad when I was offered the legal services job in Columbia.

Legal services work was stressful. I had too many cases, and I was not even saving the world. The high point of practicing law with legal services in Columbia, South Carolina, was appearing in family court before the Honorable Harold R. Boulware. Judge Boulware had been the local NAACP counsel in *Briggs v. Elliott* and of course his name appears on *Brown v. Board of Education*. Judge Boulware regaled me with stories of his NAACP work and Thurgood Marshall. He was a great judge, but my fondest memories are of his generous spirit.

After three years of working at legal services, I joined the faculty at USC law school. I had some expertise in consumer law and was writing a book on truth in lending. I had already taught as an adjunct for a year and had been exposed to Bea Moulton and Gary Bellow's work on lawyering skills. I have now been a law teacher for twenty-five years, and *Brown* has been an inspiration for my philosophy of both teaching and scholarship. In clinics and other courses, I try to help my students become both competent and compassionate lawyers, using Thurgood Marshall, Harold Boulware, and other brave lawyers as models for my students to emulate. My scholarship and research of the past decade have been overwhelmingly influenced by *Brown*. Virtually all my papers, articles, chapters, and books are related to Reconstruction, the civil rights movement, and *Brown v. Board of Education*.

In my work, I have had the privilege of working with Judge Robert Carter, Judge Constance Baker, Joseph De Laine Jr., and others involved with *Brown* and civil rights. Frankly, I feel extraordinarily lucky to have been able to live a life so different from that of other white boys from Mississippi. I cannot really explain why, but I know that in 1954, *Brown* started me on a path that no one living in the housing projects in Laurel, Mississippi, could ever have imagined. The supper table in my home is much different from the one I grew up at. Yes, there is a mother who is both spiritual and an advocate for social justice. We also have far too much broccoli and cauliflower and not nearly enough biscuits, let alone tomato gravy. Yes, there is a father at the table who rants about the president. But there is no question that everyone at the table knows the true meaning of *Brown v. Board*. Our daughters think nothing of having a sleepover with or going out with black friends. Our whole family marched with forty-seven thousand other people, mostly African Americans, against the Confederate flag flying over our statehouse. We have all demonstrated against the death penalty. I never did become that civil rights lawyer, but *Brown* has changed me and my family forever.

W. Lewis Burke was born in Meridian, Mississippi, in March 1948 and attended elementary and secondary schools in Laurel and Gulfport, Mississippi. He is presently a professor of law at the University of South Carolina School of Law in Columbia.

16 A Journey of Conscience

Samuel M. Davis

The year was 1956. The scene was a social studies class in Pascagoula Junior High School in Pascagoula, Mississippi. I was in the seventh grade. Our social studies teacher, Mr. Dunnam, also was a state senator in the Mississippi Legislature. He proudly announced in class one day that the legislature had just voted to repeal the state's compulsory school attendance law, and he further announced that the reasoning behind the repeal was to thwart implementation of the Supreme Court's decision in *Brown v. Board of Education* two years earlier in 1954, or as he put it, so we would not have to go to school with colored children.

From 1956 until 1977, when the compulsory school attendance law in Mississippi was reenacted, Mississippi was the only state in the Union without a compulsory school attendance law.

I have little memory of how I felt at the time. My best recollection is that I felt nothing one way or the other, primarily because I did not fully understand the import of what our social studies teacher had told us. Moreover, I did not feel that it would alter my life in any respect. The latter certainly proved to be the case, because as we know in retrospect, the *Brown v. Board of Education* decision, which the Court had ordered be implemented "with all deliberate speed," was met with massive resistance in the South. Even in 1956, however, change was on the horizon.

Higher education in Mississippi was integrated in 1962 when James Meredith enrolled at the University of Mississippi, an occasion attended by violence, the deaths of two persons, and an extended occupation of the campus by federal troops. At my own college, however, in the fall of 1962 no black students enrolled. In fact, no black students enrolled during my four years there. Only when I entered the University of Mississippi School of Law did I have black classmates. Some of my professors in college, particularly political science and history professors, raised my consciousness about *Brown v. Board of Education* and civil rights generally, but not until I entered law school did I have occasion to explore the legal bases of *Brown v. Board of Education* and other cases and legislation dealing with racial discrimination.

On a personal level, I developed a friendship with one of my black classmates that continues to this day, as well as with a student in the third-year class who became the first black graduate of the University of Mississippi School of Law in 1967. He later became an associate justice on the Mississippi Supreme Court, was elected president of the Mississippi bar, and today is a senior partner with a major law firm in Jackson, Mississippi. I found that through those friendships I grew as a person in a way that would not have been possible without changes brought about by the *Brown* decision.

Those were magical years at the University of Mississippi Law School. The dean was Joshua M. Morse, who had been a longtime, well-respected practitioner in tiny Poplarville, Mississippi, before being named dean. His father, also a lawyer, had shared office space at one time with another Poplarville native, the infamous Theodore G. Bilbo, who served Mississippi as governor and U.S. senator and who was a well-known racist. Surely, when Josh Morse was named dean of the law school, the expectation was that he would maintain the status quo and the conservatism that had long characterized the school. The bar, alumni, and other Mississippians must have been as surprised at what Josh Morse became as President Eisenhower was surprised at how Earl Warren turned out as chief justice of the U.S. Supreme Court.

In his first year as dean, Josh secured a leave of absence to attend Yale Law School as a Sterling Fellow to obtain an LLM degree. His stay at Yale proved to be an epiphany. In fact, for many years a connection had existed, and still exists, between the University of Mississippi Law School and the Yale Law School. For example, one of the most well respected faculty members at Yale, the late Myres McDougal, received an LLB from the Ole Miss Law School in 1935.

Josh was determined to broaden the perspectives of law students. He obtained a huge grant from the Ford Foundation that was used, among other purposes, to create a new course: Problems of Public Law brought professors from other law schools to the law school for two weeks each to teach the course. The first group was from Yale and included Dean Louis H. Pollack and Professors Eugene Rostow, Alexander Bickel, and Myres McDougal.

The next semester brought faculty from Harvard Law School, including future solicitor general Archibald Cox. During the following two semesters, faculty from New York University School of Law and Columbia Law School taught the course. The Ford Foundation grant also was used to fund scholarships for minority and other students. It also brought additional faculty to the law school, including recent Yale graduates Walter Dellinger, Michael Horowitz, Fred McLane, Joseph Chubb, Michael Trister, and George Strickler.

The young Yale professors collectively brought an exciting, dynamic atmosphere to the law school. Students in their classes looked beyond Mississippi to the country as a whole, seeing the policy issues of the day, including the growing civil rights movement, in a broader perspective. At the end of our first year, several of us were sent all over the country—from New York to Chicago to Oakland—to summer clerkships in the Office of Equal Opportunity (OEO) and other programs, an experience that also opened my eyes to the world beyond my provincial upbringing. My own experience took me to New York City, where I worked for the Vera Institute of Justice in its bail reform project, work that brought me into contact with John Amos, then an up-and-coming part-time actor and former football star who later became well known in his role as the father, James Evans, on the TV sitcom *Good Times* and more recently as General Percy Fitzwallace, the chairman of the Joint Chiefs of Staff, on *West Wing*. Working daily in the Tombs and in the New York court system, and simply traveling around the city, I also realized that summer for the first time that racial discrimination and injustice were not exclusively Southern phenomena.

My days at the Ole Miss law school were a defining time for me. My experience in the summer internship with the Vera Institute of Justice encouraged me in my second year of law school to join the first group of law students to enroll in a new course, Legal Problems of Indigence, that in addition to a weekly classroom component required us to spend twenty or so hours a week in a new OEO Legal Services Office in Oxford, working with indigent clients. Most, but not all, of our clients were black, and all of them represented the destitute, the downtrodden, and victims of injustice and discrimination. Inevitably, however, the work of the Legal Services Office drew attention and criticism, most of it directed against Dean Morse for his "liberal" innovations and his efforts to change Mississippi. Ultimately, such criticism of Dean Morse, especially for bringing the left-wing Yalies to the law school, brought about an end to his tenure as dean. The year I graduated from the law school, 1969, also marked the departure of Dean Morse from the law school.

The University of Mississippi is a far different place today than it was in 1962 when James Meredith enrolled in the midst of violent protest. Sadly, former dean of the law school Robert J. Farley and former professor Bill Murphy, who had the temerity to suggest that perhaps James Meredith had a right under the U.S. Constitution to attend the University of Mississippi, were practically driven from office. Only two and a half years after the violent confrontation, Senator Robert F. Kennedy, who as attorney general during the integration crisis had presided over James Meredith's enrollment at Ole Miss, accepted an invitation from the law school student speakers' bureau to come to campus to speak. He and his wife were welcomed by a capacity crowd at the university's Coliseum, where they received an enthusiastic standing ovation. "You have no problem the nation does not have," the senator told the crowd. "You share no hope that is not shared by students and young people across the country. You carry no burden they, too, do not carry."

Senator Kennedy's assessment is still true today. Although the university now is home to the William F. Winter Institute for Racial Reconciliation, named for former governor William Winter, who was a member of the Commission on Racial Reconciliation appointed by President Bill Clinton, Mississippi today is no more a model of racial harmony or the object of scorn than any other state.

During 2002 and 2003, in a yearlong celebration, the University of Mississippi commemorated forty years of integration of higher education in Mississippi. The occasion was inaugurated by a reunion of students who were in school at the time, university faculty and administrators, and former U.S. marshals and National Guardsmen who had maintained the peace and protected James Meredith during his stay at Ole Miss. It closed at the end of the year with a speech by former attorney general Nicholas Katzenbach, who had been the personal representative of Attorney General Kennedy in 1962. One of the great ironies of both the opening and closing ceremonies was that James Meredith, who lived in a world of silence during his days as a student, except for the conversation with the U.S. marshals who guarded him, could not enjoy a moment alone at the celebration. People constantly surrounded him, seeking his autograph, wanting to have a picture made with him, or simply wanting to say hello.

In that junior high classroom in 1956, little did Mr. Dunnam know the impact his comments would have on his students. *Brown v. Board of Education* was one of the great watershed cases of the twentieth century, and its legacy is still felt today. It helped assure that the future of race relations in the United States would be shaped not by the likes of my seventh-grade teacher and state senator, but by the likes of his students and the students in the all-black junior high school on the other side of town.

Samuel M. Davis was born in Pascagoula, Mississippi, in November 1944 and attended elementary and secondary schools there. He is now dean, director of the Law Center, professor of law, and holder of the Jamie L. Whitten Chair of Law and Government at the University of Mississippi School of Law in Oxford.

17   Promise and Paradox

Charles E. Daye

Monday, May 17, 1954, would have been anticlimactic if I had known then what happened. It came three days after I celebrated my tenth birthday. As I learned much, much later, that day the U.S. Supreme Court announced its great decision in *Brown v. Board of Education*. It was a day as unremarkable as any other ordinary day in the life of a black boy on the farm in rural Durham County, North Carolina. Back then, May heralded a favorite time—the time for rites celebrating the end of the school year. Pageants and outdoor events dominated our anticipation. In one event, widespread throughout the area, we "wrapped the Maypole" with bright pastel crepe streamers. Ten boys and girls marched clockwise meeting ten boys and girls marching from the opposite direction. Each boy or girl, in turn, went over then under the streamer of a classmate coming from the opposite direction, going round and round and round until the crepe, attached at the top of the pole, came down and down, in smaller and smaller circles, until it reached the bottom of the pole, fully wrapping it. Little black girls marched in pressed white dresses, white lacy socks, and fine patent leather shoes. Little black boys wore their best white short-sleeve shirts, blue shorts, and Sunday shoes. The shoes took a beating in the dirt and dust. But we didn't worry about that. We had a majestic appearance, with each child wearing a glossy red ribbon draped across his or her chest. In May 1954, schoolchildren of both races all around Durham County engaged in these activities—at their solidly segregated schools—that signaled summer soon coming and the end of a school year.

School year's end was bittersweet. It was sweet getting out of school for the summer. It was bitter missing one's buddies and friends all summer. Many black youngsters—drawn from distant and even isolated enclaves from all over the southern part of the county—might not see each other again until school resumed in the fall. Missing was literal. Most didn't have electricity or telephones. Without phones there was no distant contact. All contact was real, live, in-person, except for the occasional letter, of the many we promised to write, which few did. Those who wrote didn't write much, or many times.

★ ★ ★

The mid-1950s was a different time in a different world. Amid the school's end activities of May 1954, in my fourth-grade class, we were anticipating going to the fifth grade in the fall. When we did go to fifth grade, we fully expected to go to our same Pearsontown school; to ride the same school bus along the well-known rural dirt roads, driven by customary sixteen-year-old student bus drivers; to go to class with our same buddies, friends, classmates; to be taught by familiar homeroom and subject teachers, art teachers, music teachers, and physical ed teachers; to be coached by the regular coaches; to be drilled in School Safety Patrol precision marches by the same assistant principal; and to be served lunch by our favorite cafeteria "moms," who would reward us by sneaking an extra square of vanilla cake onto our tray when we showed them a report card with good grades. Everybody—literally, everybody—at the school was black. To a fifth-grader in rural Durham County, going to school this way was the way it was and, for all we knew, the way it had always been.

In those halcyon days in a rural, black, ten-year-old fifth-grade boy's life, news traveled slowly. In my world, it would have been Monday night, at the earliest, listening to news on a battery-powered radio, before anyone in my household would have heard that something had been decided by the U.S. Supreme Court way up there in far-off Washington, D.C., about "desegregation" of the schools. "Desegregation" and "integration" were big, hard-to-pronounce words, with no discernable meaning to a ten-year-old black boy, but rather an unfamiliar, if not strange, diction. It is doubtful that I or any one of my pals had ever heard them anywhere, certainly not at home, and certainly not in any context that gave the words a reality suggesting that they might actually affect us in some direct, personal, intimate, important way. The day after *Brown* was decided, May 18, 1954, the Tuesday newspaper doubtlessly would have had some notice, if not a headline. The paper was delivered about 6:00 AM. But I would have been awakened about quarter to 7:00 AM to wash, dress, eat, and catch the school bus at about 7:25 for the forty- to fifty-minute ride to school. The bus went all around the main roads and dusty, dirt backroads of the southwestern part of the county to reach Pearsontown School in the central southern part of the county. Pearsontown School only went up to the eighth grade. So the high schoolers transferred to another bus to continue a cross-town trip of about fifteen miles, through the city of Durham, to the far northeast corner of the county to the Merrick-Moore School.

Bus rides were not dreaded events. It was a time for talking and playing, teasing and pleasantries—from the first-graders just getting started to the high schoolers who would graduate at the end of the year. None of us thought riding the bus was drudgery or disliked it, except maybe the timid "somewhat backward boy" whose hat somebody was always grabbing and throwing out of a bus window.

We had no appreciation that we were fortunate to have a serviceable school bus whose heater actually worked on cold winter days. This was not like the days of yore we heard about from elders in the community: "Boy, you know we had to walk five miles each way to a one-room shack of a school when the white boys and girls rode on their brand spanking new school bus. They rode right past us, poking their heads out the window laughing at us, throwing stuff *at* us and *on* us, if they could."

Ten-year-olds, therefore, did not read the newspaper until they got back home from school—and then they only read the funnies page, as soon as they could wrest it from a sibling. I am quite certain that for some indeterminate period after May 17, 1954, I did not read a solitary word about anything called *Brown v. Board of Education*. Somewhere, sometime, somebody along the way—maybe a teacher, the preacher at church, or even one of my folks—might have said something about the schools getting integrated and that maybe blacks and whites might go to school together. To a person, I am certain, the boys and girls in my ten-year-old cohort wanted nothing to do with "this integration stuff." We liked our present school world—secure, sane, affirming, safe, nurturing, and, of course, all black. Indeed, we liked it just the way it was, the way it had always been in our short lives, and maybe the way it always should be. If asked, although nobody did that I recall, we would have said, "I like *my* school. I don't what to go to any white school."

"This integration stuff" could be unsettling for a ten-year-old. But mostly it was just too much to fully contemplate. If we worried about any impending change, we didn't worry much and we didn't worry long. Because for the longest time, nothing—and when I say nothing, I mean *absolutely nothing*—happened to change the way students went to school in Durham County. I don't recall that we worried; but if we did worry, it was not much. In truth, any worry about going to a white school or whites coming to our school would have been a terribly wasted emotion. From the ten-year-old-student's perspective, nothing happened in Durham County, North Carolina, about white and black boys and girls going to the same school. I graduated in 1962 from my still all-black county school. In an assessment of the initial effect of the case in its first eight years, it would be honest to say that *Brown* didn't *even* change my school.

★ ★ ★

Almost four years after *Brown*, as an eighth-grader in the spring of 1958, I went with my mother to the Parent Teachers Association meeting at my still 100 percent black elementary school. I cannot recall the reason I went. But it was not a major or unusual matter. Students went with parents to a PTA meeting when their class was presenting a skit or had something else to do, such as sing in the Glee Club. There might have been another reason, but I hope I was not there because I had acted out and my mother had been summoned to a conference about my conduct! If that was the reason, I have repressed it in my memory.

A speaker was at PTA that night. Floyd B. McKissick Sr., who was destined to become a national figure in the civil rights movement, was already a civil rights fighter in Durham, although I didn't know it at the time. He had been a civil rights fighter even before he got out of law school. As a law student, he became a named plaintiff in the lawsuit that, in 1951, had banished de jure exclusion of blacks from the law school at the University of North Carolina at Chapel Hill—*McKissick v. Carmichael*. The case was actually initiated by other students then enrolled at the North Carolina College School of Law, but one graduated and another was found not to be a North Carolina resident. McKissick, Sol Revis, James L. Lassiter, and J. Kenneth Lee were substituted as plaintiffs. The basis of the lawsuit was that in 1950, the law school at North Carolina College, hastily created after *State of Missouri ex rel Gaines v. Canada* to serve blacks—wholly excluded from attending the University of North Carolina—was not, as required by *Sweatt v. Painter*, capable of providing an education equivalent to the law school at the University of North Carolina because it did not have comparable resources, facilities, library materials, faculty, status, or history. By the time the Fourth Circuit Court of Appeals decided the case, McKissick, however, had already graduated from the North Carolina College School of Law in Durham and he only enrolled in UNC Law School's summer school in 1951. Over two decades later, in 1972, I would become the first black professor to hold a tenure track position on the law faculty at the University of North Carolina.[1]

At the time he was speaking at the PTA in the spring of 1958, McKissick had been out of law school some seven years. Now, here he was speaking to the parents about justice, desegregation, equal education, and constitutional rights. He was talking about bringing lawsuits against the Board of Education to enforce the *Brown* dictate against the procrastination and downright foot-dragging resistance to desegregating the Durham County Schools. His speech was electric. Everybody got excited. As he spoke, the audience response of "Amen, brother!" "Tell it like it is!" "You sure enough telling the truth!" acclaimed his every call of emphatic declaration. McKissick's voice, powerful and resonant, rose and fell like a preacher's, with insistent staccato cadences and irresistible high-pitched tones of persuasion. (Though he would become one later in life, McKissick was not yet a preacher.) The speaker's passion and conviction conveyed a message stronger than, and independent of, the precise substance of his oration. That speech made such an impression that I later asked my mother, "Who did they say that man is?" She said, "That is Lawyer McKissick."

Right then and there, that very night, I decided: I am going to be a lawyer. Now, I didn't have the first clue what a lawyer did, no idea of what it took to become a lawyer, and not even the foggiest idea how I could accomplish such a feat. Yet I never wavered, never even considered *any* other career choice. What other things I might have done, whatever other fate might have awaited me, I cannot say. On that night at Pearsontown Elementary School, in the spring of 1958, in my view, it would be fair to say that while the law of *Brown* was unable to change even my school (which I did not want anyway), paradoxically, the promise of *Brown* changed my life.

★ ★ ★

In my time, like so many other African Americans, I have celebrated *Brown's* legal, political, social, and economic emanations even as I lamented its detriments along these same dimensions. These are some among many other promises and paradoxes.[2] *Brown* offered enormous and incalculable uplift and promise to African Americans. In an initial burst of enthusiasm that proved to be unwarranted, an analyst could read *Brown* to represent a fundamental turning point in U.S. jurisprudence. Its words that "segregated schools are inherently unequal" could, and did, send an affirmation of black peoples' worthiness. *Brown's* broader emanations, somehow, could be understood as affirming black people's humanity at a fundamental sociopolitical level. It offered us uplift and validation as citizens after centuries of denial and oppression premised on our unworthiness as human beings. Upon discerning consideration, and as I grew mature, I, like others in my community, saw *Brown* as an affirmation of aspects of our most basic and profound yearning for justice. We might even have believed that *Brown* meant that equal protection required equality in fact in the educational opportunity afforded to black children. We could have stretched this to mean that segregation was unlawful not for the practical or empirical reason that separation imposed by white supremacists between black and white always turned out to be unequal for blacks, but for the moral and ethical proposition that unequal education was unjust.

   Brown decided nothing of that sort. It was not based on any articulated or explicit moral or ethical principle. In its context, we have no trouble recognizing the unspeakable dilemma the *Brown* Court confronted. The country stood on the brink of a potential massive explosion in reaction to a decision for the black plaintiffs in *Brown*. The justices could reasonably have perceived a real danger to the Court as an institution. It is understandable, in political respects, therefore that the Court did not explain the result on any principled, or doctrinally neat, ethical or moral ground. Undoubtedly, that was unthinkable. Neither the framers of the equal protection clause nor the Supreme Court ever manifested either an egalitarian ideal or moral or ethical clarity favoring equality in fact for black citizens. How can *equal protection* not mean *equality in fact?*

   It takes a lawyer to explain best how things can be legally equal but not equal in any factual sense. A case must be interpreted based on the issues raised by the facts. The issue before the Court in *Brown* was whether the states' intentional imposition of unequal education on the basis of race violated the equal protection clause. The issue had three distinct elements. First, school segregation was intentionally imposed by agents of the state. Second, the segregated schools were always unequal. Third, the inequality of schools was premised on race. Thus, the issue of unequal education in the absence of *intentional* state conduct was not presented. The question of unequal education, even if intentionally imposed, but on *some basis other than race*—such as geography or family income—was not raised. The issue of educational quality *for the sake of educational quality* for black citizens was not raised.

In all the cases in which all three *Brown* elements do not coexist simultaneously, the Court has refused to find a violation of equal protection. If black schools are unequal for reasons not intentionally imposed by the state or its agents, there is no constitutional violation. If black schools are unequal because of funding variances on some nonracial basis, such as the wealth of a school district, there is no constitutional violation. If black schools are unequal and black students do not have access to advanced resources, new physical plants, or experienced teachers, but we cannot show that the state did this intentionally on the basis of race, there is no constitutional violation. In this way *Brown*'s enormous, even spectacular, promise eroded away in legalisms that diminished it. That is a paradox. It is also a pity.

When *Brown* did result in integrated schools, the blessing was not unmixed. Indeed, the reasons for fighting so hard for integrated schools had nothing to do with the belief that black *and* white or black *or* white children learned better or more when they sat in the same classes. Rather the fight for *Brown* was about equalizing educational resources between white and black schools. The logic was that the ingenuity of white supremacists in forestalling resource equality between separate black and white schools was so inexhaustible that the only real answer was for blacks to go to the same schools with whites. The quest for educational resource equality resolved into an attack on segregation itself as a last-ditch, and somewhat desperately chosen, surrogate for a thrust toward equal educational material and human resources for black kids. Here paradox is too real: *Brown* meant that African American parents in a quest for improved resources had to send their most tender children to be taught in schools with white supremacists' children.

And this burden was not without significant costs. We blacks of the *Brown* era whispered to each other about this paradox. *Brown* had been so affirming in fundamental ways. We could not go about openly criticizing any aspect of *Brown* without feeling embarrassed and fearing to seem ungrateful or even racially disloyal to those who fought so hard, for so long, and risked, and sometimes lost, so much—including their fortunes and their lives—to get us, indeed, as far as *Brown* had brought us. Some blacks did speak out about it. Some who did were called separatists. Some who did, like Malcolm X, were labeled militants. Some, like those who advocated "community control of schools," were labeled as unrealistic and were marginalized, socially and politically, even in our own communities. But there was widespread concern about the critically diminished ranks of black principals; the demotion, firing, and exclusion of black teachers; and the interest white rank-and-file teachers might not have in educating our sons and daughters. In consequence, we watched and we worried over the welfare of our children at the hands of at best disinterested, at worst hostile, white teachers.

We feared, rightly, pernicious benign neglect. This could be evidenced in subtle things. An incident that happened to our daughter in junior high illustrates what I mean. As we were wont to do, her mom and I one day shortly after a new term started, asked our daughter, "How are things going in school?" "Oh, fine," she allowed. "Tell us what you've been doing in your classes," we asked. She proceeded to relate things about each. Then she got to a subject and said, "Well, we don't do anything in that class." More inquiry revealed that our daughter and five or six other black girls in the class were allowed to sit in the back of the class to talk or play or do whatever they wanted to do, so long as they did it quietly, while the teacher taught the white girls in the class. The next morning we were at the school before the bell sounded. We told the school officials emphatically that we wanted our child to be involved in learning whatever the teacher was supposed to be teaching and that it was unacceptable to us that the black girls were allowed to be nonparticipants in the class. We worried about the loss of adequate black role models of success with the loss of examples of blacks actually in charge of something in the schools, instead of forced to traipse around as a phalanx of "assistant principals" and minor officials. We worried that white students also internalized images that "blacks cannot be in charge of anything" and had to have white supervision to do stuff right.

Brown's costs included the loss of teachers who went to church with us, who "took us personal" and would communicate with our parents when something seemed amiss. In the first grade after a few days of class, my teacher noticed that I did not have lunch as we lined up at 12:10 PM to go to eat. She inquired, "Charles, where is your lunch?" I replied, "I don't have any lunch." "Well, let's get in line to go to the cafeteria." "But I don't have any lunch money," I told her. "You just come along," she said. Now lunch was maybe only a quarter, but Mrs. Dawson paid that quarter for my lunch. The next day the same thing happened. At the end of that second day, Mrs. Dawson handed me a note and told me to put it in my pocket and to be sure to give it to my mama when I got home. I did. Upon perusing the note, my mama seemed sort of upset. "I fixed your lunch. I had a nice bologna sandwich in your lunch bag. Did you lose it? Did you leave it on the bus? Did somebody take it?" She posed these insistent queries. "No, ma'am," I told her. "What on earth happened to it?" she wanted to know. "Well, I got hungry and I ate it at recess," I told her. She knew recess was at 10:30 AM. "When did you start doing that?" I told her, "Yesterday and today when I got hungry." I imagine such incidents still happen. But such an incident was nothing special back then. Rather, it was part of the traditions of that time and place.

Teachers were icons who devoted careers to trying to get us to live up to our potential, and they nurtured, cajoled, berated ("Stop it. You're acting *stupid*."), spanked and paddled when necessary, and loved us like parents away from home. We lost some of that in a more formal, postintegration world. But there is a bit more that we lost. Back then schools, even those quite a distance, were actually a part of the community's fabric. The community took "ownership" of the schools, which were regarded as a form of communitarian property. These were not just places where students went to learn; these were places that belonged to the community as a source of pride, leadership development, and acculturation. Teachers took extra care to teach well beyond "the book" in English, and geometry, and French. They taught us life. They taught us values. They taught us cultural materials well beyond just the books—how to dress properly, how to hold a fork at a formal dinner (which none of us had ever attended), how to have manners, how to care about ourselves, how to have ambition, and how to exhibit good citizenship.

★ ★ ★

The promise of *Brown* has not yet been fulfilled. Schools in the North and South are resegregating at alarming rates and the gap in educational achievement between whites and minorities persists. Inequitable funding of public education remains associated with race, economic status, and educational attainment. Even so, the promise of *Brown* continues to represent a national commitment to social justice, political fairness, and human rights. That is *Brown's* paradox.

Our nation needs a time of innocence for the children who, after all, are its future. We need to provide a time for childhood without the burdens of segregated education. To accomplish this enormous but vital task, the nation must continue to draw its inspiration from *Brown*.

NOTES

1. Charles E. Daye, "People—African American and Other Minority Students and Alumni," in *The University of North Carolina School of Law: A Sesquicentennial History*, 73 N.C. L. Rev. 675 (1995).
2. I have discussed this question more fully elsewhere. See Charles E. Daye, "Justice Byron R. White in 'Contributions of the Warren Court to Equal Protection,'" *North Carolina Central Law Journal* 12 (1981): 260.

Charles E. Daye was born in May 1944 in Durham, North Carolina, and attended elementary and secondary schools in Durham County, North Carolina, from 1950 to 1962. He is now Henry P. Brandis Distinguished Professor of Law at the University of North Carolina School of Law in Chapel Hill.

18 A Different Kind of Education

Davison M. Douglas

The world of my childhood—Charlotte, North Carolina, during the 1960s—was almost exclusively white. All my early childhood friends, whom I met in the neighborhood, school, church, the YMCA, and Boy Scouts, were pretty much like me—white and from a middle-class background. During my grade-school years, I encountered few black people except those who cleaned homes or performed yard work in my neighborhood. I never had a black schoolmate until eighth grade. I was vaguely aware of the civil rights movement, but it didn't mean much to me as a child.

My family possessed a deep commitment to education. My mother had been a schoolteacher and later taught at a local community college. My father had grown up on a college campus where his father and uncle were professors. My parents encouraged my brothers and me from an early age to excel in school. But until school desegregation began in Charlotte in earnest in 1969 (when I entered eighth grade), I did not understand that education involved much more than successfully completing one's assignments.

The city of Charlotte had confronted the desegregation mandate of *Brown* earlier than most Southern cities. In 1957, Charlotte had been one of the first cities in the South to desegregate its schools (though this desegregation involved only three students and remained token for several years thereafter). The city's leaders shrewdly used this early desegregation to promote Charlotte as a city with a good racial climate and hence an attractive place to do business, in contrast to cities such as Little Rock and New Orleans that had bitterly fought school desegregation efforts. Mindful of the detrimental effect of racial conflict on economic development, Charlotte was also one of the first Southern cities to desegregate its public accommodations in 1963, one year before the Civil Rights Act of 1964 made such desegregation mandatory. Over the course of the 1960s, the newly consolidated Charlotte-Mecklenburg School District, one of the largest in the nation, converted to a pupil assignment plan based on residence. Though residential segregation preserved the racial identity of most of the city's schools, by the late 1960s, a higher percentage of black students in Charlotte attended a racially mixed school than in almost any other city in the United States.

In 1968, in response to the Supreme Court's landmark decision in *Green v. New Kent County* that required Southern school districts to "convert promptly to a system without a 'white' school and a 'Negro' school, but just schools," NAACP lawyers filed suit to further desegregate the Charlotte-Mecklenburg schools. The federal district court judge, James McMillan, who presided over Charlotte's school desegregation litigation, was initially skeptical, noting that the Charlotte-Mecklenburg School Board had "achieved a degree and volume of desegregation of schools apparently unsurpassed in these parts, and . . . exceeded the performance of any school board whose actions have been reviewed in appellate court decisions." McMillan later observed: "The Charlotte schools for many decades had been models of excellence. Many black children were going to 'white schools.' In the rural areas, . . . a few schools were genuinely desegregated. . . . I could not understand how anybody should complain about the Charlotte-Mecklenburg schools or insist that stronger measures were necessary to afford equal opportunity to the black children."[1]

But over the course of the litigation, McMillan took a dramatically different view. Because of the large number of all-white and all-black schools in Charlotte (due to residential segregation), McMillan concluded that the school board had not satisfied the Supreme Court's desegregation standards articulated in the 1968 *Green* decision and hence ordered the board to develop a desegregation plan that would thoroughly integrate *every* school in the Charlotte-Mecklenburg school system. In the fall of 1969, a partial desegregation plan was implemented while the school board continued work on a more complete plan.

I arrived for eighth grade in September 1969 to a wholly new environment. School buses brought scores of black children from poor inner-city neighborhoods to attend "our" white middle-class school. Most of the students at my middle school had never gone to school with a person of a different race or from a vastly different economic background. The response of the white students was at best indifference and at worst hostility. By the same token, many of the black students expressed frustration at being sent to an alien environment where they were clearly unwanted. Fistfights were frequent. Bathrooms were particularly unsafe. Although due to the "tracking" of students based on perceived ability I encountered black students during that initial year of desegregation primarily in gym class and the school cafeteria, I had firsthand experience with the inevitable conflict that arose from the adjustment to wide-scale integration. In a series of scuffles, I was razor bladed; a good friend of mine lost one of his front teeth.

In the meantime, Judge McMillan remained insistent that every school in the Charlotte-Mecklenburg system be thoroughly integrated and in early 1970 ordered the most ambitious school-busing plan in the nation. McMillan's actions provoked bitter reactions throughout much of the city, and the school board appealed his busing order all the way to the U.S. Supreme Court. In April 1971, the Court vindicated Judge McMillan and affirmed his ambitious busing plan. In the process, the *Swann v. Charlotte-Mecklenburg* case defined for the nation the obligation of urban school boards to use busing to overcome residential segregation. As it became apparent that McMillan's insistence on a thoroughly integrated school system could be thwarted neither legally nor politically, many of my white friends left for private schools. Though my parents worried that the frequent disruptions might affect my education, I remained in public schools through graduation. In time, the violence receded as both black and white students struggled together to make things work. I became a proponent of desegregation, defending its virtues to some of my more skeptical friends. I wrote a letter to the local newspaper urging the defeat of an antibusing school board member. My high school biology teacher, who had a poster of Robert Kennedy on her door, expressed gratitude for my letter, though others were not so supportive.

Although my high school academic classes were largely segregated due to tracking, I developed friendships with several black students outside the classroom, particularly on the debate team, on the basketball team, and in student government. The debate team traveled widely. Long hours on car trips forged friendships born of common experiences and aspirations. My time on the basketball team and in student government afforded similar opportunities for new friendships and a deeper understanding of those whose life experiences had been so different from my own. When I graduated from high school in 1974, I realized that I had received an education far richer than I could have ever imagined. I had learned as much outside the classroom as I did inside.

Without question, the trajectory of my professional life has been influenced in significant measure by my experiences as a student in the public schools in a city undergoing dramatic racial change. I wrote my PhD dissertation on the history of school desegregation in Charlotte and eventually returned home to North Carolina to practice civil rights and employment law before entering the legal academy in 1990. As a professor of constitutional law and history, my scholarly interests have centered primarily on issues pertaining to race.

Charlotte, I think, fared better than most cities in the desegregation process. A 1987 report prepared by the U.S. Commission on Civil Rights concluded that of the nation's 125 major school systems, the Charlotte-Mecklenburg school system had achieved the greatest amount of racial mixing between 1967 and 1985. The system did lose about 20 percent of its white students between 1969 and 1983, but those numbers were smaller than those of almost every other major city in the nation. By the same token, educational achievement levels rose in Charlotte. In 1968, one year before busing began, the city's sixth-graders possessed reading and math skills one year below the national average; by 1981, sixth-graders' reading and math skills were one grade *above* the national average. But the achievement gap between black and white children, though narrowed, did remain. Desegregation also contributed to a political shift in Charlotte. During the late 1970s, Charlotte elected its first black school board chair, Phil Berry, and during the early 1980s, its first black mayor, Harvey Gantt, both with broad biracial support. As one white political leader said of Gantt's election, "I would say to you that prior to school integration, we couldn't have done that, regardless of how good he was."[2]

In recent years, Charlotte has abandoned its school-busing plan, contributing to a reduction in racial mixing. Moreover, in 2007, the U.S. Supreme Court ruled that the Constitution does not permit school districts to consider race when making pupil assignments, even when the goal is to expose schoolchildren to classmates of different races. The decision will likely contribute to greater racial separation in America's public schools, which, from my point of view, is a real loss.

NOTES

1. Davison M. Douglas, *Reading, Writing, and Race: The Desegregation of the Charlotte Schools* 128, 135 (Chapel Hill: University of North Carolina Press, 1995).
2. Ibid., 246, 251.

Davison M. Douglas was born in Charlotte, North Carolina, in 1956 and attended elementary and secondary school in Charlotte from 1962 to 1974. He is now the Arthur B. Hanson Professor of Law at the William and Mary School of Law in Williamsburg, Virginia.

19 Sacrifice, Opportunity, and the New South

Mildred Wigfall Robinson

In 1954, I was enrolled in the fourth grade in the Berkeley County Training School in Moncks Corner, South Carolina. The Berkeley County Training School was the public school that educated all the Negro children, grades one through twelve, who resided in that county.

I remember quite clearly the day that the *Brown* decision was handed down. I recall the image of my father, the school principal, ringing a handbell while standing on a little hill that was just outside of his office. He rang that bell daily to signal the beginning of the day's classes and the end of recess. We had been outside enjoying recess in the late spring sunshine and assumed that he was signaling its end. We quickly noticed that this was not his intent—he was beckoning us to him. We ran to him. He announced with great excitement that the Supreme Court of the United States had just held that segregated schools were unconstitutional. He explained to us that there were no longer to be separate schools for white and colored children. The decision was, of course, *Brown v. The Board of Education of Topeka, Kansas*. His excitement was infectious, and so we children all became excited. We ran around and generally acted out that excitement. We did not, of course, understand all the ramifications of the decision. We could not know that widespread resistance to the appropriate implementation of the decision would ultimately lead to the firing of beloved teachers, the closing of facilities so much a part of life in black communities, and the fragmenting of the support and protection that those communities provided to their young. Nor could my family know how much the dismantling of the dual school system would demand of us personally. On that day, we celebrated the decision.

And then, nothing happened—at least insofar as public education (for that matter, anything else!) in South Carolina was concerned. The schools were not desegregated. There were, of course, the "Impeach Earl Warren" billboards alongside the highways. But in most ways large and small, it was as though the case had never been decided.

My family moved in the summer of 1954 from Moncks Corner to New-berry, South Carolina, where my father became the principal of the brand-new but still unequal Gallman High School—the school that served all the Negro students in Newberry County. Local newspapers carried no civil rights news, nor did local radio stations, which routinely signed off at the end of each broadcast day by playing a thumping rendition of "Dixie." Most homes did not yet have television. My family remained informed of current events through a black weekly newspaper published in Pittsburgh, the Pittsburgh Courier (I was the local newspaper girl). And of course we subscribed to *Ebony* and *Jet* maga-zines—publications that also reported current (sometimes, even to my young mind, horrific) events as the national struggle continued. But I suspect that many black families in our town existed in a news vacuum.

The years passed. I remember that those of my schoolmates who lived in outlying parts of the county rode a fleet of school buses (driven by fellow stu-dents) for hours each day in order to attend school. Pursuant to an arrange-ment struck with local landed white farmers, our school days were truncated year after year (in by 7:45 AM and out between noon and 12:30 PM) during spring planting and fall harvesting, as my father sought to avoid having stu-dents drop out of school entirely during those periods. As violence or the threat of violence tore the South asunder, my parents cautioned my brothers and me against rash statements or actions that could bring undesirable atten-tion to our family. Through it all, our principal (my father) and our teach-ers (including my mother) constantly exhorted us to work hard in order to prepare for the day when we would finally be a part of the larger society—a day that they assured us would come. I studied (How could I do anything else when every teacher in the school was poised to report the least instance of misbehavior to my father?), practiced piano when I absolutely could not avoid doing so, played clarinet in the high school band (first chair in my junior year in high school!), practiced the sultry look and walk of my favorite female teacher, and developed a killer crush first on the new mathematics teacher in town and then on the equally unavailable star of both the football and basket-ball teams.

There was one significant change in the pace of local life during my sopho-more year in high school. My high school band was invited to participate in the local Christmas parade as one of the parade units, thus becoming the only nonwhite parade entry. The members of my high school band and our coun-terparts in the local white high school band eyed each other warily on that cold December day, but the parade went off without incident. We marched proudly along Main Street, receiving cheers of approval from members of the black community and, at best, polite applause from the local white citizens. But for that event, my high school contemporaries and I continued along our separate ways and we all graduated from segregated schools in the early 1960s.

Well, I really didn't graduate with my class. In the fall of 1961 on the strength of my performance on standardized tests, I left high school after the eleventh grade (leaving my heartthrob behind) to enter Fisk University in Nashville, Tennessee. I did not attend integrated classes until I entered Howard University School of Law as a first-year student in the fall of 1965.

The educational experiences of my brothers, all younger than I, reflect the changes then taking place across the South. My oldest brother graduated from the all-black Monroe High School in Cocoa, Florida, in 1966 (my family had relocated twice by this time). My second brother was selected to attend the formerly all-white Cocoa High School after his sophomore year in high school. In doing so, he became one of seven black students in a student body of twelve hundred. There were no black teachers or administrators at the school during his two years there. He graduated from that high school two years after his older brother graduated from Monroe. My youngest brother attended high school in Atlanta, Georgia, to which my parents relocated in the summer of 1967—their last move. My family was only the second black family to move into their sprawling, southwest formerly all-white Atlanta neighborhood. When my brother entered Therrell High School in Atlanta, he became one of fifteen black students in a class of four hundred. Over the next four years, For Sale signs sprouted like crabgrass on the lawns of white homeowners in block after block in that area. By the time he graduated with his predominantly white class four years later, the freshman class was overwhelmingly black—the result of four years of white flight.

Meanwhile, as the racial barriers fell (or were pushed over), my father's former students—graduates of Gallman High School in Newberry, South Carolina—succeeded as military and law enforcement officers, as graduate students and scholars, as nurses and doctors and teachers. They successfully pursued careers in the larger society that had previously been closed to them.

★ ★ ★

I don't know what my father ultimately came to think about *Brown*. I know that in his later years he marveled at the obvious signs of progress in the South. Indeed, as I have indicated, he could see evidence of change within our family. He cheered the academic and career achievements of family, friends, and former students. In 1962, after a brief stint in higher education administration at a small historically black college, he sought to again attain employment as a high school principal. He was able to gain employment only as an assistant principal in the newly desegregating local high school, thus becoming second in command to a white principal less well trained and with fewer years of experience than himself. As such, he shared the fate of numerous other black administrators and teachers. From 1954 to 1972, over 90 percent of black administrators and more than forty thousand black teachers were either fired or demoted. Shortly thereafter, my father left public education administration permanently. He had been a talented teacher and administrator, dedicated to and loved by his students. In his later years, his work afforded him only tangential contact with everyday school life. I know that he deeply missed that contact.

My mother was not one of the hundreds of black administrators and teachers fired during that period. In fact, she spent her entire professional life in the public schools of South Carolina, Georgia, and Florida, first as a teacher and in her later years as a guidance counselor. However, even having succeeded in pursuing her chosen career, she too experienced unanticipated and unwarranted pain.

The last years (1967–1988) of her long career as a teacher (1954–1988) were spent in service in the public schools of Atlanta. I asked her what it was like initially to be assigned to teach in a formerly all-white school in Atlanta, an assignment that she received early in the 1970s. She described to me one early experience. She and one of her new white colleagues were standing in one of the school windows early in the school day. As they stood there, they watched school buses arrive, load white children, and depart to take the children to other area schools that remained overwhelmingly white. I can only imagine the pain of watching those children depart, fully aware that she was one of the reasons for that departure.

She told me of another early experience illustrative of the challenges of establishing authority in the changing environment. The mother of a young white teenage girl who had proven to be a disciplinary problem for my mother stormed into my mother's classroom early on one school day demanding to know why my mom had reprimanded the teen. My mom reports that she calmly turned to face the irate parent and asked whether the teen had reported her own behavior. As one would expect, the parent admitted that the teen had not. By the time the conversation ended, a chastened—newly respectful—parent departed. My mother reports that the child's behavior improved dramatically. This is a small story, but it is illustrative of the many ways in which those who stayed the course learned of and from each other.

In moving around the Atlanta community with my mother, I have seen that there are many former students, both black and white, who love and respect her. Because of the massive firings of black teachers and administrators that took place across the South during those years, this mutually important opportunity to learn respect and, with luck, to share mutual affection was denied to residents in far too many communities. Those black teachers who received assignments to formerly white schools were themselves often stretched to the max as they sought to establish themselves in new educational settings in the face of hostility from peers, disrespect from white students, and the needs of black students for support and, occasionally, intervention. As these pioneers retire, they have not been replaced—a failure that has contributed directly to the present dearth of minority teachers in public schools. In sum, I think it accurate to say that for many of them, including my father, *Brown* meant sacrifice—a loss of the personal and professional relationships that had existed for them prior to (realistically for most of the South) 1964.

For me personally as an adult, *Brown* has meant professional opportunity. Unquestionably, I would not have had the career as a legal academician that I have enjoyed had it not been for the changes that flowed from that decision.

I began teaching in September of 1972, several years after graduating from law school, dabbling briefly in the business sector and returning to Harvard to earn an LLM. My father greeted my decision with relief. I had gone to law school determined to pursue a career other than teaching, a decision with which my father, to put it mildly, was not pleased. It was quite one thing to admire and appreciate the careers and accomplishments of Thurgood Marshall, James Nesbitt, Oliver Hill, and the other civil rights giants of the 1940s and 1950s. It was quite another for the apple of his eye to become a part of a profession that was quite emphatically white and male, offered very limited career opportunities for black attorneys in general ("You won't be able to support yourself!"), and placed at risk the lives of those who actively engaged in civil rights work. Teaching, on the other hand, seemed to him an ideal way in which to put my legal training to use. From his perspective, law teaching was highly respected, placed me at no risk of physical harm, and was remunerative—I would be able to make a decent living. And it probably didn't hurt that I was following in the footsteps of many in my extended family. From my perspective, teaching would allow me to expansively explore the area with which I had become intrigued during my time at Harvard—the pervasive impact of our system of public finance on the everyday lives of American citizens. This lifelong study implicated questions that I viewed as going ultimately to the heart of fairness issues. Could a taxing system appropriately both raise money and provide incentives? What kinds of incentives? Who would pay? Who would not? How would such policy decisions affect both private and public spending decisions? How, ultimately, should the burdens as well as the benefits of government be best allocated?

I have found attempting to negotiate social acceptance more daunting; there was no natural social niche for me among my white male colleagues. I was one of the relatively small cadre of female faculty (consistently roughly 10 percent of the overall faculty) and the sole black woman on my faculty for twenty-seven of my thirty-four years (as of this writing). I would have welcomed a book of racial etiquette as a source of snappy responses to defuse potentially charged moments when, for example, an invitation to dinner early on was graciously accepted with a declaration that we "have never visited a black home before."

Surely this social unease is the inevitable outcome of our childhood seg-regation. Most of my generation still lives apart, worships apart, and socializes apart. We did not grow up together; rather we have learned to work together as a result of legal necessity. I confess that I, too, remain somewhat entrapped by the vestiges of our unhappy racial history. Even now upon meeting a white South Carolinian (or any Southerner, for that matter) of my age, the barrier of racially charged common memory persists. Our mutual discomfort is poten-tially disabling.

I think that I glimpse what might be through the lives of my three chil-dren. From birth, the children have lived in integrated settings. My life experi-ences have clearly affected my approach to parenthood; I have never been able to assume that our environment was benign. Early on, I was on constant alert for racial overtures, for some sign that my children were racially threatened. This vigilance led me, at one point, to call the mother of a child who had invited one of my children to a sleepover to inquire whether she knew of my child's race. "My child is black. You do know that, don't you?" I succeeded in embarrassing both of us mothers, though the children were, happily, unaware of this little drama.

Despite my concerns, I feel that my children have fared well education-ally. They are all products of the college preparatory track in their public high schools. I too was tracked during my high school years. My father expertly deployed the resources available to him to construct a challenging course of study intended to prepare as many of us as possible for college and life be-yond. Thus, I fully expected my children to avail themselves of the best that their schools had to offer. I am concerned, however, at the racial isolation that resulted from the pursuit of their high school programs. Each child was frequently the only black child (at best, one of only two or three) in his or her honors and advanced placement classes. Further, teachers of color were virtu-ally absent from those classrooms. In twelve years of high school—six courses per year for a total of seventy-two teachers—my three children were taught by a total of ten nonwhite teachers: three each for two of the children, four for the other. Teachers by virtue of their positions of authority underscore the legitimacy of what is being required of students and reaffirm the range of pos-sibilities available to those students. I believe that the presence of persons of color in positions of authority is symbolically important for *all* children during these formative years. In short, I have come to believe in the importance of role models.

On a more positive note, I see the ease with which my children associate with their white friends (here in Charlottesville, a majority of their friends are white). They share similar likes and dislikes—as have friends across time. I admire their mutual love and acceptance and want very much to believe that I am witnessing the forefront of permanent national change. In sum, my children seem to me to be moving through life aware of race but not unduly burdened by it.

It is finally clear to me that my children view race differently than I. What I now share with you was written in 1999 by my eldest daughter. She was required to prepare an essay as a part of an admissions process. I use this with her permission:

> Our legal system has proven itself capable of fostering generalized social change over the long-term and for this reason I will always be in awe of its power. Growing up and living in Charlottesville, I have been sheltered from a great deal of racism. However, Charlottesville's history tells a very different story. In the years following *Brown v. Board*, Charlottesville public schools were closed for roughly one year to avoid integration. Some of my friends' parents were unable to graduate from Charlottesville's public high schools because the school system was shut down. The reaction of local city and state officials evidenced the widespread hostility that the Supreme Court's decision encountered in the south. And what local officials fought against vehemently then, my friends and I, both black and white, can still only look back [upon] in disbelief. It is this disbelief that I love. With regard to race relations, we differ so radically from our parents that we are unable to truly understand or appreciate the events of their lifetimes. And these differences run far deeper than a simple generation gap. *Brown v. Board* not only represented a legal change but for many residents of Charlottesville it catalyzed a social metamorphosis that has come of age in my generation. That is awe inspiring.

"*Brown* catalyzed a social metamorphosis that has come of age in my generation." That was one young person's view at a moment in time forty-five years after the *Brown* decision was handed down.

My father died when my first two children were relatively young and before my third child was born. I know that he would be astonished by the South through which his children and grandchildren move.

Or would he?

Mildred Wigfall Robinson was in the fourth grade in Moncks Corner, South Carolina, when *Brown v. Board* was decided. She received her elementary and secondary education in the state's schools, which remained segregated, then graduated from Fisk University. She is Henry L. and Grace Doherty Charitable Foundation Professor, University of Virginia School of Law in Charlottesville.

20 Crossing Invisible Lines

Linda A. Malone

I was born the year that *Brown v. Board of Education* mandated that schools desegregate "with all deliberate speed," yet until I went to college, I never had a class with a person of color, Asian American, or Hispanic. In that first year of college, 1971, I left the South and my hometown of Chattanooga, Tennessee, for the first time and moved to New York, motivated in large part by my naive belief that I was leaving this culture of racial discrimination behind.

"All deliberate speed" was not an acceptable term for the South in which I grew up, particularly when it came to the elimination of racial discrimination. By "the South," with a capital S, I am not referring to a region following state boundaries or below the Mason-Dixon line. Northern Virginia, for example, was not part of my South—it was too fast, too slick, too mainstream American. American culture had not been as thoroughly homogenized as it is today by corporations, television, and the Internet. It still felt as if everything moved more slowly in the South, from the words on our lips to the changes in our cities and towns. Slowness was a virtue, delay an acceptable method of avoidance, and more polite than outright refusal. It is no coincidence that the filibuster was elevated to an art by Southern politicians.

Even as a child I was not surprised when nothing changed in my elementary school in the years following *Brown* and all the adult talk of integration. I knew how deep and immutable the resistance to change would be. My parents were racists by any definition. My father told me that African Americans had short foreheads because they are more closely related on the evolutionary scale to apes than white people are, and therefore less developed in their intelligence. Of course, he had never seen the high, elegant forehead of a Masai warrior or an Ethiopian woman, and he didn't say "African Americans," much less the then progressive term "Negroes" or even the commonly used "colored people." My parents used the N-word, a word to this day I cannot say or even write. Today I go to hip-hop concerts with my daughters and involuntarily flinch every time the word is used, which is often. I understand that people of color have adopted the word as their own, using it with each other to diminish its evil power.

I wonder how many children and young people today have any understanding of the intensity and commonality of racism in the 1950s. I think my own daughters associate it exclusively with the Ku Klux Klan and skinheads, not really appreciating that there were ordinary-appearing people who believed unbelievable things then, and still. My children go to integrated public schools and think nothing of it. Teenagers today aspire to black culture, mimicking the dress, the talk, the gestures of their favorite black singers or rappers, just as their favorite white performers Justin Timberlake and Eminem do. *Brown* was a judicial thunderbolt to the South, thrown straight at the core of racism in the teaching of children. Delay was an effective but ultimately unsuccessful weapon against the Supreme Court decision, and other methods of resistance and avoidance would take its place.

I noticed no change in racial relations in my limited universe until 1964. I was in the fifth grade of my all-white public elementary school, Lookout Mountain Elementary. Anyone who has gotten anywhere near Tennessee knows Lookout Mountain, a tourist destination and Civil War battlefield with massive, multiple billboards (a thing of the past in most states) lining every interstate and commanding drivers to "See Rock City!" "See Ruby Falls!" "Ride the Incline!" The Incline is a cable car that runs from the base of the mountain to the top, filled with tourists during the summer but running all year round. I lived halfway up Lookout Mountain, on a tiny, very rural, residential street with four or five houses that for some inexplicable reason had the only stop for the Incline other than those at the base and the top of the mountain. During the school year the only passengers were two or three students and the African American maids, nannies, and yardmen riding on the closest thing we had to public transportation to the top of the mountain to work at the homes of the wealthiest white families.

The topography of Chattanooga directly reflected the deep social and economic stratification of the city. The city itself is in a valley of the Chickamauga River, surrounded on all sides by Lookout Mountain, Signal Mountain, and Missionary Ridge. The wealthy white families lived on the summits, in monumental homes looking down on the lights of the city. My own home's location reflected our unclear social standing. My parents weren't poor, but lower middle class was the best we could claim. I was lucky to be sent to the elementary school on the top of the mountain, a far better school than the school I would have attended going down the mountain. Some of the wealthiest and most prestigious families of the South lived on the top of Lookout Mountain. Many of them were from "old Coca-Cola money," the creators of the original Coca-Cola formula and the founders of the Coca-Cola bottling plant in Chattanooga, the first in the world.

The station at the top of the Incline had public restrooms labeled "White" and "Colored." Never having set foot in the "Colored" bathroom, I can only assume it was identical to the "White" bathroom, with separate doors inside leading to the men's and women's bathrooms. The white and colored bathrooms each had a water fountain at their entrance, also separately labeled "White" and "Colored." I had seen public facilities labeled like this for all of my short life and thought nothing of it—except when "Whites Only" facilities were not accompanied by facilities for anyone else, I always wondered where they could go to the bathroom or get a drink of water.

One day the racially divided bathrooms were there, and the next day when I went to school the "White" and "Colored" signs were replaced with "Men" and "Women" on the outside entrances. There were no signs above the water fountain. The "White" bathroom was now for women, and the "Colored" bathroom was for men. I saw over the next few months how difficult it was for the "colored" people, many of whom I knew well from our morning and afternoon Incline rides, to walk into a bathroom with a white person. Many of them seemed to wait until no one else was in there before going in. For the next two years while I finished elementary school, the specter of those signs hung over the water fountains, with whites and blacks still using the previously assigned fountains on the basis of race, with the exception of the tourists who could not see the barriers they were crossing. The outward signs came down elsewhere— on buses, hotels, and restaurants. The inward signs remained up—with the seating on buses and in restaurants just as racially segregated as the schools and employment would remain for some time.

> Well they passed a law in '64
> To give those who ain't got a little more
> But it only goes so far
> Because the law don't change another's mind
> When all it sees at the hiring time
> Is the line on the color bar.[1]

It made me sad to see my adult black friends hesitate outside those doors. They were good, kind people who joked with me, complimented me on my schoolwork, and shared their food with me on the afternoon rides. Despite everything I had been taught at home, and the segregated world I inhabited and saw on TV, I felt in my heart that there was something very, very wrong at the bottom of that momentary hesitation outside invisible doors. For me, that was when the walls of racism that had been so carefully constructed around me as a child began to crumble.

I had been watching the evening news with my parents during dinner for several years, but it wasn't real and personal to me until the civil rights movement got the attention of the entire nation in 1963. My parents voted at every opportunity in every presidential race for George Wallace, governor of Alabama and self-proclaimed racist. I saw the fire hoses and snarling dogs unleashed by him on black and white protesters in Selma, Alabama, and thought simply, as a child would, that it was a terribly mean thing to do to somebody who isn't trying to hurt you. My parents thought Wallace was doing the right thing. Martin Luther King didn't think so, and was shown saying so more and more on the evening news. It was impossible not to listen to Martin Luther King. His voice was musical and powerful, with the unmistakable imprint of hundreds of years of Southern churches in its cadences and crescendos. I also heard a gentleness to what he said, a word not often used to describe his speaking style. He seemed so confident that what he was saying was right and good, that there was no need to beat someone over the head with it, as Wallace or Malcolm X did. His demands for fairness, better jobs, better pay, and better schools were exactly the things my own parents said we needed. I couldn't figure out why they thought they had more in common with the wealthy white families on the top of the mountain than with the poor white and black families in the valley whose needs were so similar to theirs. What King said simply made sense to me—more sense than what I had been hearing at home. With a child's certainty I divided people into good people and bad people, and even in my limited world those categories didn't correspond to blacks and whites. As strongly as my parents disagreed with Martin Luther King's position on integration, the only personal comment I remember them making about King himself was that "he was going to get himself shot." When they listened to Malcolm X, they said that "he should be shot." They both would be shot, of course, along with George Wallace. Before that would happen, I was listening to what Martin Luther King had to say, until one day, August 28, 1963, he spoke to me personally:

> I have a dream that one day down in Alabama, with its vicious racists, with its governor having his lips dripping with the words of interposition and nullification—one day right there in Alabama little black boys and black girls will be able to join hands with little white boys and white girls as sisters and brothers. . . .
> And so let freedom ring . . . from Stone Mountain of Georgia.
> Let freedom ring from Lookout Mountain of Tennessee.
> Let freedom ring from every hill and molehill of Mississippi—from every mountainside.

Brown was beginning to have an impact on our local public high schools. There were no middle schools in our city—elementary schools went to sixth grade and high schools went from seventh grade to twelfth grade. I assumed I would be going to a public high school for seventh grade. Instead, I was told by my elementary school principal that a private donor who gave scholarships to low-income students for high school had offered me a scholarship to go to Girls' Preparatory School, the female counterpart to the two private military boarding schools for boys in Chattanooga, Baylor and McCallie. All I had to do was to pass the entrance exam for GPS and meet with the donor to pass whatever personal test she utilized in these meetings with prospective scholarship students. I had no trouble with the entrance exam but was terrified of the meeting. I shouldn't have been. The donor was a kind, elderly woman putting her husband's old Coca-Cola money to a good use supporting educational opportunities in high school and college for students without the financial support necessary. She would pay my pricey high school tuition for the next six years.

All five hundred or so GPS girls met every morning together for chapel. We had four years of required Latin, one year of required Bible study, and an excellent education in everything except science and math (deemed more important for boys than for girls). Typing wasn't offered because, we were told, GPS was not a vocational school. We were all white. As the public schools slowly integrated, I heard parents speak with approval of our school's segregation and the entrance exam, which many parents saw as a safeguard against racially open admission if there was ever a black family who could afford the tuition. GPS was not a boarding school, but Southern families sometimes sent their daughters to live with relatives in Chattanooga to attend the school before college and marriage (in that order), probably even more often after *Brown*.

As we went through all my high school yearbooks a few years ago, my daughters and I laughed at the undeniably absurd uniforms, with twelve front pleats, a black ribbon tie, eighteen tiny buttons, brown leather belt with the GPS buckle, white crew socks, and saddle oxfords or loafers. Occasionally in town I would see African American girls my age or younger wearing a GPS uniform, and I would know that they were wearing clothes given to their mother by her employer. No one would wear that ugly uniform unless she had to, and I felt sad and deeply ashamed for reasons I couldn't explain.

I couldn't explain much of what I was feeling. I couldn't discuss my discomfort with segregation and racism with my teachers or my friends, and certainly not with my parents. I couldn't imagine raising it with the few African Americans I knew, who probably wouldn't have been comfortable discussing it with someone white, and my age, under any circumstances. I lived in a segregated society and no one I knew who was white seemed to have any significant problem with it. Television shows still didn't depict interracial relationships or situations in ways that might offend viewers like my parents. I kept my feelings and opinions to myself, afraid of the consequences if anyone found out what I was thinking. How could I be so sure that segregation was wrong when everyone else I knew personally seemed to think it was all right or at least an acceptable way of life?

Once again, some much-needed affirmation came from an unexpected source. This time, Huck Finn spoke to me. Given a choice between reading Mark Twain's *Tom Sawyer* or *Huckleberry Finn*, I checked out *Huckleberry Finn* because it was available and everyone else was waiting for *Tom Sawyer*. I couldn't stop reading. I thought the book was the most subversive thing I had ever read. The transformation of Huck's views on racial relations, which no one around him seemed to share, brought about through the kindness and dignity of Jim, mirrored my own experiences and sense of isolation. Mark Twain is a respected Southern author—did my teacher, the librarian, or any of the other adults not know what was in this book? Did they not recognize what Huck concluded—that his Southern upbringing was flat-out wrong when it told him not to associate with a black man like Jim just because he was black? I felt empowered to believe segregation was wrong, and someday even to say it. I had no less traditional Southern white icons than Huck Finn and Mark Twain on my side. When I first learned many years later that some community groups want *Huckleberry Finn* taken off reading lists because it reinforces racial stereotypes, I wanted to proclaim the brilliance of a book that can so accurately depict those stereotypes in order to destroy them, so that even an uneducated, unsophisticated child like Huck Finn, or me, could see through them. It is the Mark Twain equivalent of a rapper using the N-word to eradicate its evil power. Our discomfort in either context is, I hope, part of the healing process.

In my last year of high school, one African American girl was admitted to seventh grade. I never knew her name, but I looked for her every morning at chapel from across the gym. Seniors rarely crossed paths with seventh-graders, and I never met her. Nothing is worse for a teenager than standing out from the crowd in a socially unacceptable way. As a teenager I imagined the courage it took for her to come to school every day—her or any of the other children who crossed those frightening, invisible barriers to education in those years. As a mother now, I can't imagine the strength and torment it must have taken a mother to send her child into a vicious battle the child would have to fight on her own, in a building and a world beyond a mother's reach and protection.

Coca-Cola stock thrived, and I went to Vassar College on a wave of soft-drink consumption. My parents were horrified I was going "up North" for college but were mollified by a vision of a sheltered Seven Sisters college that bore no resemblance to the real thing, which after two years of coeducation was almost half men and brazenly radical in every respect. Fearful to the last minute that they wouldn't let me go, I signed up to live in Main dorm because it was all women and I had read about it in Mary McCarthy's famous book,

The Group. I soon learned that racism was not limited to the South. A woman in my dorm who had gone to a Brooklyn high school torn apart by gang wars spoke openly about her hatred for blacks and Hispanics. Yet, for the first time in my education there was diversity in the classroom, and I can testify from experience what a dramatic improvement it made in the classroom experience. It was an absolutely vital transition to living in a comprehensive world.

While I was reveling in this diversity, there were movements on campus for separation that took me by surprise. Many alumnae and students thought the college had lowered its admission standards in order to admit men, an accusation the college vehemently denied. More compelling was the argument that Vassar should have remained exclusively a women's college to provide an environment in which women could lead and be educated without the constraints of male predominance. My friend Jamaica and I joked about how little contact with boys we had had in our high schools and agreed that, for us at least, dealing with the other half of the species seemed a fairly important educational initiative.

Jamaica was not her actual name. She lived across the hall from me in one of the few single dorm rooms. She had heard me talking to my roommates in the hall with my Southern accent, and come running out to ask where I was from because she too had been singled out by her accent. From that day on, she called me Chattanooga, or Chatt for short. In return I called her by her home, Jamaica. We became close friends over the course of our freshman year. In the spring, she broke up with her boyfriend, and we spent many nights for several weeks going over every aspect of the breakup, as college friends will do. Then suddenly she seemed to be avoiding me and my calls. After several weeks when the pattern was unmistakable, as she went into her room I confronted her to ask what was going on. She told me that her friends who were black ("black" being the identification chosen by them in the 1960s and 1970s, rather than chosen for them as in the past) had told her she was spending too much time with me—a white girl, and even worse a Southerner. They had suggested that she should spend more time and share her problems with them instead.

I understood, all too well. We were both outsiders at Vassar and oblivious to the political and social dynamics for others of our friendship as outsiders in this radically different environment. She needed their community and support more than she needed my friendship, and I would have made the same decision in her place. We parted good friends, and the next year she moved into the small and beautiful dorm that was almost entirely filled with African American students. It wasn't de facto, reverse segregation as some of my classmates suggested, but a necessary separation to find an identity and cohesive community of support for the difficult social transitions they were confronting at the time. I did hope, however, that this need for separation would be a temporary transition and not a permanent solution for her, myself, or my country.

> This Court has long recognized that "education . . . is the very foundation of good citizenship." *Brown v. Board of Education*. . . . For this reason, the diffusion of knowledge and opportunity through public institutions of higher education must be accessible to all individuals regardless of race or ethnicity. . . . Effective participation by members of all racial and ethnic groups in the civic life of our Nation is essential if the dream of one Nation, indivisible, is to be realized.
>
> . . .
>
> Just as growing up in a particular region or having particular professional experiences is likely to affect an individual's views, so too is one's own, unique experience of being a racial minority in a society, like our own, in which race unfortunately still matters.
>
> —Majority opinion by Justice Sandra Day O'Connor in *Grutter v. Bollinger*, upholding the diversity admissions program of the University of Michigan Law School, decided on June 23, 2003

NOTE

1.   Lyrics from "The Way It Is" by Bruce Hornsby, copyright by Zappo Music, 1986. Reprinted by permission.

Linda A. Malone was born in June 1954 in Chattanooga, Tennessee, and attended elementary and secondary schools in Lookout Mountain, Tennessee, from 1960 to 1971. She is now the Marshall-Wythe Foundation Professor of Law at the College of William and Mary, School of Law, Williamsburg, Virginia.

21 Segregation in Memphis

Phoebe Weaver Williams

Among the first wave of baby boomers who arrived after the World War II veterans returned home, I was born during 1946, in Memphis, Tennessee. My father, Alonzo Weaver II, had served in the all-black Ninety-third Signal Company of the U.S. Army. Serving his country with distinction in battles at New Guinea and the Solomon Islands, Dad earned two bronze stars.

Military service interrupted Dad's education since he was among the many men drafted after the December 1941 bombing of Pearl Harbor. At the time, he was a senior attending a historically black institution, LeMoyne College (now LeMoyne-Owen College), in Memphis, Tennessee. While attending college, he worked nights to help support his mother. Fortunately, the draft did not defeat Dad's efforts to secure a college degree; he had completed sufficient credits to graduate during the previous semester. The draft, however, prevented Dad from participating in his college graduation ceremonies.

Dad's mother, Ruth Weaver, appreciated the value of formal education. A progressive woman in other areas as well, Ruth even permitted her children to refer to her by her first name. Ruth decided to forego the income that Dad, her oldest son, could have provided to help support her family of eight children. Instead of sending my father to work after he completed elementary school in Wynne, Arkansas, she sent him to live with an aunt so that he could attend Dunbar High School in Little Rock. There was no high school for black children in the Wynne township. Later, Ruth left Wynne, separating from Lon, my grandfather, and moved the family to Memphis, Tennessee. Prior to moving there herself, Ruth boarded some of her children with an accommodating woman in Memphis so that they could attend the black public high school there. As a result of Ruth's initiative my aunts and uncles (with one exception) attended and graduated from Booker T. Washington, the first black public high school in Memphis. By the time I was born, Ruth had already succumbed to some mysterious illness, so I never had the opportunity to know her. Nevertheless, Ruth's efforts to educate her children helped inculcate in my family a strong respect and desire for formal education. When Ruth attended the 1942 LeMoyne College graduation, walked across the stage, and accepted Dad's diploma, she must have felt both sadness and joy.

During his stint in the military, Dad returned home for a one-week leave, during which he married his college sweetheart, my mother, Claribelle Howard Weaver, on June 14, 1943. They would not see each other again until he returned to the United States during September 1945.

Dad seldom spoke about his childhood. We never really knew or appreciated what it must have been like for him to grow up poor in a rural Arkansas community that separated its black and white citizens so thoroughly that they lived in separate townships. Under the Southern incarnation of apartheid, whites resided in Forrest City and blacks resided on the other side of the railroad tracks in Wynne. Dad seldom spoke of his military experience or how he felt about risking his life for a country that separated its military forces based on race. Neither Dad nor Mom complained about the discrimination or the racism that they experienced while working as teachers in rural county schools outside Memphis, Tennessee. When I questioned Mom about litigation to equalize the salaries of black and white teachers, she explained that they all knew that county teachers earned less than city teachers, and black county teachers earned even less than white county teachers. Yet, they never dwelled on the racial inequities.

The few instances when my parents discussed racial discrimination were memorable. Dad told me about the discriminatory treatment he received after returning to the States from World War II. Dad was with a group of soldiers assigned to escort German prisoners of war to a detainment center. The group stopped at a restaurant and attempted to purchase some refreshments. The white restaurant owner refused to serve the black soldiers, stating that he did not serve Negroes. He, however, noticed the German POWs standing outside and stated, "You [the soldiers] can bring them in," but "you boys will have to wait outside." Both anger and sadness came over Dad when he told me this story. Dad was obviously frustrated by the depth of racism that could be harbored by some people. That restaurant owner would have rather served meals to the enemy than to black soldiers. The subject of racial discrimination surfaced again after the Supreme Court issued its historic decision in what I would later learn was *Brown I*.

★ ★ ★

Brown I was one of two Supreme Court decisions my father ever discussed with me. Another case decided in 1952, *Brotherhood of Railroad Trainmen v. Howard*, had involved my maternal grandfather as the named plaintiff in what I would later learn was a significant duty of fair representation case. The latter decision, however, was not brought to my attention until much later. As educators, the *Brown I* victory for equal educational opportunities may have meant more to my parents. I was one month away from age eight when the

Court announced its decision. Nevertheless, the discussions that ensued left a lasting impression.

Initially, May 17, 1954 was not an unusual day. I ran to meet Dad as his car pulled into the driveway. He was then teaching eighth-graders at one of the rural black schools in Shelby County, Tennessee. That evening, Dad seemed unusually happy and animated. I understood the reason for his excitement after he explained to me that the Supreme Court, the highest court in the land, had announced that segregated schools were against the law. Even at that young age I understood what Dad meant by racial segregation. I had already learned that our family did not enjoy the same privileges as did white families residing in Memphis. So, when Dad announced that the Supreme Court stated that segregated schools were unlawful, I expected immediate improvements. I peppered Dad with questions. Unlike many parents of his generation, my father encouraged my inquisitiveness with answers. I asked, "Does this mean that you are going to send me to the white kids' school?" He hesitated. "Well, no, I don't think so. We'll have to see." I pressed further. "Dad, does this mean that the white kids will come to my school?" "I don't know." "Does this mean that we will get to go to the zoo and the fairgrounds whenever we want to?" Again, he was not sure. He finally stated that we would have to wait and see what would happen.

As I reflect on the questions I posed, I can understand why the victory in *Brown I* engendered such hope for change. As an almost eight-year-old, I wanted and expected change immediately. When I reflect on how long I waited for *Brown I* to make a difference in my life, I can appreciate the frustration of those who still wait and hope. I waited not realizing that the following year the Supreme Court issued *Brown II*, a decision Dad never bothered to mention—a decision that government officials, members of the judiciary, and private citizens would use to evade *Brown I*'s mandate for a number of years.

★ ★ ★

As a child living in Memphis, Tennessee, I quickly learned that racial segregation resulted in unequal opportunities. During our school outings at the Overton Park Zoo we were greeted with a sign at the entrance that announced that certain days—Thursdays, I believe—were colored days. (Colored families could visit the zoo only one day of the week.) Most working black parents could not take their children to the zoo on colored days. They relied on school field trips to expose us to cultural opportunities. Our parents financed these ventures, paying additional fees for transportation and entry to the zoo park grounds

When I rode the bus, it was obvious that the few seats designated in the back of the bus for colored were only a fraction of those available for white patrons. As the colored section filled with riders, we appropriated seats toward the front of the bus that were designated as belonging in the white section. When the white section became crowded, the customs of segregation required that colored riders offer their seats to white patrons. I often saw black men and women give their seats to white persons, who took them. I gave up my seat as well. Unlike Rosa Parks, we got up from our seats in Memphis.

During shopping trips downtown with my maternal grandmother, Magnolia Howard, I followed her down back corridors past what appeared to be an elegant white dining facility to the small room designated as the restaurant for "colored" patrons. Many times Grandmother and I traipsed past white facilities marked "Ladies' Room" located near shopping areas to the restroom designated for us: "Colored Women located in the basement." I often wondered why black women were not considered ladies.

Despite these experiences, sometimes I refused to accept the extent to which eating establishments were segregated in Memphis. A Mexican restaurant opened in the vicinity of my home and I was attracted to the large sombrero at the entrance. There was also an Italian restaurant on a major thoroughfare that Mom and Dad frequently used to reach our home. Intrigued by the exterior décor of both these establishments, I asked my parents why they never took us to eat at either of these restaurants. I recall my Dad remarking that those restaurants refused to serve black patrons.

On occasion, Dad brought home food from a Chinese restaurant, a treat that our family enjoyed. However, that stopped after my father explained how humiliated he felt going to a back window reserved for colored patrons to purchase the Chinese takeout food. When I questioned my father about why we never ate out at restaurants, he explained that, as far as he was concerned, the assault on his dignity when dining at segregated facilities was not worth the dining experience.

Nevertheless, when it came to pursuing educational advantages, dignity concerns gave way to more important ones. Both my grandmothers had appreciated the value of an education, instilling in my parents those same values. My maternal grandmother, Magnolia Davenport Howard, had graduated first in her class from one of the oldest high schools established in Memphis. Upon graduation, Grandmother declined an offer from her mother's employer to work as a domestic, insisting that she planned to secure employment as a teacher in the Memphis public school system. According to family legend, Grandmother was hired after a white member of the Board of Education heard her valedictory speech and was impressed by her performance. During the early 1900s, teachers were not required to have college degrees. Nevertheless, Grandmother attended college during summers and on weekends until she earned her bachelor's degree. She was well into her sixties when she finally graduated from college.

As a family we patronized the Colored Branch of the City of Memphis Library. It was located in a small building in a black neighborhood. The City of Memphis employed black librarians to work there, and they were courteous and kind to us. Yet, I knew that white children had access to a much better facility. During trips downtown I could see what appeared to me a massive and impressive structure that housed the downtown public library, which at that time was open to whites only.

No matter how much you were prepared to spend or how well you presented yourself to department store clerks, who were always white, you were not treated as well as white customers were. I often noticed my grandmother's frustration and that of other black patrons as they waited for sales clerks to serve all the white customers before serving them. Some of the clerks would mask their discriminatory conduct by pretending that they had not noticed the line of black customers waiting for service. After serving all the white customers, they would casually turn to the black customers and ask, "Who's next?" My grandmother greatly resented store policies that prohibited black women from trying on hats before purchasing them. She protested against this practice by purchasing the hat, trying it on at home, and returning it if she did not like it. We made many trips to the hat department. She explained to me that despite store policies, some white woman would eventually wear a hat that had been on the head of a black woman.

★ ★ ★

The summers I spent missing my parents while they were away in Nashville attending the historically black Tennessee A & I State University were some of the most frustrating experiences caused by segregation policies. As educators, my parents appreciated the advantages that graduate degrees would provide to their careers. However, when I complained about them leaving us at home during the summers in the care of my grandmother, my mother explained that in order to earn their degrees they would have to attend a university, and none of the universities in Memphis admitted black students for graduate work. Therefore, they had to travel three hundred miles away to attend school in Nashville. Their room at the college dormitory was barely large enough for them. When they were away, the summer days seemed to drag and I really resented segregation for taking my parents away from me.

I attended all-black schools until I entered Marquette University as an undergraduate. During kindergarten and for the first few years of elementary school I attended a Lutheran private school. My first teacher, Mrs. Smith, was a white woman. However, the rest of the students and the teachers were black and, despite her token presence, I knew I attended a black school. My interactions with Mrs. Smith did little to dispel the negative messages I received from racial segregation. Mrs. Smith, while kind in some respects, demanded much from the four- and five-year-olds in her charge. If lessons were not completed properly, we were reprimanded. If the child's response was tears, Mrs. Smith had the offender stand in front of the class and sing with tears streaming down his or her face, "When You're Smiling, the Whole World Smiles with You." As a four-year-old, I found this brief interaction with a white person at times both confusing and frightening. I worked to avoid any reprimands or the disgrace of having to sing before the class. As a reward for my efforts, after a short period Mrs. Smith promoted me to the five-year-old group and I entered first grade at the age of five.

Upon entering the sixth grade I transferred to the neighborhood public school, Hamilton Elementary. Even though I had not witnessed any progress toward integrating the small Lutheran private school I attended, I still believed that circumstances might be different at the larger public school. So, for a while I waited for integration, which meant that I expected that one day white kids would attend my school even if it was not feasible that I would attend theirs. I did not then realize that by that time, the State of Tennessee had passed its Pupil Assignment Plan, a meaningless gesture that resulted in no black children transferring to white schools. I shared my plans to monitor school desegregation with no one. Rather, I examined each light-skinned black child very carefully to see if its presence represented an end to segregation. Gradually, my hopes for change diminished as I watched the news events on television portraying Southern resistance to desegregation. The violence surrounding the black children who attempted to enroll in the Little Rock schools was frightening and discouraging. I realized that no white kids were coming to my school and I would not be going to theirs.

I had never entered a white public school, so I could not adequately compare the white public schools in Memphis with the school I attended. Yet, I sensed that they were better. Further, I knew the condition of some of the black rural county schools where my parents taught. There were distinct differences between the three-room schoolhouse where my mother taught and the school I attended. I often visited black rural schools with my mother, since classes were held at those schools during summer breaks when the city schools were not in session. Black rural schools were closed twice a year so that black children could work during the cotton-chopping and cotton-picking seasons. During the summer they made up some of the classes missed. Because they were black and poor, these children suffered even greater disadvantages. Even the unkempt barely lit colored restrooms in the department stores were better than the outhouses that served some of the black rural schools.

When I reached high school, our science teacher explained to us that we were not receiving the same educational advantages as white students. I learned that the test scores of students attending black schools in Tennessee were among the worst in the nation. Mr. Wilkerson, a science teacher, often expressed frustration over the discarded textbooks we were issued for our science instruction. We knew that we were using textbooks that were no longer considered good enough for white students. It was customary for a student to enter his or her name in the textbook. By the time we received the science books, they were worn and had four to five names in them of students who we knew were not in our school. Mr. Wilkerson directed our attention to the copyright dates in the textbooks and complained that his job was made more difficult by the outdated textbooks. Occasionally, our lessons were infused with the tension and anger he felt because those in authority thought secondhand, outdated materials were good enough for us. We knew our education did not matter as much to those in authority as that of the white students. Mr. Wilkerson persisted and supplemented the outdated material, expecting the best from us despite the obstacles.

We had a music teacher who taught us to sing a variety of musical selections. However, she explained to us that we would have to learn "Dixie," "Old Black Joe," and other Old South songs because if there were white visitors from the Board of Education, they would expect us to know those songs as well. As I reflect on that experience, I find it ironic that the segregated system we were under denied us equal resources and expected us to celebrate the cultural traditions that supported that racial inequality as well. We understood both our teacher's message and the cultural messages of the Old South songs. We sang "Dixie," but not with any enthusiasm, performing it well enough so as to not embarrass our teacher in front of white visitors.

★ ★ ★

In *Brown I*, the Court concluded that segregation when sanctioned by law could generate such feelings of inferiority in the hearts and minds of black children they could lose their motivation to learn. Further, as noted earlier, the messages of inferiority came from more than segregated educational facilities. Segregated museums, libraries, zoos, fairgrounds, parks, and restaurants also generated feelings of inferiority.

How did we overcome those feelings of inferiority? Our teachers motivated us to learn, supplementing the required instruction about Tennessee history with black history as well. Some of my high school classmates are college professors, professionals such as physicians and lawyers, and otherwise accomplished individuals. To the extent some of us overcame those feelings of inferiority, I credit the efforts of our parents and black teachers to undo them. Their messages to us were that we were talented students and with hard work we could compete. They expected us to succeed and, as one teacher stated to me, accomplish great things. We were taught that we were not inferior. Rather we lived and studied under an inferior social and educational structure—one that condoned racial segregation and inequality.

During high school we were tracked, based on ability, into different classes for English instruction. Under the direction of Mrs. Hunt, an English teacher assigned to teach students in the accelerated track, I was exposed to a Socratic method of instruction. Mrs. Hunt assigned readings from Thoreau, Emerson, and other authors. We were not only expected to read the assignment but also challenged to think about it and analyze it. What was most intimidating about that class experience was that we were expected to discuss our assignment from a podium at the front of the classroom. During the presentation both the teacher and students posed questions. Further, we could not be certain when we would be called to present our assignments in this fashion. I was told that the teachers were demanding in the other classes as well. So prior to attending law school, I was exposed to the tension of being on call to stand and deliver. The experience in Mrs. Hunt's class was only one example of how our teachers worked to undo the messages of inferiority sent by racial segregation.

★ ★ ★

My maternal grandfather, Simon L. Howard Sr., challenged racial discrimination while working for the Frisco Railroad as a train porter. He along with other black porters sued the Brotherhood of Railroad Trainmen union and prevailed when the Supreme Court ruled in their favor and they were reinstated in their jobs. That decision was the only other Supreme Court decision my father brought to my attention. He explained that for a period of time my grandfather refused to cash his checks from the railroad, thinking that to do so would compromise his case.

Yet, the successes against segregation were always gradual and incremental. As a result of my grandfather's employment with the Frisco Railroad, my grandmother had a pass and could travel free of charge on the Frisco line. Together, we took the train often. Nevertheless, when we boarded the train we were still treated like Homer Plessy had been back in 1896—shuttled to the colored car with the conductor standing on the platform directing the passengers to cars according to their color. Black cars were often crowded and on occasion when we would walk through a white car we would notice that there were empty seats. Colored waiting rooms at train stations remained noticeably inferior to those designated "Whites Only."

Racial segregation permeated other aspects of life as well. At some point during my childhood, my parents chose to use the services of a Jewish physician who decided to challenge the Southern custom of separating his black from his white patients. I have vague recollections of the incredulity we initially experienced when his receptionist invited us to wait in the larger more comfortable waiting room that formerly had been reserved for his white patients. For a while the patients still held to the habits of segregation, sitting in a segregated fashion in the former white waiting room. Whites sat on one side of the room and blacks sat on the other. We often waited in silence, facing each other. It appeared that each of us was wondering what the other was doing there. The doctor did not take appointments. Some black patients left in anger when they saw white patients who had arrived later called before them. Despite this accommodation, the doctor would still have to pay for his transgression against Southern customs. We saw his practice change from one that served mostly white patients to one that served only black patients. I did not realize it then, but I was witnessing white flight—a private response whites would effectively use to oppose integration.

The Bellevue Park was only two blocks from my parents' home. Yet, it was off limits for me as a playground since it was reserved for whites only. For that matter trips to any Memphis Park were infrequent. The colored parks were not conveniently located near our home. Memphis is on the banks of the Mississippi River. Occasionally on Sundays after church we would stop at a park area to look at the river. We knew, however, that we were relegated to the Tom Lee Park area. An inscription on a monument at that park which I understand has now been replaced described the heroic efforts of Tom Lee, a black man whom the city officials had designated "a truly worthy Negro." From the inscription on that monument we learned that Lee was honored because he rescued a number of white folks from the river after the steamboat on which they were traveling sank. The white community measured our worth by how well we served them.

On occasion during the summer my cousins from up North would visit with us. Unaware of Southern segregation customs, one of my male cousins from Chicago succumbed to the temptation of the swings and playground at the Bellevue Park and decided to visit that park. When my father discovered that he had gone to the whites-only park, he tore out of the house looking for him and severely reprimanded him. I realized later that my father feared what could happen to a black Northern boy who violated segregation laws. Another cousin from Milwaukee made the mistake of passing up the white porcelain fountain with rust stains that spewed lukewarm water labeled "Colored" for the cooler labeled as the white drinking fountain. As she headed toward the white fountain, my mother grabbed her by the collar and pulled her away, again fearing the repercussions of breaking the segregation laws.

When I grew older, I challenged my parents, questioning their willingness to go along with some of the Southern customs that appeared to only affirm our inferior status. I became particularly irritated when white Southern secretaries who worked for the superintendent of the Shelby County Board of Education referred to my father, who by then was a high school principal, by his first name. Black parents and teachers frequently called our home. However, when doing so they asked to speak to "Mister Weaver." As I grew older I resented hearing the secretaries slur forth, "Is Alonnnnnza there?" I wanted to tell them that his name was Alonzo Weaver, or Mr. Weaver, the appellation customarily used by his black professional associates. But I knew that my parents would never tolerate that type of defiance. I also sensed from them the reprisals they would experience if I had acted on my feelings. I had heard my father complain that during the sit-in demonstrations that were joined by young black college students from his alma mater, the county board of education passed over qualified black LeMoyne graduates who were perceived as possible "protestors."

I knew that my parents' fears for us and for themselves were not unfounded. I had hidden a copy of the *Jet* magazine in my room that showed the picture of Emmett Till in his coffin, and I often reread the article and stared at the grotesque picture of his body in the casket. I knew that even black children were not immune from racial violence. Later, when I saw on television the angry white faces shouting at the black children who attempted to integrate the schools in Little Rock and heard about the murder of the little girls attending Sunday school in Birmingham, I knew that as children we would not necessarily be spared from racial violence.

★ ★ ★

When the main library finally opened to black patrons, trips to that facility became adventures. Visits to the public museum, the Pink Palace—a facility that for many years I observed from a distance—were filled with victorious excitement. We were not oblivious to the sacrifices made by those who challenged segregation. Nevertheless, testing the integration of public facilities became for us a recreational activity. Some of my early dates involved going to places to test the reality of integration. We were disappointed with our visit to the Pink Palace. All we saw were Confederate uniforms, swords, and Civil War memorabilia carefully preserved and displayed in glass cases. Racial integration of museums did not address the problem of what our community valued as history worth preserving.

Segregation in the City of Memphis school system persisted. No white kids came to Hamilton High School and the promises of *Brown* remained unrealized. At least that was the case when I graduated in 1963.

Eight years later, my younger sister, Phyllis Weaver, and her classmates registered some of the same complaints we had about the inequality in resources given to black schools. Textbooks were still outdated and black schools were still overcrowded with makeshift buildings being used to house black students. Under the gradual and incremental approach the lower courts tolerated as a remedy for constitutional violations, Memphis City and Shelby County Schools remained segregated and unequal. Eventually, the Board of Education undertook a two-week experiment with integration. A few black teachers, including my mother, who by that time worked as a librarian for the Memphis

City Schools, exchanged places with white teachers. My sister deemed that experiment a miserable failure. The white teacher assigned to her class continually expressed surprise at the ability of the black students to understand the assigned readings. Phyllis and her classmates realized that their white teacher assumed black students were inferior. Sensing their distrust she attempted to relate to them by discussing Dr. Martin Luther King. Her efforts came too late to establish a rapport; they were met with cynicism and distrust. A short-term teacher exchange could not erase years of racially stereotypical thinking about the intellect and abilities of black students or black students' perceptions that white teachers were racially biased.

After more than a decade of delay and under court order, the Memphis and Shelby County schools made a tolerable effort to desegregate. During July of 1965, an interracial group of ten representatives from the Shelby County school system joined ninety other individuals from various Southern states at a Desegregation Institute sponsored by the George Peabody College for Teachers at Vanderbilt University. Dad was among those who attended the Institute. I am indebted to Mrs. Lovelle Jenkins, a retired African American librarian who attended the Institute and shared her recollections and records with me.

According to Institute reports, Memphis and Shelby County had made no progress with integrating the schools. Like so many other jurisdictions, they avoided complying with *Brown I* by implementing a freedom-of-choice plan of desegregation. Voluntary plans of this kind placed the burden of desegregation on black parents and students to seek transfers to white schools. However, if black parents requested transfers, they subjected their children to testing and themselves to administrative denials that would lead to fruitless appeals. Under that plan no black student had applied to transfer to a white school. Under orders from federal officials, Mrs. Jenkins removed her children from the black county school and enrolled them in the white school in her neighborhood. While their attendance was not met with the turmoil of Little Rock, her children nevertheless experienced the stresses of attending school under the microscope of desegregation. Mrs. Jenkins reported that after the Institute the county schools stopped their practice of closing the schools to accommodate the cotton growers. Further, through field trips to white schools Mrs. Jenkins learned of the extent of the inequality in resources afforded the black Shelby County schools. Unlike the white schools, there were no libraries or science laboratories in the black elementary schools.

By 1968, the black citizens of Memphis had completely lost patience with gradualist approaches to desegregation. The strike of the black sanitation workers brought years of unexpressed frustrations to the surface. Even though the issues concerned recognition of the sanitation workers' labor union, black students saw the treatment of the sanitation workers as just another example of the racism that had pervaded the city. By that time I had left Memphis.

My sister, however, has vivid memories of the "Black Mondays" when black students were encouraged to not attend school and join in the protest demonstrations. Black teachers and administrators were clearly at the divide. The Board of Education expected them to come to work, teach and keep order in the schools. Members of the black community recognizing the significance their support could offer the movement wanted them to stay at home or better yet join the protests.

The tensions from the strike along with the other frustrations with segregation blacks had experienced in Memphis reached their boiling point on March 28, 1968. Phyllis recalled that as she and a couple of other students approached Hamilton High School, a black minister standing on the corner told them that they were "damned fools" for coming to school that day. Nevertheless, Phyllis went to school, apparently more concerned with our parents' reaction if she skipped school than with the minister's response to her attendance. From the window of her classroom she and the other students watched the ensuing violence that began at Hamilton and later would spread to the other black high schools in Memphis. Phyllis recalled students forming crowds outside the school. Some of them threw bricks at cars and later at a garbage truck. Her teachers were instructed to lock the doors to the school buildings. The police moved to disperse the students, some of whom attempted to get into the school. Police cars, a police helicopter, and ensuing violence created a frightening scenario. Rumors circulated at the school that a girl had been killed in the melee between the police and the students. Phyllis feared for her own safety as well as that of our younger brother and our parents. A few days later, a student attending the school where my Dad served as principal was killed. That tragedy was followed by the assassination of Dr. Martin Luther King during his visit to Memphis to support the efforts of the black strikers to form a union. Black Memphians were no longer willing to wait for change.

Phoebe Weaver Williams was born in June 1946 in Memphis, Tennessee, and attended elementary and secondary school there from 1950 to 1963. She is now an associate professor of law at Marquette Law School in Milwaukee, Wisconsin.

22 What I Learned When Massive Resistance Closed My School

Richard J. Bonnie

I grew up in Norfolk, Virginia, in the 1950s. With a population of three hundred thousand and a thriving naval base, Norfolk had become the largest city in Virginia. Mine was a typical 1950s upbringing—very quiet and stable, with a Leave-It-to-Beaver flavor. I lived an insular life with a highly predictable routine—walk to school, walk to Hebrew lessons, wait for Mom to pick me up to take me to baseball games and piano lessons, then perhaps to Toastmaster's Club, Children's Theater, and so on. (In fact, baseball should be at the beginning of the sentence, since that was the most important part of my life—I even had to hide my Wildcats baseball uniform in the garage when my mother forbade me to play because the practices left too little time for homework.)

My life typified growing up in the white professional class of the urban postwar South. I hardly ever saw any black people except the maids and gardeners who worked at my house and elsewhere in my neighborhood. There were certainly no black people in Granby Elementary School. My father, a dentist, had some black patients whom I would see on Wednesday afternoons after piano lessons, and on Saturday mornings after piano theory class. Aside from these occasional exposures, though, it was a lily-white existence.

It was worse than that, really. It was a socially blind existence. I was oblivious to the world outside my extended family and the Jewish community. I didn't notice the signs Whites Only or Colored on the restroom doors, in the movies, or over the water fountains. I never thought about the fact that our maid, Elsie, and the other maids slept in the hot upper floors of my house and all the neighboring houses. I never rode a bus at all, so I never noticed the segregated seating patterns. I don't remember hearing about the Supreme Court's decision in *Brown v. Board of Education.* (I was in the fourth grade at the time.) Time passed, and I graduated from Granby Elementary School in June 1958.

Then I grew up.

In the late summer of 1958, the governor of Virginia, J. Lindsay Almond Jr., closed the white secondary schools in Norfolk rather than succumb to the directives of the federal courts. One of the schools closed was Northside Junior High, which I was scheduled to attend as an eighth-grader in the fall.

I was thrust into the maelstrom of Massive Resistance at the very time that I was opening my eyes to the world around me and becoming conscious of my own identity—and of my responsibilities to others and to my community. I was scheduled to become a Bar Mitzvah in October 1958, so I was engaging in the sort of introspection that becoming a Jewish adult is supposed to invite. I did not realize it then, but I was being transformed. No longer did I aspire to become Mickey Mantle's successor in centerfield for the Yankees. Now I wanted to become a lawyer. And I also wanted to leave the South. I now hated being a Southerner.

How did this happen?

Despite an initially muted response to the *Brown* decision by many of Virginia's leading politicians, including Governor Thomas Stanley and then attorney general Almond, strong opposition eventually emerged after U.S. senator Harry F. Byrd Jr. condemned the Supreme Court for striking a "serious blow" against the rights of the states. In August of 1954, Governor Stanley appointed a thirty-two-member commission (all white members of the General Assembly), chaired by state senator Garland Gray, to recommend a course of action in response to *Brown*. In November of 1955, the Gray Commission proposed that the General Assembly enact a pupil placement statute vesting plenary authority in the local school boards to assign pupils in a manner consistent with local welfare, providing that no child should be required to attend an integrated school, and authorizing tuition grants for parents who enrolled children in private schools to avoid integration.

In the fall of 1956, a Special Session of the Virginia General Assembly rejected the Gray Commission's approach—which would have allowed local school boards to adopt integration plans while allowing white parents to opt out of them—in favor of what became known as its Massive Resistance Plan. The legislature found that school integration anywhere in the state constituted a "clear and present danger" to the health and welfare of Virginia's children, and set up an intricate plan for preventing any local board from integrating its schools. It vested ultimate authority for pupil placement in a State Pupil Placement Board appointed by the governor, displacing the traditional authority of local boards. The criteria that the state board was directed to apply effectively prohibited assignment of white and black students to the same school. The legislature also appropriated funds for tuition vouchers for students whose schools were closed to avoid integration. In addition, the governor was directed to seize control of white local schools to which black children had been assigned, and was empowered to reorganize them on a segregated basis, such as by eliminating grades or classes to which black children had been assigned. The governor was permitted to return control to the local school board, but if the schools were reopened on a nonsegregated basis, state funds for their operation would be withheld.

In November 1957, J. Lindsay Almond Jr. was elected governor on a segregationist platform. In his inaugural address in January 1958, Almond took a hard line, declaring that integration would not be permitted to occur on his watch. With Virginia's Massive Resistance Plan in place, and a governor prepared to implement it, the focus of attention then shifted to the local school boards and the federal courts.

During the fall of 1956, ninety-six black schoolchildren had filed suit in the federal district court to desegregate the Norfolk public schools. In February 1957, Judge Walter Hoffman had declared the state's new Pupil Placement Plan unconstitutional, and had directed the Norfolk School Board to develop a plan for desegregating the city schools. This decision had been affirmed by the Fourth Circuit, and the case had been remanded back to Judge Hoffman. The pace of the litigation now pointed toward desegregation during the fall semester, 1958. On June 7, 1958, Judge Hoffman ordered the school board to desegregate the schools when they opened in the fall. (School boards in Charlottesville and Arlington were under similar orders.)

On July 17, the Norfolk School Board adopted a pupil assignment plan governing cases in which black applicants requested reassignment to formerly white schools. Under the plan, these requests would be assessed on a case-by-case basis taking into account ten factors, including academic test performance, the applicant's health and safety, place of residence and proximity to the school to which assignment had been requested, physical and moral fitness, social adaptability, emotional adjustment, and cultural background. Applicants were required to take the written tests and undergo personal interviews.

About 46,000 children, including me, were expected to enroll in Norfolk's public school system in the fall of 1958—28,500 in elementary schools, 11,000 in junior high schools, and 6,500 in high schools. About 70 percent of the school-age population was white. Over the course of the summer, 151 black students applied for reassignment to the city's three white high schools (Granby, Maury, and Norview) and three of its four white junior high schools, including Northside. Although 88 of the applicants took the tests and were interviewed as required by the plan, 63 students refused to do so on the ground that the plan was unconstitutional.

On August 18, about two weeks before the schools were scheduled to open, two justices of the Virginia Supreme Court—acting on a petition from the parents of two white students—enjoined the school board from reassigning any black students under the plan. That same day, the school board rejected all 151 transfer applicants. A week later, Judge Hoffman ruled that several of the criteria considered by the board (e.g., fear of racial tension and isolation of transferring students) were legally impermissible, and directed the school board to reconsider all 151 cases. Four days later, after Judge Hoffman threatened its members with a contempt citation, the board (acting under protest) assigned 17 of the black students to white schools. Judge Hoffman denied the board's request for a one-year delay in implementing the reassignment, whereupon the board postponed school opening until September 22.

The expected clash between the federal courts and the state's Massive Resistance Plan began to materialize. On September 12, the U.S. Supreme Court handed down its important decision in *Cooper v. Aaron*, strongly reaffirming its ruling in *Brown* and refusing to allow Little Rock to delay integration because of violent resistance that had been fomented by the state's political leaders. *Cooper* strengthened Judge Hoffman's hand in his refusal to grant the stay requested by the Norfolk School Board. On September 18, Governor Almond closed the Charlottesville schools, taking control of them under the authority conferred on him by the 1956 statute. Meanwhile, Judge Hoffman enjoined the state from enforcing the Virginia Supreme Court's August order purporting to enjoin the Norfolk School Board from integrating its schools. The school board immediately sought a stay in the Fourth Circuit and postponed the opening of Norfolk's secondary schools for another week.[1]

While the wrangling continued in the district court, Norfolk's children enjoyed their extended summer vacation and parents scrambled to identify educational alternatives for their children in the increasingly likely event that the schools remained closed. In my case, my parents made provisional plans to retain a private tutor, a retired Navy captain, Charles Bowerfine, who lived on Hampton Boulevard near the naval base—a long way from Riverpoint, Granby Street, and my highly circumscribed existence. I wasn't looking forward to the long bus ride, including three transfers, not to mention the intensity of one-on-one tutorials.

Norfolk's schoolchildren joined the fray on Monday morning, September 22. About seventy students, including me, assembled at Northside to sign a petition imploring the school board to keep the schools open. The petition said that we did so "not as segregationists or integrationists but as students who want an education." I do not recall who organized this effort, and I do not claim to have had any major role in it, but it was probably my first political act and represented my awakening to the cause of civil rights. The Northside demonstration, in which I participated with my lifelong friend Stuart Steingold, was recorded in an Associated Press photo that appeared in the *Washington Post* and other major newspapers.

Needless to say, no one aside from the press was paying any attention to the few students who signed a petition or to the three hundred parents who signed a similar petition the next week. After Judge Sobeloff refused to stay Judge Hoffman's order, Governor Almond "seized and padlocked" Norfolk's three white high schools and three of its four white junior high schools (including Northside) to prevent their opening on September 29. Ten thousand students, including me and Stuart, were out of school.

So what did these students do? In Charlottesville, the press reported that the public school teachers were holding private classes for 1,200 white children, but the Norfolk public school teachers refused to participate in organized private instructional programs of this kind. However, according to the *New York Times*, about 300 of the 442 teachers in the six closed schools engaged in some private tutoring. About 4,500 students were in private tutoring programs spread throughout the city in private homes, churches, and other locations; about 1,500 students had enrolled in private or public schools in other locations; about 1,000 attended evening classes in the adjacent city of South Norfolk. Approximately 3,000 students were not educationally occupied. In an important political statement, the Norfolk Education Association stated that its members would not provide private tutoring after the fall semester.

As for me, I made the ninety-minute trek to Captain Bowerfine's house three times a week. I don't remember very much about what I learned from him. But I do remember a lot about what I saw, thought, and felt as I left my sheltered environment and traveled to his house. The most vivid memories are of riding on the bus. I found myself walking to the back of the bus because I felt so uncomfortable sitting in the front with the other white passengers. I don't think this was a political statement as much as it was an expression of my emerging moral embarrassment about being white in a segregated society. I also remember thinking about the social turmoil of which I was a part, and wondering how it would affect me. But most of all, I remember thinking how much I hated being a Southerner. This feeling had a humble origin—my fellow campers made fun of the few Southern pronunciations in my vocabulary when I went to camp in Maine the summer before the school closings—but it intensified as I became more politically and socially aware over the next few years. Now I saw everything through the prism of race relations in the South. I suppose that this embarrassment was coupled with an exquisite sensitivity to discrimination and a sense of mission that I associate with being a Jew in America after World War II. These few months were a time of awakening to my own identity—as a white person, as a Southerner, and as a Jew.

I became very interested in state and local politics during my high school years, as Norfolk voters began to elect candidates opposed to the Byrd machine. I started a Young Democrats Club at Granby High and was energized by the young dissenters that were running for city council. I cannot say for sure that my personal political awakening was related to the school closing and to Massive Resistance, but I have no doubt that the Byrd machine's unequivocal hostility toward the *Brown* decision, the Supreme Court, and the cause of civil rights galvanized opposition to the machine politicians who controlled key state and local offices. Although my friend and colleague Jay Wilkinson has argued persuasively that the Byrd machine was already losing its grip before *Brown*, the moral blunder of Massive Resistance certainly accelerated its collapse and thereby helped to change the face of Virginia politics.[2]

The fissures in the machine became evident during the fall of 1958 as the clash between the federal courts and Virginia's recalcitrant politicians continued to unfold. In a referendum authorized by the city council, Norfolk's voters were asked whether the council should petition Governor Almond to return the six padlocked schools to local authorities to be reopened on an integrated basis. Many citizens were not eligible to vote in the referendum because they either had not registered or had not paid the poll tax. Even among the forty thousand eligible voters, only twenty-one thousand voted. The deck was stacked against a "yes" vote because a ballot note indicated that parents would have to pay a "substantial tuition" if schools opened on an integrated basis. Although the segregationist position prevailed, almost nine thousand voters endorsed integrated schools.

The *New York Times* editorial page lamented the result but expressed both amazement and pleasure that 40 percent of the voters favored integration, demonstrating an "increasingly strong body of moderate Southern opinion" against Massive Resistance. Of course, the *Richmond Times Dispatch* drew the opposite conclusion, pointing out that Norfolk "is a cosmopolitan Southern City where one would have supposed the sentiment would be as strongly in favor of opening the schools as any other urban center of the South." Defeat of integration in Norfolk was accordingly seen "as an index to the depth of feeling on this issue."

Bolstered by the referendum, but waiting for the other shoe to drop in the Fourth Circuit, Norfolk's machine-dominated city council voted on January 13 to close all schools above the sixth grade for the second semester. This decision would have affected thirty-six schools and seven thousand additional children, including five thousand black children. Local black leaders called this plan an "abomination" and sued to block it. This was the last gasp of Massive Resistance in Norfolk. Several days later, on January 19, the Virginia Supreme Court and a three-judge federal district court issued separate decisions declaring the state's 1956 Massive Resistance statute unconstitutional under both the state and federal constitutions, thereby putting the decision about the reopening of the Norfolk schools back in the hands of local authorities.

The fight was now between the city council and the school board. The federal court's order restored control of the schools to the Norfolk School Board, and the school board made plans to reopen the closed schools on February 2. Meanwhile the city council, backed by Governor Almond, advocated closing all the schools. In a CBS Special narrated by Edward R. Murrow and Fred Friendly on January 21, Almond insisted that private tutoring was an adequate substitute for the public schools. In response, the chairman of the school board and the superintendent of the city schools pointed out that at least three thousand students were not attending any classes, and local business leaders argued that closing the public schools would have a disastrous impact on the Tidewater economy. On January 27, Judge Hoffman enjoined the city council from cutting off funds for public education, calling the council's plan an "evasive and discriminatory scheme" denying black students equal protection of the laws. (This order was later upheld by the Fourth Circuit.)

The Norfolk schools reopened without incident on February 2, 1959, as seventeen black students enrolled in the six schools that had been padlocked by Governor Almond in September to keep them out.

These events occurred five decades ago. Has anything changed and, if so, did *Brown* have anything to do with it?

We can begin with the schools. Have the Norfolk schools changed? The integration plan in 1959 was symbolic, of course. Only one black student attended Northside, and I never met her. I don't remember ever having a meaningful conversation with the token black enrollees at Granby High during my three years there. But, what do the Norfolk schools look like now?

Norfolk is now a teeming New South city at the center of a sprawling metropolis of 1.6 million people. Although there has been substantial white flight from the center of the city, Norfolk itself is by no means an empty shell—it is a cultural and commercial center with an economically and racially diverse population. Having said that, though, the minority population, largely black, is much larger in Norfolk than it is in the adjacent cities of Virginia Beach and Chesapeake. Norfolk's school district had about thirty-seven thousand students in 2002–2003, two-thirds of whom were black. About 80 percent of the black school-aged children are in the public schools, compared with about 50 percent of the white children. Within these parameters, public education in Norfolk is fully integrated, reflecting a reasonable degree of residential integration in many parts of the city. The student body of Northside (a middle school serving sixth, seventh, and eighth grades) is about 50 percent white and 45 percent black. Granby High is about 50–50. Maury High is 60 percent black and Norview is 70 percent black, reflecting the residential composition of those areas.

Obviously these numbers tell us next to nothing about the quality of the education and the social experience of the children attending the Norfolk Public Schools. But they do tell us that the pervasive wrongs of state-enforced segregation—in the schools and elsewhere—have been acknowledged and erased, and that the children's lives have a profoundly different moral texture than the lives of children separated from one another by walls of prejudice and discrimination.

The South has changed. It's not perfect. But I now love living in the South. It's probably wrong, as a matter of historical interpretation, to attribute the extraordinary social and cultural changes in the South to *Brown*. My colleague Mike Klarman has convincingly argued that the role of *Brown* has been overstated and misunderstood. The Supreme Court did little on its own to achieve its aspirations, he says, while its edict galvanized the political energy of the forces opposed to change.[3] Norfolk's experience is a case in point. Changes on any significant scale did not occur until the civil rights movement developed steam a decade after *Brown*. Even so, for those of us whose identities were being forged in the 1950s, *Brown* was a very powerful force. It was a beacon of change, an invitation to remake the South, and a catalyst for thinking deeply about one's own place in a flawed but changing society.

I leave it to the historians to discern the role that *Brown* played in changing the schools, in fostering civil rights, and in reconstructing the South. But I am sure that *Brown* and its immediate legal aftermath had a profound impact on me and on the course of my life. And, as this book reveals, I am not alone.

NOTES

1. On Massive Resistance and Virginia politics, see: Matthew D. Lassiter and Andrew B. Lewis, eds., *The Moderates' Dilemma: Massive Resistance to School Desegregation in Virginia* (Charlottesville: University of Virginia Press, 1998); Benjamin Muse, *Virginia's Massive Resistance* (Bloomington: Indiana University Press, 1961); Carl Tobias, "Public School Desegregation in Virginia during the Post-*Brown* Decade," *William and Mary Law Review* 37 (1996): 1261–1306; J. Harvie Wilkinson, *Harry Byrd and the Changing Face of Virginia Politics* (New Haven: Yale University Press, 1971).

2. See Wilkinson, *Harry Byrd.*

3. See Michael J. Klarman, *From Jim Crow to Civil Rights* (New York: Oxford University Press, 2004).

Richard J. Bonnie was in the eighth grade in Norfolk, Virginia, when the public schools were closed to resist the Supreme Court's decision in *Brown*. He is Harrison Foundation Professor of Medicine and Law, Hunton and Williams Research Professor, and Director, Institute of Law, Psychiatry, and Public Policy at the University of Virginia.

23 Standing Up for *Brown* in Danville

Richard Bourne

I was eleven years old when *Brown I* came down in May 1954. My biggest concerns were girls (I didn't like them but secretly coveted their attention) and making the majors in Little League baseball (I couldn't hit, and so knew I would be relegated to the minors). I don't remember much about my family's reaction to *Brown*, except that they thought it was high time for the Court to rule as it had and that they were generally elated about the prospects for change it augured. The next day, because there was a delay in getting into the elementary school I attended, the kids were milling around the schoolyard. They were full of anger and resentment and suggested that integration would never come to Danville, Virginia, where we lived. When I told them I thought the decision was a good one, they called me a "nigger lover." I had never heard the term before and wasn't sure what it meant, but I knew I didn't like being ostracized.

White kids in places like Danville had very little contact with black kids. The programs open to us—the schools, youth sports leagues, the scout troops, YMCA programs, et cetera—did not include people of color. We were aware of the order of things—I remember, for instance, knowing that I could escape the gentle control of our black nanny when she took us downtown on the bus simply by moving to the front of the bus—but gave it not a thought. We accepted it as the way things were. We didn't think much about it.

I went away to prep school at Andover in September of 1957. I was the only kid from my Danville high school class who went to school with Negroes. As part of its massive resistance to federal desegregation policy, Virginia enacted legislation that allowed any parents who wanted their child educated in private schools to get a tuition grant from the local government where the child lived, with reimbursement to come from the state. The grants were rather puny, like most of the voucher payments right-wingers are trying to foist off on Americans in the twenty-first century, but they were enough to help rich people like us. My father decided to take advantage of the program to spite the system. The deans at Andover and my father got a chuckle out of the fact that I was the first kid from the state of Virginia to get a tuition grant. The local white populace was furious because we weren't using the money for the purpose it was intended—to flee integrated public schools.

The lynching of Emmett Till in Mississippi and Orval Faubus's resistance to desegregation in Little Rock were the only major national crises in race relations I remember from the 1950s, but things began heating up in 1960 and stayed that way through most of the next decade. Pressure on Jim Crow mounted nationally with the Montgomery Bus Boycott, the bombing of the Sixteenth Street Baptist Church in Birmingham, James Meredith's integration of Ole Miss, the Freedom Rides through Greyhound and Trailways bus routes across the South, and the sit-ins at the Woolworth's store in Greensboro, North Carolina. My parents got involved, in a minor way, in trying to promote reform, both on a local level in my hometown and on a regional level throughout the South. My mother helped create the Virginia Council on Human Relations, a state offshoot of the Southern Regional Council out of Atlanta, and became the Southern national vice president of the YWCA, which was more progressive than its male counterpart, and spent the next five or six years traveling around the American South cajoling women in Southern cities to desegregate their local YW chapters. During the summer of 1960, the city government in my hometown closed its public libraries rather than desegregate them, and my folks got involved in a local political scrap about the issue, which forced them to become more publicly aligned with the cause of desegregation. I became a cub reporter for a local newspaper during the summer of 1960 and covered the library story, which turned out to have its deliciously silly side. The city officials briefly reopened the library as a stand-up facility, sans desks or tables and without the right to go into the stacks. Some fool had taken seriously a tongue-in-cheek article by Harry Golden in the *Carolina Israelite* that suggested that whites could integrate all their facilities (schools, libraries, restaurants, etc.) so long as they never allowed blacks to *sit down* in white folks' presence. The city's leadership was finally forced to back down under pressure from businesses wishing to build plants in Danville but unwilling to move into the backwater Danville would become if, like Prince Edward County, it closed its public schools.

During the library crisis I also engaged in some rather silly pranksterism: three of us ole white boys fashioned ten-foot-long footprint stencils out of a cardboard container used to ship Scott toilet paper rolls. We then painted giant black footprints all the way from the center of the town's main street to the front doorstep of the home of the leader of Danville's segregationist forces, a state senator (and member of the University of Virginia Board of Visitors), replete with a twelve-foot-wide blood-red circle and huge letters printed onto the street pavement shouting, "White Supremacy—GOTCHA!" The good senator's daughter accused me and one of the other boys of the dastardly deed, but we never owned up to it. I remember driving down their street and seeing a couple of burly cops examining the footprints; one was down on hands and knees measuring their length with a tape measure. Needless to say, Bigfoot went uncovered by this newspaper reporter.

The courage of the black people, particularly the young, who integrated schools, led sit-ins and took Freedom Rides, and risked loss of life, limb, and liberty, was an extraordinary phenomenon which ultimately enthralled the American nation. The cruel antics of Bull Connor, Birmingham's public safety director, in the spring of 1963—siccing Alsatian dogs and fire-hose cannons on African American preachers and teenagers—transfixed those who saw it on television. That summer black people in city after city took to the streets to engage the local power structures with direct action campaigns of civil disobedience in an attempt to break the back of Jim Crow. My hometown—like Albany, Georgia, and Cambridge, Maryland—was one of the battlegrounds pitting race-baiting white politicians against black people whose demands were fantastically modest (they wanted appointment of one black cop, one white-collar worker in city hall, one black clerk in each of the major department stores, desegregation of the *dressing rooms* in the department stores, the elevation of a few token blacks to skilled positions at the local textile mill, and the creation of a biracial committee to promote further reforms down the road).

The divisions among blacks were over tactics, not principle (some of the more conservative middle-class leaders were afraid putting too much pressure on the white community would lead to retaliation the black community couldn't handle). In the end, however, the leadership of courageous college and high school students and African American churchmen shamed even the most conservative black business people into supporting the movement, using their homes and business property as collateral to borrow money to pay lawyers and post bonds for the kids who were filling the jails. Members of the white community knew, deep down where it counts, that the talk of "outside agitators" and the myths about the happiness of the black community with their "place" in the Jim Crow system were false, and they could not tolerate dissent lest the entire edifice collapse around them. To a large extent the race-baiters were able to silence most white dissenters with a variety of methods of coercion—economic threats, loss of jobs, social ostracism, et cetera.

I was lucky. My parents continued to respond to the movement with attempts to persuade our white neighbors to accept the changes which were upon us because doing so was the right thing to do. They donated money and contributed to the movement in a minor way by providing a safe house for a white member of the Student Non-Violent Coordinating Committee (SNCC) when the leaders of the movement indicated they were afraid the local constabulary might rough him up. (During this time, SNCC and the Congress for

Racial Equality sent "civil rights workers" into Southern communities, acting as a sort of cavalry for the movement.) Two years later, young civil rights workers Andrew Goodman, Michael Schwerner, and James Chaney were murdered in Neshoba County, Mississippi, by members of the Ku Klux Klan, including a deputy sheriff. I became a news reporter again, covering nothing but the movement.

On August 28 of that year, the movement held its March on Washington and Martin Luther King Jr. gave his famous "I have a dream" speech. The whole crescendo of voices and action which had begun that spring forced the national administration to rethink its civil rights policy and led to its promotion—and the ultimate passage—of the Civil Rights Act of 1964. King gave another speech in a Baptist church in my hometown. I will never forget it. I was the only white person in the building, a speck of salt in a sea of pepper, and I felt a little out of place. He told the crowd they should not give up, or become despondent, because victory *would* be theirs. Then, borrowing from Gandhi, he told them they would arrive when they were ready. To get ready, he said, "you must desegregate your minds; you must believe you are somebody." For the first time, it dawned on me that I had work to do to desegregate *my* mind.

The movement continued to bring change to the country. Events in 1964 and 1965—the campaign in Selma, Alabama, the murder of Viola Liuzzo in Alabama, and the lynching outside Philadelphia, Mississippi—created pressure to enact new legislation, the Voting Rights Act of 1965. The riots in Newark, Watts, and Detroit created the backdrop for the creation of the Office of Economic Opportunity (the Poverty Program) in 1966, and the 1968 riots when Dr. King was murdered in Memphis created the groundswell for the Fair Housing Act of 1968 as well as the occasion for the Kerner Commission report on how intractable were the problems of poverty, race, class, and criminality which would afflict the country for the rest of the century and beyond.

I graduated from college in 1964. After going to Cape Town on a fellowship to see the world's only other four-bathroom society, I came home and went to law school. I then became a staff attorney with the Civil Rights Division of the Department of Justice. I worked there for five years before quitting and going into teaching. I have been a full-time academic since 1973.

The changes I observed (and, in a very modest way, participated in creating) before I joined the academy were all set in motion by *Brown*. That decision was easily the most significant judicial event of the twentieth century. *Brown* began the process of setting aright the worst decision of the nineteenth century, the *Dred Scott* case. *Brown* was important because of its promise. It created expectations that, before it came down, had been all but obliterated by the disenfranchisement of blacks in the South and the rollback that began in the 1890s of most of what had been gained during Reconstruction. The great men of Howard Law School who set the legal strategy leading to *Brown* must have had doubts whether their plans would bear fruit. They did. And when African Americans began to see what *Brown* promised, they demanded that the country honor the promise, and they put their lives on the line to push the country to meet its obligations.

Though progress has been made to address the most obvious forms of racial discrimination in this country, the promise of *Brown* remains unfulfilled for millions of Americans. Dr. King's "I have a dream" speech is much remembered, but not well remembered. The part we leave out had more resonance, that hot day in 1963, than the dream sequence itself. In it Dr. King suggested that the country had given its black citizens a bad check, returned by the Bank of Justice with markings indicating insufficient funds. The failure of Reconstruction had at its heart the unwillingness of our nation's people to redistribute economic resources in such a way as to give the newly freed blacks the wherewithal to use the newly created rights that had been formally accorded them. They received the right to vote, but the call for "forty acres and a mule" fell on deaf ears. Without economic independence, our African American citizens could not sustain themselves against the economic, political, and social dominance of the larger white community, and their formal rights were shamelessly taken from them. I often worry that the Second Reconstruction, the one *Brown* set off, will end the same way. There are reasons for hope. Affirmative action has been this generation's version of forty acres and a mule, a sort of reparations in kind to jumpstart the black community so that it can sustain its entree into the mainstream of the society and its culture. Affirmative action has been hugely successful in creating a large, self-sustaining African American middle class that can support itself and its offspring for generations to come and begin, finally, fully to participate in the nation's life.

But an underclass has been left behind. It needs support. It needs intervention. It needs affirmative action big-time. And I am terribly afraid that the society will, once again, halt reconstruction before its course is done. Most white people—and a lot of the newly arrived blacks as well—seem to have forgotten three hundred and fifty years of slavery and another century of peonage and the crippling effects that these have on our least fortunate citizens. They perceive the inhabitants in our urban ghettos as "the other," not even as part of the same society we share. We seem to have no stomach for creating jobs for poorly educated, thoroughly demoralized people who do not have the middle-class background sufficient to launch themselves successfully in the American market. Support for inner city schools, libraries, and services is disappearing. The only thing we seem to do for blacks is build bigger prisons in which to warehouse their thoroughly demoralized young males. The new ideology denounces promotion of social programs as inciting class warfare, accuses champions of the disenfranchised as refusing to honor the dream of a color-blind society, and suggests as an overarching ideology an individualism which would gladden the heart of Herbert Spencer. In effect, this thinking tries to cut off the opposition with arguments as silly and shameless as my schoolmates attempted when they called me a "nigger lover."

In the end, I am not afraid. If *Brown* taught me one thing, it was not to be afraid of being called "nigger lover." Maybe I didn't understand that on the lawn of my elementary school, a half century ago. I do now. It is not a shame to receive such a label; it is an honor. *Brown* taught me that.

Richard Bourne was born in Charlottesville, Virginia, in November 1942 and attended elementary and secondary school in Danville, Virginia, from 1948 to 1957. He is now a professor of law at the University of Baltimore in Baltimore, Maryland.

24 Urgent Conversations

Earl C. Dudley Jr.

I have been thinking about the significance of *Brown v. Board of Education* for most of my life. I was in the ninth grade at Herndon High School in Fairfax County, Virginia, when *Brown* was decided. Difficult as it may be to imagine today, that part of Fairfax County—now a populous, high-tech corridor—was then very rural and *very* Southern. As was the case in most of the rural South, there was little or no residential segregation. White folks and black folks lived right next to each other, for the most part quite amicably. But everything else was segregated—not just the schools, but the restaurants, the lunch counters, the theaters, and for the most part, even the stores.

When the decision came down, it immediately became the only topic of conversation. As far as I ever discovered, I was the only student at Herndon High whose parents told him that the Supreme Court got it right. This was itself quietly remarkable, for both my parents had been born and raised in poor white families in Tidewater, Virginia. Indeed, I believe on the basis of anec-dotal evidence that, at least before World War II, my father shared all the typi-cal prejudices of his time and class. Three years in a Japanese internment camp during the war changed all that.

I can honestly say that I never heard my father disparage any person or group on the basis of race, religion, or ethnicity. And before *Brown* there had been no occasion in my family to confront racial issues directly. So when we discussed the Supreme Court decision over dinner that first night, my parents explained to me that slavery had been a terrible thing, and that Negroes had been oppressed and mistreated even after slavery was abolished. All people were equal, Negroes had a right to the same education I was getting, and there was no reason that white and black children should not go to school together.

What my parents said seemed unassailably logical and reasonable to me. What is more, it accorded with my own limited experience. Prior to the eighth grade I had attended a private school in Washington, D.C., that catered to the children of foreign diplomats, and thus I had gone to school with children of all racial backgrounds. And I had made friends with many American black children on the public buses that I rode each day to and from school. I was therefore profoundly shocked the next morning when my expression of support for the Court's decision brought down on my head a great deal of abuse from my schoolmates, most of it verbal but some of it physical as well.

I had a wonderful civics teacher that year, Patricia Alger, who decided to seize the moment to do a little educating. She spoke in quiet and reasoned tones about the decision and announced that she would hold a debate in class the following week on whether the Supreme Court was right or wrong. When she asked for volunteers for the debate, there were many for the pro-segregation side, but initially I was the only one who stepped forward to support the decision.

Mrs. Alger said she needed another volunteer because she wanted to have two-person debating teams. Finally, a very pretty and lively girl with an innate sense of fairness and the marvelous name of Dixie Lou Simpson volunteered to join me in defending the Court. Dixie's parents, who had just moved to Northern Virginia from Alabama, certainly had not told her the Supreme Court got it right, and I am quite sure Dixie didn't think so either. But she and I worked diligently together to prepare our arguments. After the debate was over, Mrs. Alger asked for a vote of who had won, and Dixie and I garnered a solid majority. I don't mean we made converts, but at least Mrs. Alger got us talking in civilized tones, and Dixie and I gave the others something to think about.

The next few years in Virginia were filled with not very civil arguments about race. Often the air was blue with racial epithets. Politicians in the state, led by then attorney general J. Lindsay Almond, made heated speeches and swore to resist integration to the end. Liberal and moderate voices were hard to hear in the din.

A little over three years after *Brown*, I went off to western Massachusetts to college, hoping and believing, very naively, that I had left ugly racism behind. It was, I think, on the occasion of my second haircut in the tiny town of Amherst that I heard two of the barbers speaking derisively of a basketball team with five "jigs" on it. As I made friends with my classmates, I began to meet some of their parents in social settings. Conversations with these parents, who were mostly from New England and New York, soon developed a wholly predictable pattern. When the parent learned that I was from Virginia, I received a stern lecture on how badly we treated our Negroes down there, as if that had not occurred to me. They were, I was told, entitled to equal rights and to go to school wherever they wanted. Of course, the parent would almost invariably add, "I wouldn't want to live next door to one or have my child marry one." The deafness of these people to their own words at first irked me, but as time went on, I decided to retaliate with a little humor, though it was seldom taken that way. Why, I would ask, were they opposed to people living where they wanted to or marrying whomever they pleased?

This approach usually produced inarticulate sputtering, followed often by the questions, "Do you have a sister? Surely you wouldn't want her to marry one?" I would tell them that yes, I had a sister, that who she married was her business, and that the only criteria I had for her future husband were that he love her and treat her well. This normally gave rise to a swift change of subject or to the parent deciding that his or her drink needed freshening.

Some legal scholars have criticized the reasoning of the *Brown* decision, and others have sought to downplay its significance, pointing out, quite correctly, that it produced very little school integration on its own. Not until Title VI of the Civil Rights Act of 1964 threatened a cutoff of federal funds to recalcitrant school districts was any real widespread progress made in integrating Southern schools.

These criticisms, to my mind, wholly miss the point. The *Brown* decision was transformative, but not in the way one conventionally thinks about judicial decisions. What *Brown* did was to elevate race from America's dirty little secret to its most urgent topic of conversation. And the Court's unanimity permanently awarded the moral high ground in the coming debate to the proponents of equal rights for all Americans. One cannot ask more from any judicial decision. True, *Brown* was resisted by all-white Southern governments, and it produced a potent political backlash. But the ugliness of the backlash itself contributed mightily to legislative changes that strongly promoted civil rights. Most important, *Brown* got people talking—incessantly, in some places—about racial issues. While it was offensive to listen to the rantings of the open racists, and irksome to listen to the harangues of those who failed to understand the nature of their own racism, this orgy of talk was, I think, ultimately quite healthy.

It gave the great spokespersons of racial progress—in Virginia, courageous black leaders such as Oliver Hill and S. W. Tucker and progressive whites such as Armistead Boothe—a spotlight and a forum, and it gave the Patricia Algers of the world a chance to educate quietly. Moreover, it exposed to those who were listening and even, I think in the end, to those who were mouthing the platitudes of segregation the banality of their own arguments, the ultimate emptiness of racism.

In some ways, the transformation came more quickly than one could realistically have expected. I shall never forget the sight of J. Lindsay Almond, by then governor, personally holding onto the Virginia standard at the 1960 Democratic Convention to prevent a few diehards from appropriating it to take part in a last-ditch pro-segregation floor demonstration.

To my mind, the decision in *Brown* both seemed at the time and has proved ultimately to be the most important single event in the United States since the end of World War II. Its message was one of hope. Obviously that hope has not yet been entirely fulfilled. But we have come a long way in fifty years, and I have faith based on that progress that the journey will continue.

Earl C. Dudley Jr. was born in the Philippine Islands in 1941 and attended public high school in Herndon, Virginia, from 1952 to 1957. He is now professor of law and director of the Graduate Program for Judges at the University of Virginia School of Law in Charlottesville.

25 Virginia Confronts a "Statesmanlike Decision"

David W. Miller

Williamsburg, Virginia, was not entirely typical of its region in 1955, the year in which I graduated from high school. It was a college town and hence had a larger element of liberal intelligentsia than many otherwise comparable communities had. Since the late 1920s, Williamsburg had been the scene of the Rockefeller-financed restoration of the eighteenth-century colonial capital. This gave the city a strong economic base and also infused an element of outside (Northern) influence.

John D. Rockefeller Jr., Williamsburg's financial angel, was a devout Baptist whose personal views on racial issues differed from the public stances taken by the organization that he funded. Rockefeller promoted racial equality in quiet ways, assiduously avoiding conflict with the established white-only ethos of the community. Thus, when the white high school (the old Matty School), which stood on the former grounds of the Governor's Palace, needed to be razed to make way for the restoration project, Rockefeller financed the building of *two* new public high schools in Williamsburg—one white (Matthew Whaley School) and one colored (Bruton Heights School). The two schools were utterly equal in physical characteristics and amenities. Both were spacious and well equipped. The Rockefeller family endowed a generous college scholarship fund for a top graduate of each of the two schools. If there was such a thing as separate but objectively equal public schools—aside from the "badge of inferiority" inherent in forced segregation—Williamsburg had them. Indeed, the black school had a more highly credentialed faculty than the white school. (It took me a while to realize that disparity resulted from limitations on employment opportunities for educated blacks.)

The Rockefeller interests did not try to confront most segregationist sentiments and practices. Thus, while the two public schools were equal in so many ways, the white school stood in a rather prominent location near the restoration project, while the black school was in an obscure location (at least from my vantage point) on the "other" side of the C&O railroad tracks. The downtown movie theater, which was owned and operated by the Restoration, admitted whites only. (The only other local cinema, a privately owned drive-in on the outskirts of town, featured a high wall down the center to separate the vehicles and persons of white and black patrons.) Public benches in the downtown area were all designated by signs as white or colored. Blacks held no public offices. The college opened to townspeople a rich cultural life, but the only time I ever saw blacks in attendance at any of the college events was when the superb choir of Hampton Institute would come to perform a concert of "Negro spirituals."

Williamsburg was also a county seat, and the surrounding area was rural, dominated by farming and fishing. There were clearly defined black and white settlements, country stores, recreation areas, and so on. But not everything was segregated. For instance, farmers brought their merchandise to farmers' markets and lined up their wagons full of produce or seafood without apparent regard to race. Black domestic workers came into town early each weekday, and at the end of the day assembled on the benches surrounding the town flagpole waiting for their rides home. They seemed oblivious to the plaque on the flagpole, which commemorated its donation by the Ku Klux Klan. (In a later era, when my father assumed an important position at the College of William and Mary, my mother covertly arranged for the KKK plaque to become accidentally lost, thus extirpating a degrading symbol that had always irked her. The rediscovery of the plaque in an obscure warehouse many years later provoked questions and speculation, but Mother never acknowledged her role in this small gesture for racial decency. Now that she is gone, I feel entitled to blow her cover.)

My school class—all white, of course—consisted of about equal parts farm kids and city kids, whose families were mostly merchants, tradespeople, blue-collar workers, and college professors. Most shared the racist views of their parents. We who were subject to more liberal influences did not broadcast dissent and certainly did not go out of our way to seek friendship with African American youngsters of our own ages. We knew them barely, if at all.

I was just finishing eleventh grade when *Brown I* was decided. I was a writer on the school paper and I aspired to be editor-in-chief the next year. I decided to try my hand at writing an editorial about the *Brown* decision. After describing the decision, the editorial opined that it would mean profound changes in Southern society. Some would resist those changes. (Oh boy, would they!) But right-thinking folks would acknowledge that the system of racial segregation was morally wrong and would work courageously toward changing that system, as the Supreme Court's decision demanded. At the same time, it would be important to be considerate of the discomfort that would be suffered by those who had grown up with the old ways. At some point in the editorial, I quoted the very early reaction of Virginia's governor Stanley, who characterized *Brown I* as "a statesmanlike decision." (I always had the impression that

Governor Stanley was a bit dull. Very soon, of course, he was gagged by the dominant political machine of Sen. Harry Flood Byrd. In his naiveté, his first words were spoken with disarming candor, for which I admired him.) After my editorial was published, some of my classmates congratulated me, others derided me, and most were indifferent, being more interested in the forthcoming senior prom, high school baseball championship, and other more immediate events. My then girlfriend read the editorial and asked me, in a troubled tone, "You don't think that we should go to school with *them*, do you?" I said that I did, and our relationship was never quite the same again.

Our senior year was quiet. Concerns about *Brown I* were overshadowed by the impending opening of a new (white) high school, so that our class would be the last to graduate from the kindergarten through twelfth grade Matthew Whaley School, which would then become an elementary school. Students in the lower grades were asked to make recommendations as to such momentous issues as the school mascot, school songs, school colors, and the like. There seemed to be little awareness that there was another whole group, now excluded, that would someday participate in the life of the new high school. By the time of the *Brown II* decision, we seniors were out of there, leaving behind the new uncertainty about the meaning of "deliberate speed." The kids who were then in elementary and junior high school would live to experience Massive Resistance, white academies, and other occasions of shame in the Southern experience in the mid-1960s.

For my part, I went off to a college in New England, where I encountered diversity that I had never known before. Despite my liberal attitudes, the first time I took a small class with a Negro classmate, I was so aware of the novelty of the experience that I could hardly pay attention to the content of the class. While I had mouthed egalitarian beliefs as far back as I could remember, growing up in a segregated society and school system had severely limited my life's experience—but not only with regard to blacks; away from small-town Virginia, I encountered for the first time in my life such exotic creatures as Asians, Jews, Hispanics, uncloseted gays, and preppies.

White guilt (or was it just curiosity?) played at least a part in my decision to seek a post–law school clerkship with Judge William Henry Hastie of the U.S. Court of Appeals for the Third Circuit. Hastie had been part of the group, including Charles Hamilton Houston and Thurgood Marshall, that engineered the antisegregation litigation culminating in *Brown*. He was the first African American federal judge. And a great judge he was. I learned so much from him that I cannot begin to catalog my indebtedness. Not the least among these, I gained much understanding of the legal and personal struggles leading to (and following) *Brown*.

I am still struck by the changes that have taken place in my hometown in the nearly half century since *Brown*. When I go there, I see blacks and whites easily working together, shopping together, playing ball together. I am amazed that most youngsters, both black and white, seem so unaware of the deep struggle that occurred only a few decades ago. This is surely a sign of progress, but the end of de jure segregation has not rooted out the prejudices that persist at so many levels of U.S. society.

David W. Miller was born in June 1937 in Richmond, Virginia, and attended public schools in Williamsburg. He is professor of law emeritus at University of the Pacific, McGeorge School of Law, Sacramento, California, and lives in Fort Collins, Colorado.

26 Brown as Catalyst

Blake D. Morant

It is well known that some counties in Virginia actively resisted *Brown's* mandate to end segregation with "all deliberate speed." To stereotype Virginia by the resistance of some would be an unfortunate generalization. A sterling example is the city of Hampton, which desegregated public schools in the early to mid-1960s and did so with little fanfare or discernable rancor.

Hampton first implemented a freedom-of-choice plan to achieve integration. Parents could send their children to any school in the city. My mother enrolled me in Thorpe Junior High, a school that had few if any students of color at the time. Mom was not alone in her decision. Approximately 35 percent of eligible African American children in my neighborhood and adjacent vicinities attended Thorpe. The majority of African American parents, however, chose to send their children to predominantly African American schools. The predominantly African American junior high school did not have any white students, suggesting that white parents enrolled their children in predominantly white schools.

Thorpe's opening in 1965 was an exciting mixture of anticipation and angst. Administrators, who sought a smooth transition from homogeneity to diversity, were vigilant and noticeably interactive with the student body. From my perspective, the administration largely achieved their goal. The school year commenced uneventfully and with an air of optimism. Curiosity was a pervasive norm. Dialogue between minority and majority students appeared objectively fluid and cordial. As an African American attending a predominantly white school, I, too, possessed a strong sense of curiosity. For the first time in my life, I had the opportunity to interact meaningfully with students of different races, ethnicities, and socioeconomic backgrounds.

I recall vividly my homeroom, which was one of the advanced placement seventh-grade classes. Sitting next to me was Keith Savage, a very bright, talented, and personable white student. Keith and many other white students in my class were open to new experiences presented by integration. Keith and I worked jointly on class projects, studied together, and ultimately forged a lasting friendship. I also formed bonds with other students in the class. My eventual election as class president signaled the marginalization of race, at least within the context of my seventh-grade homeroom. The experience of other African Americans at Thorpe appeared to mirror mine. Many had beneficial relationships with students of different backgrounds. This is not to suggest that acrimonious incidents did not occur at Thorpe. Those incidents, however, were few and quickly abated.

In 1968, the City of Hampton took a decidedly aggressive step to integrate its schools. The school board replaced freedom of choice with a system that required students to attend schools in specifically drawn geographical zones. Unilateral assignment to schools had dramatic effects. Predominantly African American schools in the city suddenly disappeared. Self-segregation was negligible in the period during which Hampton instituted zoning.

Prior to the 1970s, the city's housing patterns, while homogenous within individual neighborhoods, were fairly diverse over a broader, geographical area. Although there was little integration along individual streets, large grids or sections of streets where African Americans resided were adjacent to areas where whites resided. For example, the neighborhood where I lived as a child was predominantly African American and situated within a fifth of a mile of a predominantly white neighborhood. This pattern of living was relatively common in Hampton and contributed to a geographic integration that, at that time, obviated the need for busing. Compulsory attendance to schools within a particular zone seemed truer to *Brown's* mandate to desegregate. After 1968, however, racial shifts in housing patterns prompted the city to create unusually shaped zones to sustain integration in many schools.

The city's implementation of zoning coincided with my enrollment at Hampton High School. Hampton High was far more integrated than Thorpe Junior High and fostered greater racial interaction. High schools, with larger student populations and more numerous course and extracurricular offerings, naturally provided greater opportunities for socialization. This certainly was the case at Hampton High. Extracurricular and group activities broke down barriers and prompted students to expand their social spheres. Homecoming courts and student organizations became reflective of the school's demographics and racial makeup. My associations and friendships with students of various backgrounds transformed my high school experience. I achieved leadership roles in the marching and concert band, and became vice-president of the student body as the result of a campaign based upon student unity. Gratifyingly, my experience at Hampton High was not unique. African Americans achieved leadership positions in many organizations including, but not limited to, student government, academic clubs, and athletic teams.

One friendship that I formed at Hampton High led to the selection of the University of Virginia as my college of choice. Michael Elmore, a white friend who was a year ahead of me in high school, communicated with me frequently during his first year at Virginia. In a particularly memorable conversation, he stated: "Virginia's atmosphere has changed and will continue to change for the better . . . I believe you could contribute to this new atmosphere and thrive in the process." Mike's advice became a prophecy and our friendship became an invaluable asset during my years at Virginia.

Despite its benefits, integration and the socialization it facilitated were certainly not trouble-free. Some schools in Hampton reported disturbing incidents with racial overtones. One example during my sophomore year in high school was a student government election in which an African American candidate failed by only a few votes to be placed on the final ballot for president. A physical altercation between white and African American students ensued in an isolated part of the building. While that incident initially inflamed racial tensions, its lingering effects appeared minimal. Regular dialogue among the parties defused tempers and reestablished civility. As a result, subsequent elections for student government positions took place without animosity or resentment.

My experiences in Hampton's secondary schools and ultimately at the University of Virginia anecdotally support the *Brown* court's underlying belief that integration facilitates broadened exchanges and enriching relationships. Keith Savage, whom I met in the seventh grade, is a successful theatrical performer who remains in close contact. My friendship with Michael Elmore, who is a college administrator, endures despite the divergent paths our careers have taken. The integration of secondary schools also enables individuals to think meaningfully about the conundrum of difference. Modification of negative attitudes regarding race and the abandonment of stereotypes occur *only* when individuals confront and reevaluate the reasonableness of those beliefs and generalizations. For those touched directly by *Brown's* mandate, the reevaluation of racial attitudes is inevitable, and this landmark case's impact is indelible. Indeed, forty years after our meeting at Thorpe Junior High, Keith Savage can still recall the names of each African American student in our seventh-grade homeroom. *Brown's* impact on him and my other Hampton High classmates, whom I see when I visit the city, remains palpable and lasting.

The benefits of school desegregation as mandated by *Brown* are, in my view, multifaceted. Education encompasses more than the study of facts, figures, and rules. The learning process must be a holistic enterprise in which diverse students are exposed to challenging disciplines and encouraged to engage in civil debate. This intellectual exchange encourages critical thinking and enhances reasoning and analysis. *Brown's* mandate ostensibly furthers this integral objective in secondary schools.

Of course *Brown* is not a panacea. Forced integration does not necessarily translate into voluntary, social interaction—a point emphasized by the critics of *Brown*. Yet integration's benefits, which include the equitable distribution of resources to schools, the maximization of opportunities for interaction between diverse individuals, and the reexamination of racial beliefs, appear to outweigh potential detriments.

As social psychologists suggest, any meaningful change in deep-seated beliefs requires stimuli that prompt a cognitive reassessment of those beliefs—an often lengthy, time-consuming process. *Brown's* mandate has been a stimulus that compelled many to reassess their attitudes on race and, in many cases, accept integration as a societal ideal. While *Brown* may not be solely responsible for this attitudinal shift, the decision undoubtedly contributed to it.

In his century-old and timeless book *The Souls of Black Folk*, W. E. B. DuBois opined that "the problem of the Twentieth Century is the problem of the color line." If DuBois presents a societal challenge, the *Brown* mandate should be considered a seminal strategy to meet it. Society's gradual acceptance of integration and the social interaction it fosters remain fundamental and enduring constructs of *Brown's* profound legacy, and secure the decision's place as a landmark in American jurisprudence.

Blake D. Morant was born in Fort Eustis, Virginia, in November 1952. He attended elementary and secondary school in Hampton, Virginia, from 1959 to 1971. He is now dean and professor of law at Wake Forest University School of Law in Winston-Salem, North Carolina.

27 Equality and Sorority during the Decade after *Brown*

Taunya Lovell Banks

I learned that my elementary school was racially segregated when a television newscaster announced that the U.S. Supreme Court ruled for the petitioners in *Brown v. Board of Education*. It never occurred to me before May 17, 1954, that there were no white teachers or students at my school. For almost ten years my parents shielded me from the ugly reality of de jure segregation—as Guido Orefice, the father in the Italian film *Life Is Beautiful*, shielded his son from the horrors of Nazism.

Nothing immediately changed for me after that day. My parents never mentioned the decision. To discuss the implications of *Brown* would undo their hard work shielding me from the psychologically debilitating experience of U.S. race-based apartheid.

The public schools in my Southern hometown, Washington, D.C., desegregated the following fall. I arrived at school in September 1954 to find many of my schoolmates gone. They were now attending formerly white schools closer to their homes. Gone too was our annual celebration of Negro History Week, as well as our May Day celebration. Nevertheless, my elementary school, Neval Thomas, remained all black due to racially restrictive residential patterns. Some school systems, anticipating the ruling in *Brown*, started building new schools deep within single-race residential areas; others adopted this tactic after the *Brown* decision.

Desegregation did bring us new opportunities. My school was selected to appear on a local television show where elementary school children visit and report on historical sites in and around the city. The school was assigned the Custis-Lee Mansion, the home of General Robert E. Lee! Although none of the teachers said anything to us directly, I distinctly remember hearing them talk among themselves about the insult imposed on us by having to visit the home of a Confederate general.

I was among the students selected to appear on the show, and I remember our visit to the mansion, which still had slave quarters. My sheltered background did not allow me to fully appreciate the horror of the quarters. Instead,

I remember commenting that the slaves must have been very small to have lived in such low cramped places. After the visit I lost interest in the assignment and was bumped from the group for not preparing my part. To this day I do not know whether subconsciously I realized our assignment was terribly inappropriate, or whether my teacher's lack of enthusiasm wore off on me.

Despite the desegregation of Washington's public schools after *Brown*, I did not attend an integrated school until junior high school. *Browne* Junior High was only nominally integrated when I arrived in the fall of 1956 and quickly became all black again. The children of Jewish merchants who serviced the community, and of the few working-class whites who remained in the area, quickly left the school by the following fall. Their flight from Browne and the neighborhood mirrored white flight from public schools and urban areas around the country in the post-*Brown* era. The only white person left in my junior high school was the band teacher, a nice man who introduced me to the French horn.

When I entered Georgetown's Western High School in the fall of 1958, I found myself in an integrated school where blacks were in the minority. The students came from varied backgrounds; children of Congress members, cabinet officials, and diplomats mingled with children from Chinatown and children of the genteel poor, writers, artists, civil servants, black domestics, and black professionals. Other than a classmate from Texas who commented in gym that she had been taught that black people had tails, high school life was fairly conventional. There were the usual cliques. The high school sororities and fraternities excluded black students, which I expected, *and* Jewish students as well.

I remember walking down the hall behind two affluent white sorority girls who were speaking openly and unashamedly in derogatory terms about some Jewish students I knew. To my surprise they continued their discussion knowing I could overhear them. Patricia Williams writes about the simultaneous horror and delight of being allowed to overhear and be a passive party to such conversations. In a sense you are allowed to be a party to the "othering" of someone else. Rather then feeling like a member of the in-group, I felt invisible, not important enough for people to act civil in my presence.

I had only one black teacher in high school, a woman with a PhD who taught me biology. Her advanced degree was not unusual at Western High School. There were several other women teachers at the school with PhDs, most in the sciences. Only later in life did I realized that sex discrimination in higher education probably caused me to have such highly trained teachers in high school. Those women teachers with doctorate degrees probably could not get jobs in any of the area colleges or universities.

Unlike elementary and junior high, in high school I encountered teachers and counselors who harbored low expectations of black students. When my mother asked my French teacher why I got a C when the college-level tutor my parents hired said my comprehension of French was excellent, the teacher replied: "Why are you concerned? She's not going to college anyway." My mother told me many years later that she drew herself up to her full five feet three and a half inches and told the teacher that she, my father, my paternal grandfather, and my great-grandfather were college graduates. I never got a C in French after that conversation.

Senior year when I received a letter from the University of Pennsylvania asking me to submit my portfolio of drawings to the Museum School, my counselor advised me not to respond since I already had been admitted to Syracuse University. At the time, my father was on a Fulbright in Japan and my mother was not knowledgeable, so there was no one to counsel me otherwise. I was only sixteen, so I took the counselor's advice. Belatedly, I learned that white teachers and counselors could not always be trusted.

I came of age in post–World War II America, with pictures of the bombing of Nagasaki and Hiroshima and of the survivors of Nazi concentration camps planted firmly in my memory. Naively, I thought that we had learned important lessons about tolerance from these experiences. But, high school taught me that discrimination came in all forms—race, religion, ethnicity, income, gender, sexuality, ideology—and was not limited to black Americans.

Life seemed decidedly less beautiful by the time I entered college seven years after *Brown*. In college I learned that integration could isolate you from your own community as well. Granted, in high school the few black students were separated by class, so isolation from the early 1960s overwhelmingly working-class black community in Syracuse was not totally surprising. A few people within that community were especially kind to the small number of black university students, unlike the sole black professor at the university. In hindsight, as a college professor myself, I realized how overwhelmed he must have felt sitting untenured in his attic-like office at a white university. What really surprised me was how acceptance by certain white institutions could isolate you from your fellow black students.

Out of a combination of curiosity and pragmatism, I entered spring rush, the annual effort by sororities and fraternities to select new members from the freshman class. Syracuse offered women three options: you could rush Christian sororities, Jewish sororities, or both ("mixed" rush). At the time, there were no black sororities or fraternities on campus. A few black women and I chose mixed rush, thinking it our only opportunity to see all the sorority houses. In the end I was selected by two sororities, a local sorority and a national Jewish sorority. Two years earlier another Jewish sorority had broken the color barrier, admitting an accomplished and attractive black woman who also was the girlfriend of a nationally prominent black college football player. Ever the pragmatist, I chose the Jewish sorority because it was more prestigious and, more importantly, offered better housing and food than the local sorority. That decision cut me off both physically and emotionally from the few other black students at the university, most of whom spent all their college lives in dorms.

It was difficult trying to function in both worlds. Each had its own orthodoxy. You were part of one or the other, but not of both.

Belatedly I learned that my race had been the subject of so much concern among the sorors that the national office was consulted before I was asked to join the sorority. This fact was hidden from me by the senior and junior sorors, who warmly welcomed me. In hindsight I wonder about the reaction of the women who formed my pledge group. Surely they did not expect to have a black soror. The full implication of this fact became apparent the next year.

In the early 1960s Syracuse randomly assigned roommates, and I ended up my freshman year with an Italian American woman from Scarsdale. I did not understand why my mother remained sitting nervously on my bed until my roommate and her family arrived. My mother knew, but my father never mentioned to me, that as a student at Northwestern University in the 1920s he was not permitted to stay in the dormitory because he was black. When my roommate arrived and everyone was civil, even friendly, my mother breathed a sigh of relief and left.

I detected no problems between me and my roommate until I returned from Christmas vacation and found that I had been shifted to a single room. No one in authority spoke to me about this change, and my roommate lamely commented that she and the white woman from northeast Pennsylvania who previously occupied the single had decided to room together. Lee, my roommate, could never fully look me in the face again. It is one thing to attend classes together, but another altogether to share the same living space with a black girl.

My sophomore year roommate, a Jewish woman from my pledge class, failed to arrive. No one bothered to tell me that she had decided not to return to school. Once again I had a single room. That spring room selections were made for the sorority house. I had first choice for my class because two senior women brought me into the house during the spring semester after their roommate graduated in January. Despite my having picked a prime room and being on friendly terms with my sorors, no one volunteered to room with me. After an embarrassing moment of silence, I was asked to leave for a bit while my "sisters" spoke among themselves. When I returned, room selection was complete and I had two roommates I vaguely knew from my pledge class. The incident was never discussed again. I was expected to go on as before and forget that the incident ever occurred. I was to assume that I was an equal like all of the other "sisters." It is hard to forget those things.

That fall, my junior year, the closeness between my two roommates left me feeling like an outsider in my own room. They got to live in the sorority house together in exchange for having to room with me; they, like me, were pragmatists. Recently I saw both women together at the Baltimore train station. It seemed clear that they thought they recognized me too, but we did not speak to each other. I know why I did not speak to them, but I wonder why they chose not to speak to me.

Things were a bit better my third year. I roomed with two juniors. Unlike my pledge group, their class joined the sorority knowing that they'd have a black soror.

Overall my experiences at Syracuse were positive. I got a good education, was very active in campus politics, and even got elected to a class office. Yet, I did not realize how bitter my experiences at Syracuse left me until many years later when I was asked to return for a reunion. My bitterness stems not from these and other racially tinged incidents, but rather from the refusal of people to be honest about the prejudices apparent during that period. They were too willing to paper over their own racism and expect you to overlook and forget it as well. People want to think well of themselves, and when their actions reflect racial prejudices, they are embarrassed and ashamed. No one seemed to think about my feelings. Access to some of the benefits long denied blacks was my reward.

Taunya Lovell Banks was born in February 1945 in Washington, D.C., and attended elementary and secondary schools in Washington, D.C., from 1949 to 1961. She is now the Jacob A. France Professor of Equality Jurisprudence at the University of Maryland School of Law in Baltimore.

28 "What Are You Doing Here?" An Autobiographical Fragment

Louis Michael Seidman

I was born in 1947 in Washington, D.C. My parents were strong racial liberals. They refused to attend the National Theater because of its segregated seating policy and would not permit us to go to Glen Echo Amusement Park because it did not admit blacks. I do not remember my parents actually having African American friends, however. The only black I had regular contact with as a child was our maid, Jesse, who came once per week to clean our house. She was a large, strong woman of indeterminate age—strikingly muscular, yet extremely gentle. She was cheerful and friendly but also reserved, proud, and, on some level, deeply mysterious.

In winter 1954–1955, my family moved to New Rochelle, New York, a suburb of New York City. Jesse decided to come with us and ended up as our "live-in help" for much of my childhood. My parents were quite formal people. When my father came home from work (my mother stayed home during my childhood), Jesse would serve them dinner in the dining room. My brother and I ate separately with Jesse at the kitchen table.

At the time of our move, I attended Takoma Park Elementary School, which was segregated by law, although, as a child of seven, I had no awareness of this fact. Only a few months before we moved, the Supreme Court decided *Bolling v. Sharpe*, the companion case to *Brown*, which held that segregation in the District of Columbia school system was unconstitutional. Unlike their counterparts in the Deep South, District officials decided to comply voluntarily with the decision. As part of a public relations effort, school officials arranged for black and white D.C. students to visit a northern, successfully integrated school system. By coincidence, they choose New Rochelle. Hence, there was an odd parallel between my personal move and the symbolic movement of the District of Columbia to the new reality represented by New Rochelle.

When I arrived in New Rochelle, I attended Roosevelt Elementary School. It was integrated in name, but to the best of my recollection the only African Americans actually in attendance were the children of an African ambassador to the United Nations. A different school—Mayflower Elementary School—

was closer to my house and had a substantial number of African American students, but district lines were drawn in such a way as to place my house within the Roosevelt district.

In 1957, three years after *Brown* (and, of course, three years after our move), the first successful Northern desegregation suit was brought against the New Rochelle school system. The district court found that years ago, school lines had been gerrymandered so as to segregate African American children. As a result of the court decree, some school district lines were redrawn, but I continued to attend Roosevelt Elementary.

Sometime in the early 1960s, I remember my parents strongly urging Jesse to register to vote. She returned to our house too humiliated at first to recount what had happened: She had not been permitted to register because she had failed the literacy test. At about the same time, my parents decided that they should stop paying Jesse under the table and insisted on registering her for Social Security, although they offered to pay both halves of the tax. Perhaps for this reason (although I do not know for certain), Jesse suddenly disappeared. I never saw her again.

New Rochelle had only one high school, so it was integrated—after a fashion. The school was divided into three parts: the college preparatory track, which was predominantly Jewish; the vocational track, which was predominantly Italian; and the non-Regents track, which was predominantly African American. The "integrated" portion of the curriculum consisted of homeroom, gym, and lunch, where these groups confronted each other in uneasy silence. I do not remember having a single African American friend.

In the summer of 1963, my brother and I wanted to attend the March on Washington. My parents were uneasy about our going alone but ended up being strongly supportive. They arranged for us to stay in a hotel in New York City near where the bus departed and to be awakened at 3:00 AM to begin the trip. We were at the Lincoln Memorial when Martin Luther King gave his famous speech. My recollection of the event is quite different from the version one commonly sees on newsreels. It had been a very long afternoon, people were restless and tired of listening to the speeches, and many people were beginning to leave as King began to speak. It was hard to hear. Neither I, nor any of the people around me, had any inkling that we were listening to one of the great speeches in U.S. history.

After graduating from law school, I returned to Washington, where I clerked for J. Skelly Wright on the U.S. Court of Appeals for the District of Columbia Circuit. Years earlier, while serving as a district judge, sitting in the Fifth Circuit, Judge Wright had ordered the desegregation of the New Orleans public schools and received death threats for doing so.

Robert Kennedy wanted to appoint Wright to the Court of Appeals, but Senator Russell Long informed Kennedy that Long would never again win an election in Louisiana if Judge Wright were appointed to the Fifth Circuit. Kennedy compromised by appointing him to the D.C. Circuit instead.

Judge Wright thought that his days of dealing with integration were over, but he turned out to be wrong. Shortly after his appointment, Julius Hobson, a local activist, brought an action alleging that the D.C. schools remained unconstitutionally segregated. At that time, the federal district court was charged with the appointment of the local school board, whose members were named as defendants, so all the district judges were forced to recuse themselves. Chief Judge David Bazelon, aware of Wright's prior experiences, appointed him to serve as the trial judge. Judge Wright entered a series of sweeping orders, mandating an end to tracking in D.C. schools and an equalization of resources between the predominantly black and white schools.

By the time my own children were ready to enroll, D.C. public schools were thoroughly segregated. Perhaps in part because of Judge Wright's orders, only a handful of whites remained in the public schools, and they were concentrated in a few schools located west of Rock Creek Park. We lived in a middle-class, integrated neighborhood. My children received some of their elementary education at a predominantly white but integrated school that was west of the park, but we then placed them in private schools, where they remained until college.

Living a few blocks from our house was a large, white family that was somewhat disorganized. There was no father in the house, and the mother could barely keep track of her kids. As the story was told to me, when the time came to send her oldest child to high school, she simply packed him off to the local public school without thinking anything about it. This school had not seen a white student in years. When the kid showed up, the homeroom teacher immediately recognized that a mistake had been made and shipped the kid off to the principal's office. The principal, in amazement, said, "What are you doing here?" or words to this effect and promptly got on the phone with his counterpart at Wilson High School, the only D.C. high school with more than a token number of white students.

Within hours, the student had been successfully transferred to Wilson. These events occurred two generations after the Supreme Court's decision in *Brown v. Board of Education*.

Louis Michael Seidman was born in Washington, D.C., in February 1947 and attended elementary school there during the 1953–1954 school year and elementary and secondary schools in New Rochelle, New York, from 1955 to 1964. He is now the Carmack Waterhouse Professor of Constitutional Law at the Georgetown University Law Center in Washington, D.C.

PART III

De Facto States

29 Brown's Ambiguous Legacy

Alex M. Johnson Jr.

I was born in 1953—a year before the seminal decision in *Brown v. Board of Education*. I started my schooling in 1958 as a kindergartner at West Vernon Elementary School in South Central Los Angeles. I was that rarity as a student (or, more accurately, I should say my family was pretty unusual) in that I didn't move during my first seven years of formal public education and ultimately graduated from West Vernon, where I had some wonderful teachers. (Indeed, the teachers at West Vernon made a lasting impression on me, because they convinced me that I could go to college even though neither of my parents graduated from high school.)

Serendipitously, my family moved the summer following graduation—1965—during the summer of the initial Watts Riots. I attended John Muir Junior High (grades seven through nine) and graduated from that temple of learning in 1968. (I actually remember very little about junior high school. Maybe it is because junior high school occurs at that odd time in one's life between childhood and adolescence. I do know that I entered crazy about sports and graduated crazy about girls.) Last but not least, I attended and graduated from (in 1971) George Washington High School in South Central Los Angeles.

Thirteen years of public education in the Los Angeles Unified School District at three schools. What is important, however, is that the two neighborhoods I grew up in, the first at Forty-seventh and Broadway, the second at Florence and Vermont (a scant five blocks from Florence and Normandy, which Reginald Denny later made infamous when he was pulled from his truck and attacked in the riots that followed the acquittals of the police officers charged with beating Rodney King), and the three schools I attended were almost exclusively black.

Now we may have then been called Negro (I do remember that), later Afro American (it was during this time period that it was insulting to be called black), and even later African American (which I find hilarious and ironic today because when I was a boy growing up an even greater insult was to be called "African" anything—if someone called you an "African" whatever, fighting ensued) or black, but whatever we were called over these years, there was one constant: We were all called the same thing because we were all of the same race or ethnicity—those descendants of individuals who at one time or another had been enslaved and/or subject to discriminatory laws based solely on skin color.[1]

Although I am plumbing the depths of my memory, my recollection is that there was only one white student—named Robert Kennedy, believe it or not—and one Hispanic, Gloria Aguilar (I had a schoolboy's crush on her, and boy, was she smart) in my class of thirty-five to forty students who attended West Vernon Elementary School and more or less spent the six years together before leaving for junior high school (most of them went to John Adams—as noted, my family moved, so I went to John Muir as a result). The important point is that all the other students were Negroes, as we were called then. Many, although not all, of the teachers were as well. I do recall Mr. Salisbury, the avuncular fifth-grade teacher, and Mr. Becton (whom to this day I believe is related to General Becton), the strict disciplinarian who taught us "seniors" in the sixth grade and would make Sidney Poitier portraying Mr. Thackeray in *To Sir with Love* look like a wimp, were both Negro males who served as my role models. I must also note that my fourth-grade teacher, Mr. Tomaki Nakayama, is the reason I am where I am today. It was Mr. Nakayama who spent time with me, mentored me, and convinced me that I was smart enough to go to college and who instilled in me the confidence in my abilities to excel academically. It was also Mr. Nakayama who first took me to the campus of the University of California at Los Angeles and correctly prophesied that one day I would attend the university, which is where I earned my JD in 1978.

But I digress. Robert Kennedy, he of the poor white Kennedys that lived behind the Junipero Serra Library, was the only white I can recall attending my elementary school, but the neat thing was he wasn't really white! We didn't think of him as white, nor did he think of himself as white. He was never regarded as a white boy because he was cooler, hipper, and as we said then, badder than almost anyone in my school. In retrospect, I know why—Robert had to become black (Negro) in order to survive. Indeed, although my parents were visibly shocked when I first brought Robert home for a sleepover (as we were wont to do back in those days), by the end of the fourth grade Robert was as welcome in our home as a favorite cousin.

I do recall being very disappointed that Robert never invited me to sleep over at his house but somehow instinctively knew that even if he had asked, my parents would never have allowed it, as everyone in the neighborhood knew that Robert's father had a problem with alcohol and was unemployed, which is why he lived in our neighborhood. Robert didn't have a mother and no one knew why and I still don't know what happened to her to this day. I do have an inkling of what happened to Robert. While I was in high school at George Washington High School, I had the opportunity to attend a record hop (Come on, you remember record hops!) at Jefferson High School and I ran into Robert, and he was dealing (today we would say "slinging") Mary Jane, or weed. I later heard he got busted for something serious and was sent away upstate for a considerable period of time. (I hope he did not join the Aryan Brotherhood!)

The bottom line is that I went to a segregated school. Indeed, the case can be made that I went to three segregated schools. My high school, for example, had a higher percentage of Hispanics and Asian Americans (Michael Pinada, a Filipino and now a medical doctor, was my best friend in high school even though he was called racial slurs by some of my other friends because of his ethnicity) than my elementary school had but fewer than ten white students out of a total student population of over three thousand (yes, three thousand students with more than one thousand students in each class). I graduated seventh in our class of 1,090, or thereabouts, and my high school graduation was held at the Los Angeles Coliseum because it was the only venue large enough to hold the graduates and their guests. Little wonder that I experienced culture shock when I left Los Angeles in the fall of 1971 to attend Princeton University, which had a student body of less than three thousand, of whom 95 percent were white (and from my perspective, rich as well), and I was in the minority for the first time in my life.

Some thirty years after I first entered Princeton University as a freshman awed by my august surroundings, I became dean at the University of Minnesota Law School. Thus, in the fifty years following *Brown*, I traveled from largely de facto segregated schools to lead one of the premier law schools in the United States, which, although more diverse than my elementary school with over 20 percent of its students members of underrepresented groups, still had a long way to go to achieve its stated goal of attaining a truly diverse group of students that is societally representative.

When I reflect on my educational experience and how it was impacted by the *Brown* decision, I come to the conclusion that *Brown* did little if anything to change my primary and secondary educational experience. My elementary, junior high, and high schools were segregated—of that I have no doubt. Was it de jure segregation? Of course not. The *Brown* decision had little if any impact on that type of segregation, which is the product of largely segregated neighborhoods that produced de facto segregation, causing me to attend almost exclusively black schools.[2] I was not bused to an integrated school, nor were white students bused into the schools I attended, thereby leaving those schools almost exclusively minority. I was born too early to be offered the choice of magnet or, even later, charter schools as options to my largely segregated schools.

Nope, I went to my neighborhood schools, and no one complained about the fact that these schools were not integrated. Indeed, I can't recall a single significant discussion, newspaper story, or article about our largely segregated schools. Nor was there any hue and cry to change the status quo existing in the Los Angeles Unified School District that produced this largely monoracial educational experience. In fact, it never occurred to me that my schools were segregated and that I was receiving a largely inferior educational experience as a result. Quite the contrary: Later, when I was in high school and I watched the buses roll in Boston and other Northeastern cities and saw the raw hatred exhibited by whites whose schools were being "invaded" by people who looked like me, it never occurred to me that the schools I attended were just as segregated as those in South Boston and elsewhere. Furthermore, I would have been shocked if I had been told that I attended a segregated school and was receiving an inferior education as a result. After all, we didn't live in the South or the Northeast. We lived in Los Angeles—the land of opportunity and equality.

It is quite clear that my educational experience was colored by the racial dynamic that existed then and continues to exist in the United States, one that views and treats blacks as different from (inferior then, something else now) whites. Hence, at this level it could be said *Brown v. Board of Education* had little, if anything, to do with my educational experience as a product of the Los Angeles Unified School District. I could say that, but I won't.

I am also just as certain that although the decision in *Brown* had no direct impact on my educational experience—it did not produce integrated classrooms—the decision in *Brown* has had a profound impact and influence on my life. I would not be where I am today without the *Brown* decision and the changes it has wrought in U.S. society. I would not have been welcome at Princeton, the UCLA Law School, my old law firm at Latham and Watkins, and in all my academic positions had it not been for *Brown* and its revolutionary impact on American race relations and society. At one level, then, *Brown* has been enormously successful. Its impact on U.S. society has been nothing short of astounding. No one would have predicted in 1954 that an African American would lead a top-twenty law school and that this seminal achievement would largely go unnoticed (and rightfully so) from a societal perspective.

However, ultimately I keep coming back to the surprising conclusion that *Brown* cannot be viewed as having had a positive impact on American society as a whole. Indeed, to be blunt, I have come to the conclusion that *Brown* has failed, just as it failed to provide me and millions of others with an integrated educational experience. Thus, this essay concludes with a rather startling claim: Integration—both as a process and as an ideal or goal to be attained—has failed in U.S. society. If the goal of integration was to achieve the physical integration of U.S. society along any number of indices—geographical, occupational, educational, et cetera—it has been an abysmal failure. If the goal of integration was to improve the material or educational plight of blacks in U.S. society, it has failed. If the goal of integration was to establish a color-blind society in which race is no longer a viable category for classifying/stereotyping individuals, it has failed.

In sum, I represent *Brown*'s positive legacy. I grew up in a segregated city and attended segregated schools. My educational experience, although not a product of de jure segregation, was inferior as a result of the fact that I grew up in a segregated community. However, I do not doubt that *Brown* opened doors and opportunities for me.

Yet many blacks have not benefited from the social changes associated with *Brown*.

I have lost a younger brother to gang violence, an older sister to drugs, and a younger sister to AIDS. I am almost certain that none of these tragic outcomes would have occurred were it not for the institutionalized and systemic racism that still infects U.S. society. Hence, it is impossible at one level to say that *Brown* is ultimately successful. It did not eradicate racism, nor did it result in meaningful integration.

However, my siblings, all of whom died too young, grew up in the same household, attended the same schools, had the same abilities, and faced the same challenges that I faced. I chose one path; they each chose another. The thing that I do firmly believe, and for this I do credit *Brown* and its legacy, is that the path I chose would not have been available were it not for the decision in *Brown v. Board of Education*. For that, at least, I am eternally grateful.

NOTES

1. I have always chosen not to capitalize "black" in my work and previously have detailed why I prefer the lowercase "black" to "African American." For those who care, that can be found at Alex Johnson, "Destabilizing Racial Classifications Based on Insights Gleaned from Trademark Law," *California Law Review* 84:887–888, note 6.
2. For a discussion of the factors that contribute to residential segregation, see Alex M. Johnson Jr., "How Race and Poverty Intersect to Prevent Integration: Destabilizing Race as a Vehicle to Integrate Neighborhoods," *University of Pennsylvania Law Review* 143 (1995): 1595.

Alex M. Johnson Jr. was born in October 1953 in Los Angeles, California, and attended elementary and secondary schools there. He is the Perre Bowen Professor of Law at the University of Virginia School of Law in Charlottesville.

30 Public Education in Los Angeles: Past and Present

Paul Marcus

I was born in New York City, but we moved to Los Angeles when I was a young boy in the mid-1950s. We lived in a dense working-class area in the central part of the city, and I went to the Los Angeles Unified School District public schools. My neighborhood was very diverse, with many different religious groups and racial groups.

Overall, the vast majority of kids—white, black, Hispanic, or Asian—went to fairly homogeneous public schools at that time. But my school, Alexander Hamilton High School, was atypical—it geographically covered a wide range. To the far eastern poor part of the district, where I lived, there were working-class families from African American, white, and, to a lesser extent, Hispanic groups. But the far western part of the district was quite a wealthy area, Cheviot Hills (still a very well-to-do area), and in those days almost all the kids went to the public schools.

My earliest memories involve interacting with children of other races and backgrounds: in the neighborhoods where I lived, in schools, and certainly in sports. When I got a part-time job as a teen the people I worked with were of different races—Asians, blacks, whites. It was quite common playing sports in those days as a young child on teams that were pretty mixed. For me, that was very positive. I was a basketball player in high school. And there, race was irrelevant. How many points could you score? How good a defensive player were you? And the teams were made up of a variety of people. Arguably the single wealthiest person I ever met in high school was on the basketball team with me, along with other students—Asian, black, and white—whose families were struggling to make ends meet. And that was a positive and bonding experience for all of us.

The greatest tension that I saw growing up in the public schools had to do less with race than with economic differences. There was a real upper stratosphere of wealthy white kids, but the lower end of the scale was not delineated much by race; it really was defined by economics. So there would be poor white, Hispanic, and black kids, and the tension was much more between them and the children from college-oriented, well-to-do families. I graduated in 1964, and it was quite striking to me that the biggest difference I saw racially was not in the public schools but in college and law school. I went to both at UCLA, which is a very large urban public school. The number of minority students in those two settings was exceedingly small—much smaller than I had been used to seeing in high school. That I found remarkable. The mix in college was low, and it was even lower in law school; there were very few students there who were not white and generally from upper-class backgrounds, with parents or siblings with substantial educations.

As I look back, it seems to me that my comfort level for dealing with all different kinds of people is pretty high. I work in the criminal law area, so often I am engaged with people who are poor and come from backgrounds different from mine, certainly different from where I come from today, although not so different from what I grew up with, and I feel positive about that. It is an attitude I try to share with my children in their life experiences and in their work

As I reflect today on the impact of *Brown* and the ensuing civil rights movement, the positive effects can be seen in the overall changes in our national culture. In other countries it is not at all unusual, even today, to hear jokes in mainstream entertainment about race and religion. And one has the sense that the people making the jokes and laughing at the jokes simply have not grown up with different kinds of people in their schools and housing and jobs. So in that sense, in promoting an interracial culture, *Brown* was extremely positive.

There appears to have been a negative side, though, whether or not it is directly traceable to *Brown*. After I graduated from high school, but while I was in college and law school, there was a real rethinking in Los Angeles about whether our community was in fact in compliance with *Brown*—not necessarily because the district had legally barred people from different backgrounds from going to particular schools, but because the district had resegregated based on housing patterns. So major lawsuits to integrate were brought during the period I was in college and law school, principally by the American Civil Liberties Union and the National Association for the Advancement of Colored People. As I mentioned at the outset, my high school was quite mixed, but that was atypical—most schools were not, and that was at all levels. Judges directed school boundaries to be redrawn, ordered busing; there was great turmoil. There was no resistance in terms of people standing in doorways or governors or mayors saying that they were going to defy the judicial authority. But it was quite striking what seemed to happen over the twenty- to thirty-year period up until now.

The composition of the Los Angeles school district changed dramatically. I mean, the numbers are nothing short of astonishing. There was a period when I was in school when the the entire Los Angeles city school district had a white student population a little bit under 60 percent, and a black population a little bit under 20 percent, the remainder being mostly Hispanic and Asian students. Now, the white population is below 10 percent, the black population has dropped to about 13 percent, and the Hispanic population is over 70 percent. Of course, the overall population in Los Angeles bears no resemblance to those numbers. So something has happened over this period, and the anecdotal evidence I have from friends who have children or grandchildren is that many white families fearing busing and integration—and this particularly was in the 1970s but it continued in the 1980s and 1990s—left the Los Angeles school district. They left it in one of two ways.

It became socially acceptable to send children to private schools, in a way that it wasn't when I was growing up. The only children I really knew who were sent to private schools in the 1960s were kids who had learning disorders or unusual sorts of problems or came from very religious backgrounds—children who went to Catholic schools or Orthodox Jewish schools. But those were very small numbers. There were few private schools that were not linked to a religious order. That changed.

New schools were formed and schools that had been in existence expanded so that most of the upper- and middle-class people we know who remained in the Los Angeles city school district did not send their children to public schools. That was a process that seemed to transcend race and again may be more an economic than a racial issue. But the numbers changed dramatically, and I think the evidence is pretty substantial on that.

During this time, also, people simply moved out of the Los Angeles Unified School District. The integration orders were all linked to that district, which was by far the biggest in Southern California. But people were not moving out of the Los Angeles area; the metropolitan area continued to grow substantially. They were moving to cities bordering Los Angeles that had independent school districts where, frankly, the numbers were much lower in terms of minority students and there was no enforced busing. Communities such as Beverly Hills, Culver City, and Santa Monica had independent school districts and people moved there. The most striking thing occurring as a result is that property values jumped during that period. Those small cities were viewed as very upscale neighborhoods and desirable areas to live in. And one of the things that was promoted, and I remember this very well, was that the school districts there were very good. I think perhaps unstated but understood was that, because there was no forced integration as there had been in the Los Angeles schools, those cities were especially desirable.

Looking back now, it seems clear to me that the *Brown* decision had a great impact in my hometown of Los Angeles. That impact was very positive in terms of truly integrating many schools during the 1960s and 1970s, and exposing children to others not like themselves. It may also be viewed as negative, though, in the unanticipated encouraging of movement for many away from the public school system. This is the challenge we continue to face, not only in Los Angeles but also in many parts of urban America.

Paul Marcus was born in New York City in December 1946 and was educated in the Los Angeles Public Schools from 1956 to 1964. He is now the Haynes Professor of Law and Kelly Chair in Teaching Excellence at the College of William and Mary School of Law in Williamsburg, Virginia.

31 The Discrete and Insular Majority

Craig M. Bradley

I was born in late 1945 and grew up in the Chicago suburb of Downers Grove, Illinois, a town that grew from around ten to twenty thousand people during the seventeen years of my childhood there. There was only one black family in town. The father was the caretaker at a small private school. I didn't know them but, as far as I was aware, they attended the local schools without (public) incident. I, of course, had no knowledge of what private slights they might have endured. I can remember my mother pointing to them with pride if one of the children appeared in the Fourth of July parade or some other event as exemplifying the notion that blacks and whites could live together in harmony.

On the other hand, my parents spoke with considerable disapprobation of blockbusting, though it never happened in Downers Grove and surrounding suburbs. This was a practice whereby a single black family would buy a home in an all-white neighborhood. This would cause all the neighbors to become nervous that if they stayed, others would sell, driving down prices. Thus there would be a rush to sell and soon the neighborhood would be all black. This was generally thought to be the fault of the blacks, rather than of the prejudices of the whites. The blockbusters were believed to be speculators who intended to profit from this panic, rather than individual black families who simply wanted to live in a nicer neighborhood.

However, even if one were perfectly willing to have blacks as neighbors, the fear of blockbusting was real, since it could spell financial disaster to have the value of one's home reduced by 50 percent. Moreover, there seemed to be some foundation to the belief that blacks were not good neighbors. On occasional visits to Chicago, which took us through the largely black South Side (no freeways in those days to whisk you past uncomfortable realities), it could be seen that houses and lawns did not exemplify the suburban ideal of neatness and order. I don't recall anybody recognizing that this might have more to do with class than race. Of course, at that time, race was class. Very few blacks were members of the middle class.

My father exhibited the casual racism of the day, generally disapproving of blacks' lifestyle and lack of initiative, and occasionally referring to blacks without rancor in terms that today would be shockingly unacceptable. Yet, when family friends brought a black guest to the all-white swimming pool at which my father was manager, he admitted them. Although he was undoubtedly well aware of the implications of this action, he responded to complaints by shrugging and pointing out that the rules said that if a member wanted to bring a guest, he had to pay fifty cents. Period. The rules said nothing about race. Whether this was because nobody thought to include it in the rules or because the good people of the Downers Grove Pool Association balked at any such outward declaration of discrimination, I don't know. Probably some of both.

Thus there was a distinction between "our Negroes"—the unthreatening family who lived in Downers Grove, black friends of friends, et cetera— and Negroes in general, a group that was regarded with suspicion, though not outright hostility. My own feeling as a child when we drove through black neighborhoods was that these were vaguely alien beings—that it was indeed "another country," in James Baldwin's words, and a very distant and somewhat dangerous one at that. I don't recall ever meeting a black child during my entire childhood. I was, in short, a member of a discrete and insular majority.

While I don't remember the *Brown* case itself, I distinctly remember Eisenhower sending troops to Little Rock to enforce the decision there. My mother, who was more likely to express her views on political matters than my father was, thought that *Brown* was a good decision and that once blacks and whites went to school together for a few years, racial problems would disappear—a naive view that was widely shared by liberals in those days. Thus we regarded the Arkansans as unenlightened rednecks who deserved having federal troops inflicted on them. I wonder about the disconnect between this view and the attitude toward blockbusting. Perhaps we regarded Southerners with as much suspicion as we did blacks. Certainly the South was also "another country" in the 1950s, at least as much as the South Side of Chicago. Blockbusting, on the other hand, had the potential to infect *our* neighborhood and lower *our* property values.

The only incident of outright racism that came up in Downers Grove occurred at a cemetery near town in the early 1960s. The cemetery, out of sensitivity to the likely disapproval of white mourners, banned blacks from being buried there. There was a considerable outcry against this, with the local ministers, including ours in the First Methodist Church, inveighing against the cemetery, which was forced to reverse its policy. By this time, images of the brutal treatment of civil rights protesters by police in the South were appearing on television, and we Northerners were beginning to realize that the racial divide in this country was deeper and more intractable than we had previously thought.

In 1964 my family moved to North Carolina and I attended the University of North Carolina at Chapel Hill. Chapel Hill was a liberal enclave in the midst of redneck country. The university's bête noir was a Raleigh television commentator by the name of Jesse Helms, who made his reputation attacking the university as a hotbed of nigger-loving, sex-crazed Communists. But despite this reputation, which certainly didn't describe the average frat boy (except for the sex-crazed part), I was surprised to find that there were *no blacks* on the UNC basketball and football teams. In fact, there were only two in the entire ACC basketball conference, both of whom played for Maryland. Charlie Scott, who had basketball skills that his white teammates could only dream of, joined the squad as a freshman my senior year. He also became the first black invited to join a fraternity.

Of all the changes in U.S. society since the 1950s, surely this is the greatest. Southern cities have black mayors and police chiefs, the military has black generals, and blacks and other minorities are well represented in all the professions. Racism is far from dead and disturbing incidents of racial prejudice still arise. But *institutional* racism—the formal barring of minorities from schools, jobs, and positions in society—is gone. Anyone who looks back to the 1950s as a better time either didn't live through them or wasn't paying attention.

Craig M. Bradley was born in Downers Grove, Illinois, in December 1945 and attended elementary and secondary schools there from 1950 to 1963. He is now the Robert A. Lucas Professor of Law at Indiana University (Bloomington) School of Law.

32 Princess in the Tower

Elaine W. Shoben

Gearing up for the start of the new school year in 1956 was fun for me as an eight-year-old in southern Ohio, and it was uncomplicated by consciousness of national events. I had no knowledge of the Supreme Court's rulings during the previous two years in *Brown v. Board of Education* and certainly no idea that such things were relevant to life in my small town. The television—newly acquired as our family's first—brought the black and white wonder of Howdy Doody that summer and none of the dramatic images we would later see on the news of resistance to school desegregation in Little Rock and elsewhere during the years to follow.

When I went back to my previously all-white school, there was suddenly a handful of black faces in the halls. This story is about one of those children, a girl in my class named Mary, and what happened to her as a petition enrollment child whose change of school was not part of a larger school desegregation plan. In order to tell her story, however, I need to explain more about the town and to tell a bit about myself because, in the end, I managed to do a terrible thing to Mary.

Why did some black-faced children suddenly appear in my school among the sea of white-faced children that year? With a law professor's perspective now on my child's memory, I'm guessing that after *Brown* some of the African American parents in town petitioned the school board to send their children to my school. Rather than face a possible lawsuit after hearing what the Supreme Court did, the board must have granted the smattering of petitions.

School started in the hot days right after Labor Day and my friends and I had important things on our minds. We simply ignored the new kids and went about our daily lives. On one of the first days of class Ricky M. kissed me lightning fast when he passed by where I was standing in the cloakroom, and I never knew if it was on a dare or a genuine sign of affection. At eight years old, that difference is often hard to discern. My friends Beth and Melissa discussed with me for hours matters such as the kiss, but we never once mentioned to each other the presence of the new black faces in the school. I'm not sure we even noticed them at first.

The new girl, Mary P., in my class was the only African American child in the third grade. She sat in the last row and stared at the backs of all her white classmates and the white teacher at the front of the room. Mary was the best-behaved child in my class. She always came to school dressed impeccably in a starched dress. All the girl students and female teachers were required to wear dresses or skirts and blouses in those days, but Mary's attire was always especially well kept. She never caused trouble and she kept to herself as much as possible. With hindsight, I'm guessing that her parents impressed upon her the precariousness of her situation. She was very careful of every step she took. She was very smart and rarely needed to be told anything twice. No doubt her parents were impressed with her abilities and wanted to offer her the chance of an education to develop her potential. Surely they knew the danger that she would be abused verbally or even physically at the white school, but they probably felt that they could prepare her to face open racism. What they apparently miscalculated was the cost of a more subtle kind of social isolation.

The racial segregation in that southern Ohio town was not salient to a child like me. The people who were called "Nigras" (in polite talk) did the menial jobs and kept a low profile. For me they were just as much a part of the background as the silos in the countryside. I didn't see either one very often because I led a sheltered life as a member of a professional family in town. The social order was stable and invisible for my friends and me, so we went about our lives in ignorance even that the community was governed by it.

On the playground the third-graders divided into groups and did all the mean-spirited things to each other that children do to those below them in the popularity pecking order. People went in and out of favor on the whim of the social leaders. I was fortunate to be "in" more often than not, and sometimes I even got to pass judgment on my peers. Once I thought that Larry K. was a good kid, until I discovered that he was left-handed and actually used that hand to write. My clique decided that was just too weird to let him be in our good graces.

Mary and I happened to form a friendship. I say "happened" because from my end it was quite accidental. I was not trying to be friendly to her in particular, but I also wasn't trying not to be friendly. Some of my classmates acted like she didn't belong in the class, but I didn't entirely understand that. My parents were more educated than most of our neighbors and they were also more liberal. In the 1950s, "liberal" meant being in favor of the civil rights movement. Mother taught me that race didn't matter and that only a person's character mattered. Her eagerness to teach me the liberal approach to race was so great that she chose not to teach me the reality of racial politics in the town. And therein lies the tale.

The accidental friendship between Mary and me began when I was angry at my classmates over some playground dispute and I declared that I wasn't going to play with them. I went over to Mary, who was playing by herself, as always, during recess. We played together that first time and discovered our compatibility. The second and third days after that we played together, and they were wonderful too. Then my friends told me to play with them again, and I am ashamed to say that I rejoined them—leaving Mary by herself once again. I liked her so much, however, that I'd sneak time to play with her whenever I could. Mary's exclusion from my circle of friends was never discussed by anyone; it was just a social fact that we accepted without question.

Mary told me that when she was by herself she usually pretended that she was a princess in a tower. That sounded very romantic to me and sometimes we played together that we were both princesses in the same tower. I didn't think that Mary looked very much like a princess, because every book I had seen portrayed a princess as someone very white and usually blond. I had both those princess credentials, in contrast to Mary's very deep black skin and braided black hair. I don't know if Mary thought about the book portrayals herself, but we were in a fine pretend world and we princesses made our own reality. We were hardly in the real world at all during those times. We played in a remote corner of the playground and ignored everyone else as much as they ignored us. Then I would eventually go back to my social clique and leave Mary to herself again. This pattern continued for several months.

The crisis came when it was time for my birthday party. For most children, birthdays are important social events and those in our town were no exception. The guest list for a party was a matter of grave consequence. The weekly town newspaper was even known occasionally to cover a child's birthday party in the Social Notes when the child belonged to one of the prominent families. My kindergarten party had been so noted, and I still have the clipping.

For my third-grade party, my mother told me that I could invite nine friends. We planned games and bought party favors. She helped me make the nine invitations and—here was her mistake—permitted me to distribute them at school without any supervision of the guest list.

I invited only girls; boys were not yet suitable party companions. The girls were mostly from the town's fine families, and I had socialized with them for years. Beth, the doctor's daughter (yes, there was only one doctor). Melissa, a lawyer's daughter (somehow there was more than one lawyer, like the old joke about the lawyer in the small town who had nothing to do until a second lawyer moved to town). And the daughters of men who worked in the bank or who owned local businesses. Also Suzy, a farm girl whom I liked (although the farm kids were considered inferior to the city kids). And Mary.

I vividly remember Mary's reaction when I gave her the party invitation. When I handed the invitations out to the other chosen girls, they would assume the coy look of insiders and mutter some form of thanks. Mary's reaction was very different. Initially she had a stunned look and then a look of ecstasy. I thought of her reaction years later when I was reading to my own children the story of Charlie's joy when acquiring the treasured ticket to Willie Wonka's chocolate factory in Ronald Dahl's classic tale *Charlie and the Chocolate Factory*. Like Charlie, she clutched the invitation as if it were the magic solution to her misery.

Charlie's misery was physical starvation, but Mary had her own kind of hunger that year. She had grand visions of the social feast that lay before her. She asked me every detail about the party in advance. For days in a row after that I played with Mary instead of my clique because Mary made me feel like such royalty with all her questions. She wanted to know about every game we would play and what food we would eat and, most importantly, who else had been invited. I was very happy to answer her questions without end because no one else was as interested in this big event as Mary and I were.

For those days we forgot about being princesses in the tower. We just talked happily about the party on any day when the weather was good enough to be on the playground together. On bad days we had to stay indoors and play mandatory dodge ball in the gymnasium. Mary was always the first to be thrown out in dodge ball because all the kids would aim at her until she was gone. After a few such episodes, she didn't even try to avoid the ball any more and let it hit her early so that she could get out of the center. No one talked to her inside the building, including me. There appeared to be some rule to that effect and, as a rule-obeying child, I followed the unspoken injunction. So it was only on the good-weather days in the corner of the playground that we talked endlessly about the party.

The Saturday of my party finally came. My mother and I busied ourselves with setting up the games and decorating the table. There were streamers to hang, and party favors to place at each table setting, and balloons to inflate and tie.

At some point during the preparations for the party, my mother asked me casually who was coming. No doubt she assumed that it was the same crowd of girls with whom she was very familiar. The same group came every year. Because I was allowed one guest per year of my age, however, I could add someone every year. In the previous year, I had added Suzy, the farm girl. This time I rattled off the familiar names and my mother hardly appeared to be listening. Then I finished with the new name—Mary P.

My mother stopped in her tracks. She looked at me in horror. Her sudden change in demeanor was so dramatic that I froze too. I wondered what could be wrong. This behavior was very unlike my mother.

"Oh, my God, Elaine. You invited Mary? Mary P.—the girl who was added to your class?" My liberal mother couldn't bear to call attention to her race overtly because good liberals in those days thought that a person's race should never be mentioned.

I was stunned and silent.

"You can't have Mary at the same party as the other girls, Elaine! Oh, my goodness," she continued to wail. "If Melissa's mother sees her . . . Oh, Elaine. Tell me you didn't. Oh, Elaine."

Then, catching herself, she added, "There's nothing wrong with Mary. We can have Mary here sometime by herself, Elaine, just not at the party with the other girls. Their parents don't understand. I didn't know you were friends with Mary. When did this happen? How did you happen to invite her? Did you give her one of the invitations? Oh, dear."

I'd never seen my mother like that. She was in a frenzy. And she had just given me my first lesson in racism. I finally realized what had not been apparent to me at school—what was "wrong" with Mary. I suddenly realized that the reason no one talked to Mary was different from the exclusion of other people outside my clique. She had a problem much worse than Larry K.'s left-handedness. She was a social leper to everyone at school. She was unfit to have at a birthday party. She would ruin the day because other parents wouldn't let their precious daughters stay at a party that she was attending. She was a Nigra.

I felt utterly miserable. I'd like to give myself the benefit of the doubt and say that I was miserable only because I empathized with Mary. My misery was deeper than that, however. Not only was I miserable for Mary, but also I was worried about what might happen at my party. Above all, I was unknowingly mourning the loss of my own innocence. The world would never be the same.

My mother and I had a sense of dread as the time for the party drew near. We greeted the first guests without enthusiasm as we waited for the impending storm. But Mary never came. After all the other guests arrived, we proceeded with the party and no one else ever knew that a guest was missing. Mother quietly removed the extra place setting and party favors.

After the party, I felt better because I assumed that Mary had decided that she didn't want to come to the party after all. I thought it strange that she would have had such a change of heart, but I couldn't account for why else she would have missed it. Once again, my mother provided the answer.

When we were picking up the party trash, Mother commented off-handedly that she had removed Mary's place setting and favors so that a missing child wouldn't be obvious. Then she added, "I guess her mother knew better than to let her come. I should have realized that. I'm sorry I spoke harshly to you earlier, Elaine. Of course her mother didn't let her come."

That moment was the worst of all. Suddenly I had a sense not just of what was "wrong" with Mary, but what was wrong with the town. As a newly minted nine-year-old, I had no way of articulating the nature of the racism, but I was overwhelmed with a sense that Mary's problem was not hers alone. I felt terrible for my friend and terrible for myself. Both our mothers knew what we did not know—that what we had seen at school was only the surface of a much deeper social evil.

We were indeed both princesses in the tower, but we were wrong to pretend that it was the same tower. I was in a tower that required me to keep to my own kind. Mary was in a tower that was much different. As a petition enrollment child who was not part of some larger desegregation plan, she didn't even have a "keep to your own kind" option in the school. Her status in that environment was such that she was not really allowed to participate in the school except in the most peripheral way. Whatever she could glean educationally from the back of the classroom was all that she was going to get. She was otherwise totally excluded.

I never saw Mary again. After the party, I told my mother that I wanted to take Mary's favors to her house, and my guilt-stricken mother agreed. We drove across town and found the house, and I went up to the door with the favors in hand. An older sister answered the door and guessed instantly who I was. She said that Mary couldn't see me and just took the favors. I imagined that Mary was inside crying, but I could never ask her because she and I never spoke another word. She never came back to school.

A few months later, my father got a high-paying job "out east" and my family moved. I eventually attended a great suburban high school, then a Seven Sisters college (the female version of the Ivy League, before the Ivies coeducated), and finally law school. My personal battles with schooling and with the legal profession in the 1970s all dealt with sexism rather than racism because my race has remained my privilege. I've often wondered what happened to Mary, who had both battles to fight. Is she a law professor somewhere, writing this story herself as we look back at *Brown*? Or was that Saturday in January 1957 the end of her ambition for good schooling?

I have devoted my professional career to legal issues involving discrimination. No doubt my own experiences with sexism helped to shape that choice, but I suspect that Mary was a part of that choice too. I was never able to tell her that I was sorry for how things turned out. Sorry for my naiveté; sorry for my lack of courage to open my eyes and be a better friend; sorry to have suffered so little when it was all over, when she must have suffered so much.

Wherever you are now, Mary, I hope that you eventually found the secret passage with the hidden riches that we were always talking about when we played princesses in the tower.

Elaine W. Shoben was born in January 1948 and lived her early years in southern Ohio. She attended elementary and secondary schools in a southern Ohio farm town and in suburban Boston. She is the Edward W. Cleary Professor Emerita at the University of Illinois College of Law and the Judge Jack and Lulu Lehman Professor at the William S. Boyd School of Law, University of Nevada, Las Vegas.

33   Shades of *Brown*

Charles Marvin

My sister-in-law Patricia says that Kansas can be thought of in terms of shades of brown—the earth on the ground, the dust in the air, and the burnt grass by the end of the long, hot summer. Thus my first memory of it is the picture of the scorched earth as our family arrived by train from New York City in the small county seat and university town of Lawrence in July of 1948. But my professional memory is of another Brown, my school contemporary Linda Brown, who lived with her parents in the neighboring community of Topeka, Kansas.

When we were both ten going on eleven years old, the lawsuit filed on Linda Brown's behalf was big news in Kansas and across the country, as it had been joined with lawsuits from other jurisdictions in litigation to desegregate public schools, litigation that was being heard by the Supreme Court of the United States.

Although I was young, this lawsuit caught my attention. I was a news junky, the son of a university journalism school dean in a household that subscribed to four newspapers (including the *Topeka Daily Capital*). It was very interesting to me that a lawsuit was being entertained to deal with problems of the Negro (the perceived appropriate label at the time, for which the term "black" was substituted later on) population in Kansas, small as it was.

It was not that I was unaware of minorities. On the beginning day of classes in first grade in my primary school in 1948, I had entered the classroom somewhat on the late side, and noticed that the one place on the standard double-desk seat near the front was not taken; on the other side of it sat a little Negro boy. Not thinking much about it at the time, I sat down and introduced myself to Bobby Mitchell, who was to be one of my classmates up through Lawrence High School.

By the time *Brown v. The Board of Education of Topeka, Kansas*, got rolling in the court system, the situation in Lawrence had become somewhat clearer to me. Although Lawrence had been settled in the 1850s by rabid abolitionists from Massachusetts, had become the Free State Fortress during the years of "Bleeding Kansas" leading up to and through the Civil War, and had suffered from the slaughter of its unarmed menfolk by Missouri border raiders under the hated Quantrill, by the turn of the century the town had become quietly segregated. Langston Hughes cited the pain he felt during his childhood there. By the 1930s and 1940s, the town (if not the gown) had cemented its reputation for being antiunion and antiblack. Although some children such as Bobby Mitchell went to integrated schools, there was one entirely Negro school in Lawrence, the Abraham Lincoln School. As of the 1950s, that school was in an appalling state—stinking toilet areas and a poorly maintained building, with insufficient funding for even minimally adequate educational supplies. (I am happy to say that this school was closed shortly after *Brown* came to the fore).

For the most part, the black population in Kansas kept a low profile. Its presence was not much to be noted outside of major urban areas. In fact, it was so small, it is not surprising that when my younger brother Bob first developed substantial speaking skills at age two, he should exclaim at seeing a different peer on Massachusetts Street in the heart of downtown Lawrence, "Look at the chocolate baby!"

Kansas politicians and the Kansas public did not have any desire to take flak on their public schools, so school systems across the state were integrated, at least in a formal sense, within a short period of time after *Brown* was heard a second time by the U.S. Supreme Court, and the Court unanimously, under its new chief justice, the frustrated proactive presidential candidate Earl Warren, rendered the surprising and resounding judgment overturning the old separate but equal doctrine ensconced in the law by that same court in *Plessy v. Ferguson*.

Long after the *Brown* decision came down, discriminatory practices against minorities continued in Lawrence. There were more than a few lunch counters across Douglas County (named for Senator Stephen Douglas of Illinois, of Douglas-Lincoln debates fame) where signs were still posted and acted upon that stated: "We reserve the right to refuse service to anyone." It was difficult for minority college students enrolled in either the University of Kansas or the equally locally ensconced Haskell Institute (now Haskell Indian Nations University, one of the two formerly preeminent Native American boarding schools, along with the now defunct Carlisle Institute in Pennsylvania) to find housing or employment. It took public marches, sit-ins, and other demonstrations, and the civil rights legislative and administrative revolution carried out in Washington and elsewhere, finally to get a whole series of reasonably positive results, and that only by the early 1970s.

In the meantime, I had gone on with my schooling. Upon finishing an undergraduate degree from the University of Kansas in 1964, I headed off for an internship at the Department of State. Upon arriving in the District of Columbia, I went looking for an apartment to share with a friend of mine,

Arthur Spears, a black classmate from KU who was also taking up a summer internship at State. Thirteen places in a row turned us down. Finally, at the fourteenth, the fellow who was building superintendent, a black man who was cohabiting with the white landlady, provided me and Arthur a one-room basement apartment in a building that, as was usually the case at the time, lacked air conditioning. Arthur and I spent a sweltering summer in those facilities with one little floor fan; we were not entirely alone, however, as we could share social time with a couple of young ladies, one white and one black, who both had recently obtained employment in national security affairs and who together occupied a similar apartment down the hall.

Musing upon the case of *Brown* several decades later, I sat talking with my father-in-law, Paul E. Wilson, the man who, as a young assistant attorney general, had been given orders by the attorney general of Kansas (a politician who was preparing to run for governor, and who did not want to alienate the Negro population) to take the long train ride to Washington, D.C., and represent the Topeka Board of Education versus Brown in the U.S. Supreme Court. Paul had never litigated an appellate case in his life, let alone before the federal courts, and had certainly never dreamed he would be appearing before the highest court of the land (at least not this young and in this capacity). He did the best he could in his professional capacity, and he thought his side had the more legitimate law arguments at the time; but he was not unhappy that a pro-integration decision prevailed. Indeed, the Topeka Board of Education itself had backed off the case in midstream, and it was only because of what state law authorities perceived to be the required procedural etiquette of the case that led them to carry that particular litigation forward for final representation before the U.S. Supreme Court. In any event, late in his life and long after retirement from a chaired position at the University of Kansas Law School, a position he occupied from several years after his experience litigating *Brown*, Paul Wilson wrote a book of remembrances on the case, *A Time to Lose: Representing Kansas in* Brown v. Board of Education (University Press of Kansas, 1995). In 1998, three years before he died, he gave a speech reminiscing on *Brown* at a U.S. Supreme Court Historical Society forum in Washington. I would recommend to anyone interested in the case that they read his book or watch a copy of the video of his speech.

For me, sitting in my law professor's office at the Georgia State University College of Law in downtown Atlanta, I remain with my memories of the *Brown* case, and with a framed State of Georgia document hanging on my wall:

By His Excellency Herman E. Talmadge, Governor of said State To the Honorable Paul E. Wilson

Greeting:

Know Ye, That by virtue of the power and authority vested in me as Governor of the State of Georgia, I do hereby appoint you

Honorary Assistant Attorney General of Georgia

with all the rights and privileges appertaining thereto. In Testimony Whereof, I have hereunto set my hand and affixed the Seal of the Executive Department of the Capitol, in the City of Atlanta, this thirtieth day of December in the year of our Lord, One Thousand Nine Hundred and Fifty-four.

Herman E. Talmadge

A similar tribute was paid by the Georgia governor to the lawyers representing each of the other jurisdictions joined in the case that had segregationist laws in effect for their public schools.

The state motto here in Georgia is "Wisdom, Justice and Moderation." It coexists, of course, with another old Southern motto, "Forget, Hell!" Looking North from Atlanta, in the distance one can see the mountaintops of Lower Appalachia, but whether those mountaintops trigger the vision of dogged Confederate troops retreating South one row of hills at a time from Chattanooga or the dream of Dr. Martin Luther King Jr. remains open to question.

Charles Marvin was born in July 1942 in Chicago, Illinois, and attended elementary and secondary schools in Lawrence, Kansas, from 1948 to 1960. He is now a professor of law at the Georgia State University College of Law in Atlanta.

34 *Brown* Comes to Boston: A Courtside View

Terry Jean Seligmann

It was the fall of 1973, my third year of law school, and I had just been chosen to be the law clerk for a federal district judge for the 1974–1975 year. When I asked the judge whether there were particular courses that might be helpful for me to put in my spring schedule to prepare for the clerkship, he suggested Antitrust and Securities Regulation. Reluctantly but dutifully, I signed up. In June of 1974, a few weeks before my clerkship was to begin, the judge issued an opinion, following two years of trial proceedings, that found intentional segregation in the Boston school system—*Morgan v. Hennigan*, which would be affirmed by the First Circuit in *Morgan v. Kerrigan*. For the fall of 1974, he ordered into effect a desegregation plan drawn up by the Massachusetts Board of Education under its state racial imbalance law. The judge was W. Arthur Garrity Jr. No class could have prepared me for the next year.

A law clerk occupies a unique position in the judiciary. She is not appointed to the bench and in public performs no official functions. She may sit to the side during hearings, taking notes. She may accompany the judge during recess. Few litigants know her function. The parties' focus is on the judge, not the clerk. Counsel has a greater sense of the potential of the law clerk to affect a case. Attorneys know that law clerks review the legal memoranda filed by the parties and may draft orders or opinions on motions and other matters for the judge's review. They may suspect that judges discuss cases with their law clerks, sharing their thinking and soliciting their views. But contacting the law clerk outside court can be as ethically questionable as trying to speak with the judge ex parte. So the law clerk retains an anonymity not shared by the other participants in the litigation. The clerk's loyalty is to the judge and the court. This includes a duty of confidentiality that is deeply felt and seldom breached, either during or after the clerkship. Yet the clerk both witnesses and participates in what the court does. In the Boston school case, this meant that I was about to witness and participate in major political, legal, and social events.

To many Americans, the images that represented resistance to school integration had been Southern ones—the Little Rock Nine entering Central High School in 1957 surrounded by jeering crowds; Governor Wallace blocking the doorway of the University of Alabama in 1963. Less known were places like Fayetteville, Arkansas, where the public high school quietly admitted nine black students in September of 1954 after the *Brown* decision, and where in 1948, the law school where I taught admitted Silas Hunt, the first black student, without compulsion. The attitudes of the political and community leaders, it seemed, had made a difference between peaceful and violent integration.

Boston was proud of its history as the cradle of liberty, the home to abolitionists, the intellectual "Athens of America." But its public school system entering the 1970s was far from one to be proud of. Educational achievement and opportunity had taken a back seat to racial politics. The evidence before the court had shown that school districts were deliberately manipulated to maintain racial segregation between adjacent areas. New school buildings were located to continue rather than reduce racial isolation. In white, predominantly Irish South Boston, the high school had become an icon of the community, despite the high dropout rate and low percentage of graduates pursuing a college education. For too many years, politicians had succeeded in citywide school committee elections by championing the "neighborhood school" and opposing "forced busing," with little attention to the education students were receiving. When the decision finding de jure segregation of the school system was issued, few were surprised. To most legal observers, it was an inevitable decision and one that was affirmed by the First Circuit.

In the summer of 1974, the political leaders of Boston faced the imminent prospect of children from predominantly black Roxbury attending South Boston High School under the state plan referred to as "Phase I" of the court's remedial orders. Many were shocked that the judge had adopted the state's plan; they had hoped he would defer it while remedies specifically designed to address the federal constitutional violations were designed and debated "with all deliberate speed." Political leaders took positions that distanced them from the court's actions. Those who had consistently campaigned on the antibusing platform attacked the rulings and predicted violence. But even more moderate figures temporized. Mayor Kevin White filed motions asking the court to order a metropolitan remedy that involved the surrounding suburbs, despite the clear decision earlier that same year in *Milliken v. Bradley* that a cross–school district remedy was beyond the court's authority to consider. The mayor later appeared in court personally to argue that it was the federal government's responsibility to protect and carry out the court order by mobilizing federal marshals, while President Ford voiced his disagreement with the court's order and his opposition to the use of busing. With the notable exception of the editorial voice of the city's major newspaper, the *Boston Globe*, there was little public leadership that summer directed toward healing racial rifts rather than inflaming them, or toward shouldering the responsibility for creating a new educational system of opportunity rather than defending a decayed and dual one.

When school opened, the world saw a different and far uglier Boston on their television screens, as buses of black school children were jeered by angry crowds and pelted with rocks. In December, word of a stabbing of a white youth by a black student at South Boston High School brought South Boston residents into the streets. They surrounded the school, trapping the students inside until a police decoy operation enabled their escape. Schools were closed early for the holidays and reopened with increased security measures. To this was added in 1976 the indelible image of a black man being attacked with an American flag. Theodore Landsmark, a black businessman who was crossing the Government Center plaza, encountered an antibusing rally and became the target of the crowd. Today, Landsmark is the president of the Boston Architectural Center.

The court held what seemed like daily hearings to monitor these events. The courtroom was transformed into a media center; the jury box filled with reporters. The judge's comments from the bench became the lead on the evening news. Although the phrase was not yet in common use, the judge was acutely aware that nuanced or complex discussions would inevitably be reduced to "sound bites," and worked to be sure that nothing he said would be misinterpreted. Away from the courtroom, federal monitors from the Community Relations Service and other community leaders from the churches and the black community worked with moderate white leaders to ease tensions and foster dialog.

Along with the day-to-day events in the streets and schools, the court and parties were charged with determining the scope of the remedies required to repair the damage to black schoolchildren worked by the segregated system, and to move the school system forward to one not divided by, and in practice dominated by, racial concerns. Under the Supreme Court's precedents, the responsibility for developing a remedial plan was that of the school district. In Boston this meant the five-member School Committee would be filing its proposed plan. The court set initial guidelines for this plan, referred to as "Phase II," and a deadline of December 16 for its filing. Throughout the fall, school district staff worked with their data on student enrollments and residences toward creating a proposal. But when the deadline arrived, the majority of the School Committee refused to adopt any plan that involved busing to an assigned school. Counsel for the School Committee, a respected attorney with Hale and Dorr, one of the city's premier firms, filed the staff's plan without committee authorization and then withdrew from representing the School Committee.

The court scheduled and held civil contempt hearings. At the hearings, each of the majority members of the committee testified that he would not endorse any desegregation plan which assigned children to schools beyond walking distance, while acknowledging that the schools could not be desegregated without such measures. The three were held in contempt but allowed to purge the contempt by filing a freedom-of-choice plan, of which the First Circuit later wrote: "It is inconceivable that anyone, the School Committee members or the court, could believe that the plan would be effective in eliminating and guarding against officially imposed segregation in Boston." The new counsel hired by the School Committee was a street-fighting criminal defense attorney, who treated every court appearance as a dramatic event. In the months that followed, the School Committee ceased participating meaningfully as a party in the task of crafting a remedial plan. The plaintiffs filed an alternative plan in January. Boston's Home and School Association, a parent organization closely allied with the school administration, intervened and sought to file its own plan, which argued against widespread desegregation as going beyond the identifiable effects of the school districts' intentional discrimination.

The remedial challenges of institutional constitutional cases were not completely new to Judge Garrity. He had gained public attention, mostly favorable, when he and his then law clerk spent a night in Boston's pretrial detention facility, the Charles Street Jail, in a case successfully challenging overcrowding and other conditions—*Inmates of Suffolk County Jail v. Eisenstadt*.[1] The case led to the design and construction of a new jail.

Other than general pronouncements about the flexibility of a court's equitable powers, however, there was little to assist the court in cases like the jail case or a school desegregation case in creating appropriate remedial orders, or to equip it to judge the adequacy of those measures urged by the parties. The judge used the vehicles of court-appointed experts and the appointment of masters to fill these needs. As experts, he involved Robert Dentler, dean of Boston University's School of Education, and his associate dean, Marvin Scott. These men had participated in preparing and evaluating other desegregation plans, and spoke the same language of geocodes (areas of several city blocks into which the school department had divided the city for planning purposes) and district lines as the Boston School Department employees who were the keepers of the critical student data. In February, he appointed a panel of four masters to hold hearings on the submitted plans and recommend a plan to the court. The masters were a retired Supreme Judicial Court judge, Jacob J. Spiegel; former U.S. Commissioner of Education Francis Keppel; former state attorney general Edward J. McCormack Jr.; and Dr. Charles V. Willie, professor of education at Harvard University. This panel of masters reflected academic and administrative educational expertise and veteran political instincts, as well as judicial and legal experience, and was of diverse religious and ethnic composition. The role of the masters was advisory; the court reserved to itself the ultimate responsibility to approve any remedial plans.

The plan proposed by the masters in late March was both less and more than each party sought. It involved mandatory busing, but it also left areas, in particular the mainly white West Roxbury and East Boston neighborhoods, with one-race and racially identifiable schools. And shortly after its filing, new student data became available requiring updating and revisions. At hearings, counsel for the plaintiffs and the State Board of Education attacked the plan as inadequate, while the School Committee and Home and School Association protested it went too far. The parties also debated the relevance in fashioning a remedy for the prospect of white flight, children leaving the school system for private schools or other school districts in response to changes in their school assignments. Should the reach of a remedy be moderated in order to keep whites in the system, in the hope of avoiding a shift in student population that would resegregate or create a majority-minority school population?

The court ultimately modified the masters' plan in light of the new data and redrew some of the district lines to leave fewer one-race and racially identifiable schools. In East Boston, which lay on the other side of Boston Harbor, through narrow tunnels as much as a five-mile ride away from the core of the city's minority population, the plan relied upon magnet schools instead of redistricting. West Roxbury schools, however, which would have been left 93 percent white under the masters' plan, were redistricted and included in the overall school assignment process.

Beyond the drawing of district lines, the plan offered some creative and promising initiatives to build the strength of Boston schools, to increase the number of magnet and specially oriented citywide schools, and to thus make them attractive to voluntary enrollment by Boston schoolchildren on a desegregated basis. Businesses were paired with certain schools to help prepare their graduates for careers. Many of Boston's colleges and universities pledged alliances with particular schools to build up their strengths.

A system of district advisory councils of parents and students and a citywide council were also created to monitor and to help resolve racial conflicts. The court-approved status of these councils gave minority parents and students a voice and required school officials to listen.

These and other aspects of the remedial orders looked toward schools that would reflect the ideal of the free, universal, and inclusive public school of Horace Mann's vision, and called for a "common concern with equality and excellence" by all those involved with the school system. These efforts were challenged on appeal by the School Committee as encroaching on its prerogatives to manage the schools, the School Committee arguing that the court had "no legitimate function to improve quality" of education. The First Circuit upheld these aspects of the plan in light of the School Committee's clear statements during the contempt hearings that it would not cooperate in the effort to desegregate the Boston schools, noting: "This crucial fact justifies, in our opinion, a number of extraordinary measures which might otherwise be open to question."

In June of 1975, this tumultuous school year and my clerkship both drew to a close. I never was to use Antitrust or Securities Regulation. I went on to work as an assistant attorney general, representing the Department of Education and other government agencies in public law cases. Boston schools were to continue to face changes and challenges. South Boston High School was placed into the hands of a court-appointed receiver after more violence and educational failure. To many observers, the Boston school desegregation case was an unqualifiedly negative experience for the city and its students. The personal anguish of parents and children caught up in the turmoil has been poignantly captured.[2] Like that of many inner cities, Boston's school population has become predominantly minority, and concerns with student achievement continue.[3] But in some fundamental ways, the basis of political power and the focus of politicians, educators, parents, and children shifted from race to educational quality. Initially Boston School Committee elections changed to enlarge the committee and include district representation; since 1989, School Committee members have been appointed by the mayor. Blacks have sat on the School Committee and run the school system as superintendent. Thirty years later, businesses and colleges continue to work with children in the Boston public schools.[4] Perhaps the legacy of the Boston desegregation case is that Boston can now treat education and educational quality not as an issue of black and white schools, but "just schools."

NOTES

1. *Inmates of Suffolk County Jail v. Eisenstadt*, 360 F. Supp. 676 (D. Mass. 1973), *aff'd* 494 F.2f 1196 (1st Cir. 1974), *cert. denied*, 419 U.S. 977 (1974).

2. J. Anthony Lukas, Common Ground: A Turbulent Decade in the Lives of Three American Families (New York: Vintage, 1985).

3. Following the First Circuit's holding in *Morgan* that district courts could not consider white flight a "practicality" to be accounted for in devising integration plans, white enrollment in Boston's schools plummeted. In 1973, white enrollment in Boston schools was 55 percent, but by 1980 it was 36 percent. By the 2001–2002 school year, white enrollment in Boston public schools was 15 percent. John Monahan and Laurens Walker, *Social Science in Law*, 5th ed. (West, 2001), 210.

4. Muriel Cohen, "Hub School-College Link Said to Offer Top US Benefits," *Boston Globe*, June 4, 1989.

Terry Jean Seligmann was born in New York City in January 1949 and attended elementary school there from 1952 to 1960. She served as the law clerk for the Honorable W. Arthur Garrity in Boston during the first year of court-ordered desegregation in 1974–1975. She is now the Arlin M. Adams Professor of Legal Writing at Drexel University Earle Mack School of Law in Philadelphia.

35 Checkerboard Segregation in the 1950s

Larry I. Palmer

Rocky, a summertime playmate who lived in the apartment building next door to our turn-of-the-century single-family residence, walked west to Clark Elementary School in the fall of 1953 while I walked east to Washington Elementary School. Rocky was "white" and I was "colored," in the school district's lexicon. But other black children in our neighborhood walked north to Saint Mark's Catholic School, because some cardinal had ordered those schools desegregated. My cousin, who was blind, went to the Missouri School for the Blind, which, I had discovered by attending a Christmas play, had both white and black children in the same classroom.

I used to think that going shopping had to include eating lunch at a department store restaurant or a dime-store lunch counter. I remember dressing up, riding the bus, shopping, and eating out as a preventive strike against the racial affronts in our "transitional neighborhood" on the western edge of St. Louis in the early 1950s. Perhaps my parents thought lunch out downtown would keep me from asking why we could not go to the restaurants in our neighborhood along what was then US Highway 67. But I knew that the signs, "We reserve the right to refuse service to anyone," in those eating establishments along Highway 67 were really meant for blacks.

I remember my older siblings discussing the ability of Lena Horne, the famous fair-skinned black singer, to "pass" under certain circumstances by staying at the Chase Park Plaza Hotel when she was performing there. We could not eat in the restaurant, not to mention rent a room if we had the money, in this luxury hotel less than a mile from our house on the edge of the Forest Park. City parks were not segregated in my memory, but city-owned hospitals were. This checkerboard pattern of legal segregation and private exclusion and inclusion confused my nine-year-old mind, but its purpose was clear: to denigrate my sense of self.

The family lore is that my parents migrated to St. Louis with the hope that each of their children would have the chance for a college education, which both my parents had somehow managed to obtain through the largesse of family in the 1920s. I don't know whether they envisioned a future in St. Louis without legal segregation when they uprooted their eight children from rural Arkansas three months before my birth in 1944. But my parents appeared ready for the changes that were implemented immediately after *Brown* was announced in May 1954. One of my older brothers, Harold, transferred from the black Charles Sumner High School to the formerly white Soldan High School in the fall of 1954 without much fanfare or apparent display of apprehension on his or my parents' part.

Sometime in the fall of 1954, my fifth-grade teacher, Miss Razz, announced that there were no longer "black" or "white" schools—they were all made of the same brick—but that some of the children in our school would be reassigned to other schools the following year. When she mentioned that some teachers, including her, might be assigned to another school, my heart skipped a beat. I guess my heart and soul took a recess from racial politics to develop a crush on my exotic teacher, who had lived briefly in Japan. I just could not imagine Washington Elementary without the beautiful but demanding Miss Razz. I had assumed that, given the close proximity of Washington Elementary to our house, I would not be reassigned.

My assumption was based on my observations, what I overheard adults and older siblings discuss over dinner, and what I read in the newspapers, including the weekly black press. But my ten-year-old mind could not perceive the entire plan for the voluntary desegregation of schools in the city of St. Louis. The high schools were desegregated in the fall of 1954, and the elementary schools (there were no middle or junior high schools at the time) would desegregate in the fall of 1955. The plan also included the imposition of a system of educational tracking that would begin with sixth-graders in the fall of 1955 and be fully implemented in the high schools in 1958. The elementary track was designed to divide elementary schoolchildren into two classes—the gifted, based on intelligence tests, and the remainder. Miss Razz recommended that I be one of the fifth-graders tested. My parents received a letter informing them that I had been offered a spot in the gifted class at Bates Elementary, a school in the far northeast part of town—a black section of town.

I don't remember the family decision-making process that led to the conclusion that I could make the hour-long trip on public transportation in order to attend the gifted class. But there had been a Palmer tradition of children riding the school bus, with older siblings riding the bus to school before Washington Elementary was converted to a colored school in the late 1940s. The bus trip seemed preferable to an alternative Miss Razz had mentioned: that I attempt to obtain a scholarship to one of the private schools such as Thomas Jefferson or John Burroughs that admitted highly qualified black students. I recall already at this time my name being connected to places like Washington University in St. Louis and Harvard.

I don't remember much of the summer of 1955, except a practice bus ride to Bates Elementary with either an older sibling or one of my parents. I am certain I participated in the Vacation Reading Club at the local branch of the public library that summer because I still have the certificate—thanks to my mother, who catalogued all my academic achievements—indicating I had read at least fifteen books. Technically, the certificate attested that I had checked out at least fifteen books, but I am certain that I read at least fifteen and perhaps twice as many because my mother had regularly assigned reading times for me and my younger brother each day during the summer.

I also don't recall any discussion about the anticipated racial composition of my class or the racial background of my new teacher. Enhanced educational opportunities for Palmer children seemed to have been the norm in our household. My second-eldest brother, Willie, had completed teachers' college and was already a public school teacher. Another older brother, Mac, had won scholarships to attend college upon graduation from Charles Sumner High School in 1952. My sister, Lela, had won a scholarship to nursing school after graduation from the same high school. Harold, my brother who had transferred to Soldan High, was continuing to perform academically as expected, and had one of the highest grade point averages in his class. My college-educated parents—Arkansas Baptist College in my father's case, and Lane College in my mother's—expected academic achievement from their children.

The big surprise on my first day in the post–*Brown v. Board of Education* school world was my teacher, George H. Hyram. Not only was he male, but also he had just returned from the Sorbonne in Paris where he had been a Fulbright scholar. He was in the process of finishing his doctorate in education at St. Louis University. As he began to explain how his research—teaching systematic logic to elementary school children—related to what our academic program would be like, I became very excited. French lessons, logic exercises, classroom visits from professors at the various universities in the city, trips to the St. Louis Symphony, and a lot of homework seemed what I had been waiting for all my elementary school years. He then explained that he would be our teacher until we graduated and went on to high school.

Hyram discussed the racial composition of our class—twenty-one black students and one white girl, Cynthia—implying that there had been some deliberate racial gerrymandering. All but one of the twenty-two black sixth-graders admitted into the gifted program had been assigned to Bates Elementary. Cynthia had originally been assigned to a gifted class in another school, but her parents had fought with school officials to have her assigned to our class, which was in fact nearer to her home. Cynthia's parents lived in what was then a black neighborhood in a duplex with their lifelong friends, a black couple. Without her parents' victory over the school bureaucracy and the innuendos that she—a high-IQ white girl—could not learn from a black male teacher in an otherwise all-black classroom, my post-*Brown* reassignment would have been just another Palmer child reassigned to another school in the gerrymandered lines marking the changing housing patterns in St. Louis after War World II. We had little interaction with the other students in the school, but I believe Cynthia was the only white student in the entire school.

Our entire gifted class, with Hyram as our teacher, was moved in the fall of 1956 to Washington Elementary School, transformed into a newly constructed school instead of the turn-of-the century building I had attended across the street.

Dr. Hyram—as he insisted upon being called upon receipt of his doctorate of education in the spring 1956—was clearly on a mission: to prove through his tutelage or academic dictatorship that the racist bureaucrats were wrong regarding the potential of his students. First, despite the fact we had no contact with students in other gifted classes, Dr. Hyram set the academic bar for us as being the best gifted class. It started with French. According to the school board's plans, instruction in French was to begin in the seventh grade, fall 1956. But we began our French lessons at Bates in the fall of 1955. Hyram, who spoke fluent French, had obviously studied the French educational system. He started us with the first-grade reader used in France (obtained from Paris through his contacts) and dictation in French. When Mrs. Douglas, a native-born Parisian, arrived at Washington Elementary for our first formal class in French she was obviously delighted to find a group of children who knew the rudiments of French and could say, "Bonjour, Madame Douglas," with the proper Parisian accent. She and Hyram, who spoke French to each other, must have conspired to ignore the school board's planned curriculum and moved us along to conjugating verbs, learning grammar, and taking constant dictation to develop our ear for the language.

Second, Hyram's notion of homework would make graduate school seem easy. My still lifelong friend Cynthia gave me a copy a few years ago of Hyram's notion of homework during the Easter vacation. Cynthia's schedule indicates that we were to have a Sunday off from any form of academic work during the vacation. Otherwise, we were to spend from two to four hours a day studying.

For instance, on Sunday April 12 we were to:

1   Read Article VI of the U.S. Constitution and write answers for all the questions.
2   Read part of a chapter in the textbook for history.
3   Read nearly twenty pages of the science text and make a written list of all the main ideas.
4   Read some assignment in Current Events, a weekly publication for school-age children.
5   Read a portion of a book that had been assigned for the week.

According to Cynthia's notes, the prize was no homework at all on Easter Sunday.

In retrospect, none of this seemed particularly onerous to me because Hyram had introduced the idea that I apply for a scholarship to Phillips Exeter Academy early in the winter of 1957. In one of his many talks to the class, he described the school and discussed with the entire class the academic, personal, and social weaknesses and strengths as students of each potential candidate, including me. He shared with us the outline of his tentative decision-making process for selecting which boys he would not recommend for a scholarship and which ones he would. Despite my family's lack of firm middle-class standing, he indicated that he was going to discuss the school with my parents and the parents of two other boys, one of whom was the son of a dentist.

I could not imagine why anyone, especially my parents, would question the judgment of Hyram. After all, Hyram was Dr. George Hyram, the consummate intellectual, in my eyes, who knew about the demise of colonialism in Africa from his contacts at the Sorbonne. If Hyram told my parents I could attend a party of a school friend that required me to miss their appointed bedtime, I went to the party. If Hyram thought I should go to boarding school, what earthly creature could question him? Apparently, no one did publicly, and the preparation for my application to Exeter began while a family storm erupted over Hyram's plans for me.

Hyram's plans for his academic stars meant, however, there may well have been other students who were simply terrorized by his method of taking total control over our lives. Either way, we were either the pawns or the beneficiaries of his zeal for academic achievement. Perhaps he knew what we could only surmise—that when we entered a large city high school (most of them had about three thousand students), we would be put in an academic track. The regular tracks were I, II, and III, but the elementary children in the so-called gifted class were slated to go into Track I-A, the top or super track. Either by conscious design or as a byproduct of his research and teaching, Hyram was molding us to be the top students in Track I-A, where we would finally meet some of our gifted white counterparts from other parts of the city.

Thirteen members of our class, including me, graduated in January 1958—students were allowed to enter school in either January or September in the early 1950s. So although some of us were technically in Eight High while others were in Eight Low, we had been treated the same until it came time for testing for high school placements. When the standardized test scores came back for placements in the high school tracks, the top ten scores in the entire city were in our class, with Cynthia ranked as the top student in the city. Since I was among the ten top-ranking students, I did not worry about how the other three students in Eight High might have felt. I was more preoccupied with whether I would win acceptance and a scholarship to Exeter or how I might fare in a high school with over three thousand black and white students.

A few weeks into high school made me relieved to receive my acceptance from Exeter with a full scholarship. Our Track I-A teachers were all white females who had been reassigned to high school when the two public teachers' colleges in the city had merged as part of the desegregation plan. Our French teacher resented our ability to correct her poor accent whenever she attempted to speak French to us, so she gave up trying. My English teacher seemed to respect my abilities and praised me to my parents, but presented *Pride and Prejudice* in such a way as to take out all the passion from Jane Austen. My mathematics teacher must have been fairly good or unable to destroy what Hyram had taught me because I ended up in second-year math at Exeter the next fall. But my goal was clear: Obtain Honors—the grade above A's—in my courses and escape to Exeter.

In contrast to the decision to let me go to Bates Elementary, the family decision making over whether to accept the full scholarship from Exeter was not a black and white one. My father came to see Hyram as not only stealing his son, but also sending him off into a hostile all-white-male environment without any family protection. My mother saw Exeter as the road to Harvard and professional success and was sure I could handle myself in that environment even though I was physically small. They argued constantly in my presence, with my father insisting I was not going. My two older brothers intervened on my behalf. They pleaded, begged, and in one case even cried, in order to convince my father he should let me have this educational opportunity despite the racial risks.

I took the train by myself to Exeter in the fall 1958. I would read about the Little Rock and the New Orleans school ordeals from the library of a mostly white and all-male private school in New Hampshire. Of the 125 boys in the ninth grade, there were four blacks—two of us from Hyram's class, another scholarship boy from New York, and the son of the owner of a black newspaper from Baltimore.

In retrospect, I remember some adults such as my parents and Cynthia's parents preparing their children for the post–*Brown v. Board of Education* world where there would be no legal racial segregation. But most adults in St. Louis, both black and white, were probably trying to hold on to something they thought of as precious in the pre-*Brown* world through a combination of private inclusion and exclusion as manifest in housing and social patterns. I remember some of the private institutions—the department stores in downtown St. Louis and some private schools like those in St. Louis and Exeter—doing more to break down the walls of racial exclusion than the public schools did.

I think often about how my two-and-a-half-year tutelage under Hyram changed the course of my life by providing the path to Exeter. Hyram was more like my teachers at Exeter—highly educated, demanding, and passionate about learning—but he also carried the burden of being black in an educational system designed to destroy young black minds and deprive a brilliant black teacher of his passion for learning. But in the confusing pattern of racial exclusion and inclusion of my childhood, I always try to remember that not everyone, black or white, was as protected from the emotional and spiritual bruises of racial segregation as I was by the combination of the examples of Hyram's zest for teaching and learning, my older siblings' academic achievement, and the calm demeanor of my parents as I ventured into the white world after *Brown*.

Larry I. Palmer was born in St. Louis, Missouri, in June 1944. He attended elementary school in St. Louis from 1949 to 1958 and secondary school in Exeter, New Hampshire, from 1958 to 1962. From 1975 to 2002, he was a professor of law at Cornell Law School in Ithaca, New York. From 2003 to 2007, he was the Endowed Chair of Urban Health Policy at the University of Louisville, Louisville, Kentucky. As of January 2007, he holds joint appointments in the College of William and Mary School of Law in Williamsburg, Virginia, and Virginia Commonwealth University in Richmond.

36 With One Hand Waving Free

Michael Perlin

I was eight years old and in fourth grade when *Brown v. Board of Education* was decided. There were a few black kids in my elementary school in Perth Amboy, New Jersey, and I remember being stupefied that this was even an *issue* in other places. On the other hand, I was politically aware enough, even at that age (my dad was the managing editor of the local paper, and politics was always a topic of dinner talk at home), to realize the significance of the decision. I come from a politically left family, and have very clear memories of my parents' excitement about the fact the Court had ruled as it did. But again, at that point in time, it remained abstract to me, since school integration did not appear to be an issue in the elementary school that I attended.

Over the next few years, as I moved from elementary school to grammar school to high school, I became more and more the target of anti-Semitic violence. Most such violence was initiated by classmates from Eastern European nations who had been taught that violence to individual Jews was appropriate—and even encouraged—because Jews killed Christ. The remainder was initiated, abetted, and encouraged by an especially hateful and sadistic gym teacher who literally singled out the Jewish kids for severe physical abuse. During this time, I thought about the *Brown* decision on and off and marveled at the courage of the kids my age in schools in Arkansas and Alabama and Mississippi who faced unremitting hatred and near death on a daily basis. Ironically, black kids were brutalized because they wanted to *get into* schools, while Jewish kids were physically mistreated in schools to which they had easy access.

When I was fourteen, we moved to Florida for a portion of my sophomore year in high school. We were no further south than Delaware or Maryland when I was confronted with my first example of state-enforced Jim Crow: drinking fountains at a highway roadside stop that were marked "White" and "Colored." I was amazed, mostly because we were no more than four or five hours from our home in the New York City metropolitan area.

There were no black kids in my school in Miami Beach (nor, do I expect, were there any in any public school that white kids went to in the Miami area at that time), and that was explained by the fact that there were no black families living in that town. To be brutally honest, the fact that I was finally at a high school where I could walk the corridors without fear of physical attack—from other white students—was such a relief to me that the residential segregation that led to the educational segregation was not the first thought on my mind. Some irony here: When we moved to Florida (family health reasons), Miami Beach was the only town we considered living in, because it was one of the few places in which Jews would be welcomed. Patterns of religious segregation were well known to us in the North, and we saw them as inevitable (recall the hotel ads in the *New York Times* in the 1950s and 1960s that announced, "Churches nearby," a code for "Don't bother to call for a reservation if you're Jewish").

We moved back to Perth Amboy, and then, in my junior year (1961), back to Miami Beach. One of the books assigned in our English class that year was *Native Son*. After we finished reading and discussing it, our teacher told us that he didn't know whether he was going to assign it the next year. Why? Some black families were moving to town, and there were going to be two black kids in that year's junior class. How would they feel about reading Richard Wright's uncompromising descriptions of the ravages of segregation (or, perhaps more likely, how would the teacher feel about teaching it, although that was never on the table)? Most of the kids in the class said that the teacher should no longer have students read the book, that it might be too hurtful or painful for the kids. I was one of the few who took the other side. To drop the book, I argued, would be an insult to the kids, such a decision implicitly assuming that they couldn't deal with the fact that officially and unofficially sanctioned segregation was a part of the brutishness of American life (I am sure I used none of those words then, but this was what I hoped I conveyed), and that to drop the book would make them, once again, invisible. (I had read *Invisible Man*—unassigned—before this all came up, so I am fairly sure that I did use *that* word.)

We moved back to Perth Amboy, and I never learned what happened in that English class. But the discussion has stayed with me for over forty years, since it appeared clear to me that all the participants were well-meaning and that we were all trying to project and figure out how black kids our age would react to a work of literature, something that obviously none of us could fairly do.

I went off to college the next year (Rutgers University, in New Brunswick, New Jersey), and I was immediately struck by the paltry number of black students on the campus. It was said that, in my incoming class (class of 1966), there were more students of color from Africa and Asia than from New Jersey; I don't know if that was apocryphal or not, but it certainly looked that way to a casual observer. By the time I began college, in the fall of 1962, the civil rights movement was well under way, and I recall vividly following the stories in the *Times* every day about what was happening in Alabama and Mississippi and Georgia. And it made total sense for me, in the summer following my freshman year of college, to join picket lines in Northern Virginia (where my family was then living), denouncing residential segregation (in upscale apartment buildings). I learned there that adrenalin was something real. A driver—enraged at what my picketing must have symbolized for him—gunned his motor and aimed his car at me. I saw him coming and somehow vaulted out of harm's way over a high hedge directly behind the sidewalk where I was picketing. This, of course, was nothing compared to firebombing of churches, fire hosing of children, and murdering of civil rights workers attempting to register black voters in Mississippi. But, in a graphic and heuristic way, it certainly underscored for me the level of malevolence and hatred in the hearts and souls of so many Americans.

I worked that summer for Congressman Ed Patten, a machine Democrat from my hometown (imagine Tip O'Neill, but more so), and Patten was a strong supporter of civil rights. He had been given a VIP ticket for the August 1963 March on Washington, and he gave it to me to represent him. When I went to the assigned seat, I sat down between James Garner and Brook Benton, both of whom kept asking me if I realized the magnitude of what was happening. Benton said to me: "Son, this is the turning point of American history; you'll understand it when you get a bit older."

I was mesmerized by Martin Luther King's speech, the crowd, other speakers, the celebrities, the energy, and the passion. But I was mostly struck by the authentic integration of the crowd. Someone—I have no recollection whether it was one of the main speakers or someone I spoke to in the audience—said, "Imagine. Only nine years ago, school segregation in schools was still legal," and I recall looking up and thinking about what a short time that really was, in spite of it then being nearly half my lifetime.

I first studied *Brown* the next semester in an American Government course and remember reading it with pride: The Supreme Court had finally gotten it right. There were only one or two black students in my class, but I remember sneaking furtive glances in their direction and wondering what was going through their minds.

The civil rights movement, and then Vietnam, of course, were constant companions for the remainder of my college years. I became editor-in-chief of the Rutgers student newspaper, the *Daily Targum*, in 1965, and recall editorializing about the passage of the Voting Rights Act that year, and making a connection between that bill (and the Civil Rights Act of 1964) and the *Brown* decision. Since I've always tended to the use of tortured musical metaphors, I referred to *Brown* as the "C major chord of the civil rights movement."

I started law school at Columbia in 1966 and graduated in 1969. I had Constitutional Law in 1967–1968, and *Brown*, of course, was one of the cases we had been assigned to read. Unfortunately, it was assigned for the week that students occupied university buildings, thus causing the cancellation of classes.

Few recall now that one of the precipitants of the student uprising was Columbia's announcement that it was planning on building a gymnasium on Morningside Park property that had served the needs of a mostly low-income, minority neighborhood in the shadow of the Columbia campus. How ironic that the class in which we would have studied the case that truly led to the civil rights movement was canceled because of a civil rights protest! James Meredith, who desegregated the University of Mississippi several years before, was a third-year student at Columbia at the time—I never knew him well, though we used to chat in the library a bit—and I've wondered since what *his* reaction had been at the time.

I moved to Trenton, New Jersey, after I graduated. It was, I thought, a one-year move (precipitated by a clerkship offer); we're still there. At about the same time, there was a series of "riots" in Trenton (many in the schools), and the result was, predictably, white flight, mostly from Trenton's blue-collar neighborhoods, but to some extent, from its wealthier enclaves as well. My wife and I had recently been married, and having children was far from our minds. Nonetheless, I can remember sighing and shaking my head, as I watched, year by year, the schools resegregate with furious speed.

I soon became a public defender and then director of New Jersey's Division of Mental Health Advocacy. Although my law practice was not strictly about race, in reality, of course, it was. It is almost impossible to convey my frustration as a young public defender representing an equally young or younger African American defendant in a criminal trial with a jury inevitably made up of ten or eleven of Archie Bunker's meaner and more malevolent friends, and perhaps, to avoid a constitutionally impermissible imbalance, one elderly retired black postal worker. As a public defender, it seemed to me that race was often the *only* issue of interest to the jurors (some of this comes from intuition, but also from body language, smirks, and other easily decipherable nonverbal cues and clues).

When our children were three and just born, I left law practice to teach at New York Law School (where I still am). My course load includes Civil Procedure, Criminal Procedure, Criminal Law, and six different courses in mental disability law. With the possible exception of Civil Procedure, race is an issue in each course (most significantly perhaps in Criminal Procedure, but in all the others as well), and implicitly *Brown* is also thus an issue.

During this time, we purchased a house in Trenton in a neighborhood that was then (1979) and is today authentically and voluntarily multicultural and diverse. On one side, our neighbors are Asian, on the other Latino. Across the street diagonally in both directions, our neighbors are African American; directly across the street, Armenian. We have remained in this house ever since; our two kids have thanked us many times for making this decision. It has been one of our prouder life choices.

When the time came to send our kids to school, we wanted to send them to public school (my wife and I were both public school kids). We were talked out of it, forcefully, cogently, and unanimously by friends and acquaintances, both black and white, who told us that, since such a high percentage of the five-year-olds in our district still didn't know the alphabet, the teachers were forced to spend all their time trying to bring those kids up to a level where they could think about reading. It would be, we were warned, an utter waste of our children's time, minds, and lives if we were to select the public school option.

This left us with two choices: Move to a boring, cookie-cutter suburb (as so many of our friends had done) or stay in Trenton and send our kids to private schools. We took a deep breath and opted for the latter (a religiously affiliated school for grade school, and an academically focused school for middle school and high school). And certainly, the latter was not nearly as well integrated as we had hoped. But our kids grew up in a neighborhood that was totally racially mixed. And they got to know black kids in a variety of ways that most of their peers never have.

Our youngest said that when he was in high school, many of his white classmates had never spoken to a black kid other than the few in their high school class. Growing up in Trenton, our kids have always known kids from every race and nationality and background. And that has been, without question, a very good thing.

But how does it relate to *Brown v. Board of Education*? I tell my students that *Brown* is the most important case ever decided by an American court. And I think I am right. We, thank God, cannot imagine a world without *Brown*. There have been bumps along the road, certainly. And the situation that I have described in the Trenton school system is, without question, a sad one. But, in the end, *Brown* has led to a society that is far more pluralistic and diverse and integrated than the one in which I grew up. And to a society in which all Americans can aspire to something more, something better, something different. And to which, in Kluger's words, "simple justice" is available for all. And for that I am proud and grateful.

Michael Perlin was born in March 1946 in Perth Amboy, New Jersey, and attended elementary and secondary school in Perth Amboy from 1951 to 1962 save for eight months in 1960–1961 in Miami Beach, Florida. He is now professor of law and director of the International Mental Disability Law Reform Project at New York Law School in New York City.

37 Indirect and Substantial Effect

Anthony R. Baldwin

There was no segregation by New York state law. Nevertheless, there were voluntary initiatives by the New York City Board of Education to correct segregation on account of city residential patterns. There was no desegregation order against any city school district, but the City Board of Education attempted to voluntarily desegregate single-race schools and predominantly single-race schools anyway.

I never endured the chaos, disruption, and pain from implementation of a desegregation order in New York City, but *Brown I* introduced me to segregation. In the years since that introduction, *Brown I* and *Brown II* have indirectly and substantially affected me. The story begins in South Jamaica.

South Jamaica

South Jamaica borders the north end of Kennedy Airport in the New York City borough of Queens. That's where I was born, and until the day I left for college, that's where I lived with my parents and my paternal grandparents—Uncle Thomas stayed on weekends. My home for the entire time was the same one that my grandparents, my dad, my uncle, and their siblings have called the Baldwin home since 1929.

When my grandmother and grandfather moved to Princeton Street in 1929, the Baldwins became the fourth African American family in the block. By 1954 the neighborhood was well integrated. African American, German American, Italian American, and Polish American families lived side by side. The Archers, Baldwins, Badgers, Burns, McKinneys, Sadlers, and Williams—the African American families—lived next to the Yosts, the Santellis, the Boschens, and the Dorniaks on my street. The Archers were our next-door neighbors on the north side. Six white families other than those named lived in homes side by side and perpendicular to the south and east sides of our home. All families lived in two-story frame houses distinguishable only by different siding. All of us owned our homes.

I attended Public School 160 from kindergarten to the sixth grade. Only white children went to 160 before World War II. In those times African American children attended two African American neighborhood public schools that were farther away from my block than 160. The three elementary schools were all within reasonable walking distance from the Baldwin home, but 160 clearly was the closest.

Uncle Thomas recalls that when I began kindergarten in September 1951, there still was a residue of white resistance to African American children integrating 160. I didn't know about the integration or the resistance. There were no outward indications of either that I can remember anywhere in the neighborhood. All I knew was that Eileen Boschen, my white neighbor in the second grade, walked me to and from school. Since we were close enough to go home for lunch, she walked me home for lunch as well. When I started kindergarten, 160 was about 60 percent white and about 40 percent African American. By graduation in 1959, African American children were close to 60 percent of the school's population.

I was seven years old and a second-grader when Chief Justice Earl Warren announced the Brown decision, but I have no recollection of it. The Brown with impact on me then was my second-grade teacher. Mrs. Brown rewarded good reading with cookies. I became an excellent reader in the second grade. The only other Brown I knew was Harry Brown, my second-grade classmate.

From the second to the sixth grades, I lived to play football, stickball, slap ball, punch ball, and stoopball with a well-integrated bunch of neighborhood guys. To this day, I remain in touch with Stanley and Andrew Serba, Polish Americans and two of my main ballplayers. The brothers later did all the plumbing repairs for the thirty-three years that I owned a home in Queens. The brothers did plumbing work at the Baldwin home in Queens as well.

By 1954 my grandfather was dead and my mom, dad, and I lived with my grandmother. Uncle Thomas continued to come home on weekends, and my dad's sister and his other five brothers each spent some time with my grandmother three to five days a week. Six of the seven siblings were married. Their spouses often joined them when they visited. Throughout the 1950s my dad, his sister, and his brothers heatedly discussed any number of family, local, national, or international topics in my presence. Though the discussions were abundant and lively, Uncle Thomas and I recall none about segregation or the Brown decisions at any time. Today we cannot remember any basis for the total absence of the cases from those very frequent and often heated Baldwin discussions. In retrospect we speculate that there may have been two reasons for that. My grandfather, Dad, Mom, and each uncle were in integrated workplaces. Moreover, the neighborhood in which we lived had been integrated since 1929. My aunt owned a fresh-fruit and vegetable market with her husband, but it was in a South Jamaica neighborhood that also was integrated and predominantly white in the early 1950s.

I do recall my parents' stories about incidents. My mom spoke of a train ride between New York City and Savannah, Georgia. After the train stopped at Union Station in Washington, D.C., the conductor ordered her and her stepfather to change from their seats in an integrated railroad car to an all-black railroad car on the same train. They rode segregated from white passengers from Washington, D.C., to Savannah. My dad told of an incident as well. He and his best friend came within an eyelash of being arrested in Washington, D.C., while they were on a one-day leave from their army basic training. It seems that they entered the front door of a downtown store that he called Woody's in full uniform and attempted to get served at a sales counter. They got none, and only avoided arrest by agreeing to leave the store immediately.

I recall a story my mom and dad both liked to tell involving their first post–World War II stay at Boston's Statler Hilton. Their Boston friends were stunned that they were at the Statler because African Americans "didn't stay there."

The stories always were told humorously, and my mom and dad always provoked laughs as they told them. They did seem funny, and the words "couldn't go there" or "didn't stay there" seemed no big deal in the midst of the humor. The word "segregation" never was part of the storytelling.

Whenever my dad drove us to Atlantic City, New Jersey, to meet his friend from the Woody's incident and his family for a weekend, we always stayed at the Motel Lin-Mar in Pleasantville, New Jersey. Pleasantville is about five miles and across a bridge from Atlantic City. The motel was owned and operated by African Americans. From five to nine years old, I was too happy just to be in a motel, eat at restaurants, walk or ride bicycles on the boardwalk, and play to hear or notice segregation when we traveled there in the late 1950s. Since we always stayed at the same motel, I didn't notice that Atlantic City motels and hotels were segregated.

The stories, the travel to Atlantic City, and other car trips in the Northeast and New England never raised the word "segregation" or its definition for me. My mom and dad were as mum about it in their conversations with friends as they were with my aunts and uncles during Baldwin family discussions when I was around. Mrs. Brown didn't discuss *Brown I* in the second grade at any time during my 1954–1955 school year. There was no mention of *Brown II* during the 1955–1956 year in the third grade either. Significant events involving African Americans like Charles Hamilton Houston and Thurgood Marshall were not in my elementary school textbooks; nor were they topics for discussion any place that I knew.

Nineteen fifty-five was a glorious year, but it had nothing to do with *Brown II*. My Brooklyn Dodgers became world champs by vanquishing the evil Yankees for the first time in baseball history! This eight-year-old knew more about Browns that year, but it was the Cleveland Browns in the National Football League and Jim Brown at Syracuse University, not the Supreme Court decisions.

My first recollections about the *Brown* cases were from television news reports. I watched reactions by white politicians, parents, and children to something called "desegregation orders." I particularly remember the reports about whites in front of Central High School in Little Rock, Arkansas, reported on the *Huntley-Brinkley Report*, a thirty-minute daily news program. White parents and teenagers vitriolically and vociferously supported Governor Orville Faubus as he tried to keep the high school segregated. Governor Faubus declared that the African American teenagers could not enter Central High School. The white onlookers sneered and threatened the nine African American teenagers in the face of television cameras.[1]

Matters got so nasty and violent that President Dwight Eisenhower ordered what looked to me like the U.S. Army into Little Rock so that those students could just walk to and enter their high school uninjured. The news reports made the chaos and violence seem to be about some place in America far away from South Jamaica, Queens, and New York. It certainly was nothing I knew about or saw in my neighborhood or at school.

Chet Huntley, David Brinkley, and NBC-TV news reporters from Little Rock (the late John Chancellor was one of them, I think) introduced the words "segregation" and "desegregation" to me. Although there were other stories about other types of segregation reported, white reactions to school desegregation efforts keyed my interest. I'm certain what grabbed my attention was that African American teenagers were just trying to get to their assigned high school. I couldn't believe that they had to endure resistance, threats, and turmoil from whites day after day just to enter their high school building.

Those Little Rock events were too distant to impede my focus on getting outside to play, and they didn't obstruct my joy at my Dodgers' total success in 1955. (The New York Yankees ended my joy in 1956.) Then tragedy existed for me when I learned that the Dodgers were moving to Los Angeles after the 1957 season. How could they?

Brown I and *Brown II* had an impact on me through television reporting on white resistance to school desegregation orders. Television reporters, not my parents or my family, introduced me to the word "segregation," and showed that whites in places like Little Rock desperately wanted white and black public school students to remain separate.

The segregation that reporters spoke of in conjunction with *Brown I* and *Brown II* desegregation orders became personal and real to me in 1958 during my first car journey South just six hours from South Jamaica.

In 1958, my mom, dad, aunt, and I were traveling to Charleston, South Carolina, on U.S. Highway 301 when my dad drove up to the gas pumps at a

Shell gas station. The station was thirty or forty miles north of the Richmond, Virginia, city limits. While my dad stayed with the car, my mom, aunt, and I used the restrooms. My dad went to the restroom after we returned. After he left, my aunt asked me to buy a cup of coffee for her and my mom at the diner next door. She gave me the money, and I walked to the diner. As I approached, I read a sign in the glass door entrance that I had not seen at any prior time in my short life. I will never forget the words. They were: "Whites Only."

I was shocked, but I immediately knew two things. I was not white. Since I was not white, I couldn't go inside that diner to get coffee. To this day I can feel my three emotions on seeing that sign—anger, helplessness, and power-lessness. I knew what I had to do without any prior experience. Never break-ing stride, I turned around and walked back to our car.

My dad came out of the restroom as I was walking back. He saw me, and he knew where I had been. He was incredulous, and he was angry. After he as-sured himself that I was unharmed, he spoke to my aunt briefly and tersely. He reminded her that we were in Virginia and not anywhere close to New York City. At a small, nondescript diner in Virginia, I experienced what I had seen some whites fight for in front of Central High School. There was a second ex-perience in Virginia a few hours later. After those incidents I knew segregation in a personal, defined way. I also realized that it wasn't terribly far from where I lived.

My parents never discussed with me what happened on that trip. It didn't matter. Thereafter, I personally and permanently knew and understood what segregation meant. Through Chet Huntley and David Brinkley and the report-ers on their news program, I learned the word "segregation." The word took on personal meaning after my unforgettable experiences in Virginia in 1958.

After 1958, whenever I rode with my dad and our family to visit our cous-ins in South Carolina, he always left New York City at midnight. He did that so we would have complete daylight as we drove through Virginia, North Carolina, and South Carolina. I was in high school before I understood that he wanted to avoid driving through the three states at night.

My dad always stopped for both gas and restroom breaks at Shell stations on every trip south for a simple reason that I did not realize or understand at the time. We could refuel and freely use the same restrooms as whites. In those times, gas station owners might sell gas to African Americans, but that did not mean that restrooms were available.

I saw a lot more after that whenever we traveled until about a year before Title II of the 1964 Civil Rights Act became law. In the early 1960s, my dad's best friend from the army and his family lived in Frankford, Delaware. His son, who remains one of my best friends, and I had to sit upstairs to see a movie at the local theater. My friend was bused to a black middle school fourteen miles away from home when the white school in his school district was just three blocks away. By then I knew that segregation did not stop at the Northern Virginia border.

Frankford segregation did not end at death, either. Until my friend's dad stopped the practice, African American families in the area paid the local white undertaker a similar price for funeral services as whites, but he required all of them to use the funeral home's back door. African Americans' bodies were viewed in a separate and unequal viewing room as part of the funeral service for a similar price as a white funeral. My dad's friend is buried in an all-black cemetery in Steelton, Pennsylvania. Ironically, that cemetery is across *Lincoln* Street from the white cemetery. In New York, segregation accompanied my parents' deaths as well. My dad died in 1965, and Mom died in 1971. It's now apparent to me that they are buried together in the black section of a private cemetery in Queens.

Richmond Hill

Brown I and *Brown II* had a direct impact on my life from September 1961 until June 1964. The New York City Board of Education faced increasing city-wide racial segregation and overcrowding in primary and secondary schools during the late 1950s and early 1960s in spite of its voluntary desegregation efforts. The increasing racial separation was mostly a reflection of changing racial residential patterns.

South Jamaica, my block, and my neighbors exemplified the problem. There were ten white neighbors in 1957. When I graduated from high school in 1964, there were two. All eight were replaced by African American families. Some of the African American neighbors changed in those seven years as well. Another African American family replaced each family.

To integrate and to relieve the overcrowding in public schools, the board altered city school attendance zones in each borough on its own initiative in 1958. The 1958 alterations changed my high school attendance zone. When I began high school in 1961, I went to Richmond Hill instead of John Adams. Adams had a significant plurality of African American students. Moreover, 95 percent of all of my junior high school classmates and my best elementary and junior high friends went to high school there. On the other hand, Richmond Hill had an 85–90 percent white student population from 1961 to 1964. I was far less than happy when I began attending Richmond Hill in 1961.

There is no doubt that *Brown I* and *Brown II* influenced the board and me for my high school years. Overpopulation at both John Adams and Richmond Hill caused both schools to schedule students in double sessions. Since both schools were overcrowded, overcrowding could not have been the essential basis for the change in my attendance zone. The reason for it had to be integration.

During my junior year at Richmond Hill, the board's halting integration efforts nearly produced a citywide minority student boycott. By midterm of my senior year, African American and Puerto Rican parents and white supporters inside and outside public education were angry and frustrated with the board's "deliberate speed." The anger and frustration boiled over into a one-day city-wide student boycott on February 4, 1964. That day 150,000 students were absent from the city's public schools.

I was not among the boycotting students. I felt that I should stay out of school in order to support the boycott, but my parents made it crystal clear well before February 4 that I wouldn't be absent on that day. The clarity, certainty, and strength of their position and the comparative weight and size difference between my dad and me were deterrents to disobeying my parents' order. I went to school on February 4. Few African American students were absent from Richmond Hill, and I recall no picketing there.

Cambridge and Beyond

At Harvard, I began to see *Brown* and the problem of segregation from a different angle. One of Chief Justice Warren's former law clerks taught me Constitutional Law. During that course, Jesse Choper assigned a problem that centered on the *Brown* decisions, the cases preceding the decision, and the subsequent cases up to the time. Derrick Bell, a former attorney for the National Association for the Advancement of Colored People Legal Defense Fund and the first African American faculty member at Harvard Law School, taught a relatively new course called Race, Racism, and the American Law. Professors Choper and Bell expanded my horizons of knowledge and understanding about *Brown I* and *Brown II* in their respective courses, but it was in Race, Racism, and the American Law that I learned the rest of the story. Spirited and often heated discussions were the norm on every topic that we covered in that semester, but it seemed that none produced more heat than the *Brown* decisions, public school desegregation, and, by then, public school integration. Derrick Bell conducted a learning experience that deepened my understanding about both their significance and the remaining unanswered issues through a racism hypo. (For each Race, Racism, and American Law substantive topic, we discussed a hypothetical fact pattern. Each fact pattern focused on current topic issues. The fact patterns were called racism hypos.)

The public education racism hypo was a real catalyst for me. I began to feel *Brown I* and *Brown II* after learning the rest of the story. The feel resulted from the flowing class dialogue and the discussion about the hypothetical. I still recall hearing Bell's eyewitness account about the office celebration among the NAACP Legal Defense Fund attorneys after the *Brown I* decision. I remember hearing how Thurgood Marshall warned the staff that they really had only begun their work. He predicted that difficult legal fights lay ahead.

Learning about the *Brown* cases and the *Brown* advocates continued when I began my career in legal education. Genna Rae McNeil's time at the University of North Carolina (Chapel Hill) overlapped the period during which I was at the North Carolina Central University School of Law in Durham, North Carolina. She was researching and writing a biography about Charles Hamilton Houston.[2] During our conversations, I learned much about Houston's life, his times, his experiences, and his construction of the legal strategy for sinking the *Plessy v. Ferguson* separate but equal principle step by step.

Opportunities to learn about and feel *Brown* continued. I heard Judge Robert Carter at an American Association of Law Schools annual meeting in New Orleans in the middle nineties. Judge Carter had been a member of the NAACP Legal Defense Fund team during the 1940s, 1950s, and 1960s and argued *Brown I* and *Brown II*. Hearing him declare that "separate will never be equal" with a strength and a passion belying his years was a personal glimpse of the strength, belief, and commitment to the argument and holdings in *Brown I*. That feeling remains with me.

A second golden opportunity to view that same glow and feel that same strength of commitment presented itself at Mercer Law School's 2001 symposium on *Brown v. Board of Education*. The late Oliver W. Hill was a symposium participant. Along with the late Judge Spottswood Robinson Jr. and Judge Carter, Mr. Hill represented the plaintiffs in *Davis v. School Board of Prince Edward County*, the Virginia companion case to *Brown*.[3] He shared his experiences from the case, his perspective on the Fourteenth Amendment, and his views about equal justice and the natural evolution of law in a videotaped question-and-answer hour. Mr. Hill was the highlight of the symposium for me.

Oliver Hill's clear recollections of the people and the times, his role, and his understanding of the bases for the litigation and litigation strategy were dramatically underscored by his physical and verbal response to a question at the end of the interview. Though clearly exhausted after an hour of questions and answers, the ninety-one-year-old, when asked if he thought the *Brown* decisions had been worth the fight given what had happened since 1955, lifted his head, straightened his body, looked squarely at the camera and his interviewer and uttered an unequivocal, *"Yes!"* Mr. Hill reminded the interviewer that the long fight waged was against per se, de jure segregation. He was clear and strong when, in sum and substance, he told her that the fight was the right fight because separate would never be equal.

Brown's first impact on me resulted from watching television reports about Central Park High School. I was directly influenced and affected when the New York City Board of Education changed my high school attendance zone to desegregate an 85–90 percent white high school. Learning about *Brown I* and *Brown II* in Constitutional Law and in Race, Racism, and the American Law, and then feeling the two cases through teaching about them and learning further of them from Judge Carter and Oliver Hill left a deep and enduring effect.

I am driven to have students feel *Brown I* and *Brown II* as I do. If they can, then there is some hope that there will be a personal impact from the cases on each of them. There also is some hope that one or more will contribute positively to answering the question posed by Charles Houston: whether "the system which shall survive in the United States of America . . . shall be a system which guarantees justice and freedom for everyone."[4]

NOTES

1. See Scott Shepherd, "The Legacy of the Little Rock Nine," *Atlanta Journal-Constitution*, September 21, 1997.

2. See Genna R. McNeill, *Groundwork: Charles Hamilton Houston and the Struggle for Civil Rights* (Philadelphia: University of Pennsylvania Press, 1983).

3. See *Davis v. County School Board of Prince Edward County, et al.*, 103 F. Supp. 431 pg. 431 (1952). On Hill's extensive advocacy for racial equality, see Oliver W. Hill Sr. and Franklin Stubbs, *The Big Bang:* Brown v. Board of Education *and Beyond: The Autobiography of Oliver W. Hill Sr.* (Jonesboro, AR: Four-G, 2000). For Mercer Law school's 2001 Symposium on *Brown v. Board of Education*, see volume 52 of the *Mercer Law Review* (Winter 2001).

4. See Leland Ware, "Setting the Stage for *Brown*: The Development and Implementation of the NAACP's School Desegregation Campaign, 1930–1950," *Mercer Law Review* 52: 673.

Anthony R. Baldwin was born in 1947 and attended elementary and secondary school in New York City from to 1952 to 1964. He is presently professor of law at the Walter F. George School of Law, Mercer University, in Macon, Georgia.

38 *Brown* Goes North

Michael H. Hoffheimer

> The world-old phenomenon of the contact of diverse races
> of men is to have new exemplification during the new
> century.
>> —W. E. B. DuBois, *The Souls of Black Folk* (1903)

Growing up in Clifton, a white middle-class neighborhood in Cincinnati, I knew African Americans were different because they had their own name— first "colored people" and later "Negroes." We were taught never to use the N-word anywhere. My sister, born in 1957, was not taught to call African Americans "colored people," and she recalls her confusion on first hearing the term and asking my mother if there really were people of different hues.

I have an early memory of an elderly African American woman on a park bench. I was told she had been born a slave. But the first African American I knew was Eula, our cleaning lady. She came once a week and ate lunch in the kitchen by herself. Her lunch included soup and a slice of white bread. One week she stopped coming. My older brother Dan told me she had killed her husband.

Clifton abutted an African American neighborhood, and by the time I entered kindergarten, Clifton Elementary School included African American children. But classes were tracked. Better teachers taught the high-achieving sections composed of students destined for better high schools, and these sections were almost entirely white.

Race consciousness was hardly all-pervasive. Miss Turpeau taught me in fifth grade for an entire year, and I did not know she was African American. And I do not remember the race of most of the other workers except Tom, a quiet dark-skinned African American janitor. From a newspaper article we learned that Tom once played drums with Duke Ellington.

Around 1964 the Perrys, an African American family, bought the house across the street from us. I recall the seller of the house, a Unitarian minister, being vilified for selling his house to African Americans. Their youngest son, Michael, was my age and would become a regular companion. He had a sister, Karen, a glamorous teenager who stayed in her room a lot, and an older brother, Harold, who rivaled my brother as a source of secret knowledge.

Michael's father, Dr. Nelson Perry, was on the faculty of the University of Cincinnati Medical School. I think he was a pioneer in radiation treatments for cancer. From Michael I learned about cobalt and radium. Their house was strewn with gifts from important people whose lives Dr. Perry had improbably prolonged. Michael and I once stole cigars from a dresser drawer, a gift from the president of the cigar company. (They were cheap cigars and were going to waste, as Dr. Perry did not smoke.)

One large room in the basement was devoted to racks containing thousands of issues of medical journals. A cardboard carton in this room served as the space ship on which Michael and I practiced trips to the Mushroom Planet—space fantasies fueled by the Eleanor Cameron books to which Michael introduced me.

The interior of the Perrys' home was memorably clean. The Perrys installed wall-to-wall carpeting and a stereo system with speakers in different rooms. On their vinyl disk player I first heard "Stop in the Name of Love."

Mrs. Perry sifted dirt in her garden through a screen to remove all the pebbles. She feigned amazement when I did not know what "gee" and "haw" meant. And she engaged me in serious discussions, as when a neighbor, a juvenile court judge, imposed a draconian sentence on an offender who had stolen a television set. At the Perrys' dinner table, milk was served from a glass pitcher instead of from the dairy bottle, and both parents drank large glasses of milk.

I knew that some neighbors resented an African American family on the street. One neighbor spat in Mrs. Perry's face when they moved in, and the Perrys sometimes got nasty phone calls in the middle of the night.

Michael Perry was not supposed to be on the high-achieving track. According to school rumors, he was admitted to our class only because Mrs. Perry went and yelled at the principal. Rumor had it that the principal moved him only grudgingly and with predictions of failure. Classmates resented the fact that he was included in our special section due only to the intervention of his mother.

But Michael rose to the top of our class. He proved to be good at everything, not just the science that was his passion.

Like other children in Clifton I grew up spending hot summer days at Clifton Meadows swim club. In its pool we learned to swim, and on its courts we learned to play tennis. In the days before universal air-conditioning, it seemed like every kid in Clifton either belonged to the pool or went regularly as a guest of friends who were members.

I don't know why I never thought to take Michael to Clifton Meadows.

Did I really think the Perrys preferred going to the indoor pool at the Y across town? It was our classmate Jeffrey Seeman who invited him. In my memory, the result of accumulated hearsay, Michael entered the water and angry mothers pulled their children out of the pool. According to one version, the pool was drained. According to another, the pool was closed for the day.

What actually happened was less dramatic. Jeffrey had asked Mrs. Seeman one morning if they could take Michael to the pool. Though Jeffrey was unaware of possible problems, Mrs. Seeman was concerned enough to call Mrs. Perry and explain the situation to her and get her permission to take Michael. Mrs. Seeman also called the mothers of two other classmates who supported the decision to take Michael as a guest.

When the Seemans took Michael to the pool, a young woman employee told them they could not enter. Mrs. Seeman refused to leave until she had talked to the manager and to an officer of the corporation. She and the children waited outside the fence that surrounded the club until informed by the club's authorities that club policy did not permit African American guests. At that point Mrs. Seeman expressed her regret and left. The Seemans took Michael swimming at another pool in an adjacent neighborhood. That night the Perrys visited the Seemans and brought pastries. Jeffrey's mother recalls the decision to invite Michael as "one of the most important things" she and Jeffrey have done in their lives, and something that established a strong bond between them.

The "Michael Perry incident" provoked a crisis in the white community. Until then, Clifton Meadows had not defined itself as a whites-only pool. It had never needed to identify itself racially because no African American had ever tried to join the club or use its facilities. But the lack of a public whites-only policy did not mean African Americans were welcome.

While the board vacillated, a majority of the club's members wanted a policy excluding African Americans, and the board adopted a formal policy banning African Americans as guests. The importance of race in this redefinition of the community was underscored for me by the argument advanced by the children of segregationists. They insisted on racial rather than personal reasons for excluding African Americans. Conceding that the Perrys might be fine people, they argued that, if they were, they were exceptions to racial type.

The crisis in the white community also revealed differences within our family. My father, a lawyer and member of the board, sought to avoid conflict, mediate differences, reduce passions, and change policy at the board level. My mother became active in equal housing politics and joined the NAACP, enrolling my brother, sister, and me as youth members.

I played no heroic role in these events. In anger I pleaded with my mother to quit Clifton Meadows. But we remained members, and I am sorry to say I went back to the pool after Michael's humiliation—though I was never very happy there again and stopped going entirely within a year or so.

For Michael and me this story had no happy ending. Segregation triumphed during the years that counted for us. There was no heartwarming denouement. Michael and I did not become lifelong friends. Our common anger at segregationists did not prevent us from drifting apart when we went to different schools after sixth grade. Within two years he moved to Bloomfield Hills, Michigan, with his family.

For the community, the story has a different ending. For three years members who wanted to open the pool to African Americans worked to change the club's policy. In 1965–1966 Gilbert Bettman ran for the board on an antidiscrimination platform but was soundly defeated. In 1966–1967 opponents of the whites-only policy supported the efforts of board member Teresa Mauer to effect change from within. Mrs. Mauer was a member of the Catholic Church, and her leadership was especially important because many supporters of the whites-only policy were members of her church. Although I was not aware of it at the time, it is obvious in hindsight that most of the vocal opponents of the whites-only policy were Jewish—as were most, if not all, of Michael's white friends. Sally Kamholtz (née Elder), whose family were Episcopalians, recalls her perception that the controversy pitted Jews and Protestants against Catholics. But some Catholics also opposed segregation, including Teresa Mauer and my mother.

After efforts failed to change board policy, in 1967–1968 forty families ("the furious forty") decided to resign in protest. Art Spiegel played the leading role in the legal campaign that forced Clifton Meadows to abandon its whites-only policy. He would later be appointed U.S. district judge for the Southern District of Ohio by President Carter and enter on duty on May 20, 1980. My father believes that Judge Spiegel's activity in the Clifton Meadows dispute was an important reason for his nomination to the federal bench.

Art Spiegel had graduated from the University of Cincinnati in 1942 and served in the Pacific as a captain in the Marines. He graduated from Harvard Law School in 1948. The Spiegels were members of Clifton Meadows and lived in property that adjoined it. They were known for their support of Democratic Party candidates—and as the only family in the neighborhood to own a donkey. Judge Spiegel would later explain in his memoirs how early experiences with discrimination and anti-Semitism had left him a confirmed opponent of discrimination:

I had experienced incidents of prejudice or persecution which made me have doubts about myself and which created strong, ambivalent feelings:

on the one hand, to feel that something was lacking, to accept being a loser, not to try to succeed or win with a maximum effort because of the fear or expectation of failing or losing, yet, on the other hand, to be angered and to be challenged to rise above the insults and prove my worth.

It was Art Spiegel who persuaded the "furious forty" to postpone their mass resignation while he sought legal relief. In the spring of 1968 he brought a lawsuit in federal court challenging the whites-only policy. Though victory was not assured under existing equal protection law, the litigation led to negotiations that produced a settlement. He recalls:

The newspapers carried the controversy because similar issues were facing other swim clubs in the Cincinnati area. Maybe the publicity, embarrassment, and just possibly the recognition that they may have been wrong, brought our opponents to the table.

On April 18, 1968, a consent decree was entered that "provided, among other things, for an injunction prohibiting discrimination against any person as a guest of the corporation on the grounds of 'race, color, religion or national origin.'" Disgruntled members challenged this decree, but it was affirmed by the Sixth Circuit.

In 1969, the Spiegels' youngest child, Roger, invited his Clifton School class to Clifton Meadows. Roger's guests included a few African American classmates and Miss Turpeau. Thirty-five years later, the club includes African American members, and white members regularly take African American guests.

Brown had a mixed legacy in the North. Though Cincinnati did not have a dual school system, *Brown* spelled an end to the days when Michael Perry could be excluded from important educational benefits within an integrated school on the pretext that he was intellectually inferior. Yet those benefits became available only because his mother fought for them, and they came at the cost of resentment and lowered expectations from his peers. Moreover, the triumph of integration at Clifton School was brief. A generation later, white flight has left the school unavailable for families seeking a racially diverse educational environment.

Even after the Perrys exploded the myth of inferiority, *Brown* did not mean they could swim in the community pool. On the contrary, the political culture after *Brown* authorized white communities to maintain spheres of public life that excluded African Americans explicitly on the basis of race. At the same time, the spirit of *Brown* and the momentum of the civil rights movement energized activity that eventually ended discrimination at the pool.[1]

NOTE

1.   This chapter refers to the actors as I knew them at the time—hence Art Spiegel and Mrs.
     Seeman instead of Judge Spiegel and Dr. Robinson. The facts about the Perrys are based
     on my memories as supplemented and corrected by telephone interviews conducted in
     2003. Especially helpful were interviews with my classmates Andrew Spiegel and Jeffrey
     Seeman; with Andrew's father, U.S. district judge S. Arthur Spiegel; with Jeffrey's mother,
     Dr. Joan Seeman Robinson; with my father, Harry M. Hoffheimer, brother Daniel H.
     Hoffheimer, and sister Mary S. Hoffheimer; and with neighbor Sally Kamholtz (née
     Elder). Judge Spiegel shared part of his unpublished memoirs, "Hey Kids Meet Your Dad"
     (ca. 1992). I also consulted the published opinion resulting from the litigation, *Allinsmith
     v. Funke*, 421 F.2d 1350 (6th Cir. 1970).

Michael H. Hoffheimer was born in Cincinnati, Ohio, in December 1954. He attended elementary and secondary schools in Cincinnati from 1960 to 1971. He is now a professor of law and Mississippi Defense Lawyers Association Distinguished Lecturer at the University of Mississippi School of Law in Oxford, Mississippi.

39 The Virtues of Public Education

Susan L. DeJarnatt

Brown had little immediate impact on my own education but has had a profound effect on that of my children. I grew up in a small town in the Pacific Northwest that started its civic life as a lumber company town. It is the home of what during my childhood was the world's largest pulp mill, operated by Weyerhauser. The founders of the town were Southerners who saw no place for people of color in their mill or in their town. The tiny African American community was unofficially but effectively restricted to a single neighborhood whose children went to the other high school in town. Ironically, that high school also educated most of the children of the managerial class. My classmates were nearly all white and nearly all working class.

The only relief from the all-white population was a small community of Hawaiians who were allowed to work at the mill and whose children went to my high school; a handful of Asian Americans; and the one lone African American girl who transferred in halfway through my junior year in high school, who was quiet, shy, and probably miserably lonely. *Brown* had no immediate impact on this situation because there were so few people of color to begin with. But the civil rights movement made us aware, at least in the abstract, of the impact of segregation in the United States, and the general sense I had was that most of my fellow students thought segregation was wrong and unfair. Certainly that was the value I was raised with at home—that Martin Luther King was a hero, and that Lyndon Johnson's and Hubert Humphrey's great accomplishment was the 1964 Civil Rights Act. My parents admired Johnson and Humphrey for their civil rights efforts long after I had become very dismissive of both men because of their role in promoting U.S. involvement in Vietnam.

My schools were not very strong academically. They were designed to educate the children of the working class and to prepare them to work at the mill or to marry the men who worked at the mill. The most important students were the football stars and the cheerleaders. It was not an easy place to be an openly smart, college-bound girl. I couldn't abide the limited goals of most of my classmates and they thought I was peculiar. But I shared the education experience and made friends with kids whose economic circumstances and worldviews were very different from mine. Working-class and poor people were real, not some abstract "other." I learned more about what life is like for most people in the United States in my hometown than I did in the more privileged college environment that I left home for. I learned that because I went to school with a representative cross-section of the community I lived in. No one went to private school, except for some of the Catholic kids who went to Catholic grade school before joining everyone for high school. Some kids dropped out, some got pregnant, some joined the army, some went to college, many went to work at the mill. I didn't want the limited horizons of that small-town life for my children and I did not want such a racially monotonous environment. But I did value the experience of feeling that the school was reflective of the community whose children it educated, and I wanted that for my children too.

I have lived in Philadelphia my entire adult life. I ended up here by chance but the place suits me well. It has the cultural and culinary advantages of a city with new things and new people always to be discovered, and anonymity available if you want it. But it also has a deeply rooted community and is small enough that you can feel a strong sense of connection. And it is not racially monotonous.

I have two children, one now in college and one in fourth grade. The older one went to our neighborhood school from kindergarten through eighth grade. She then moved on to an academic magnet public high school that draws students from all over Philadelphia. My kids have shared their education with the children of their community—except for most of the well-off white ones. In elementary school, they have been in the position of being in the minority, which has been occasionally uncomfortable but hardly threatening. And they have benefited from learning and playing and growing up with children from a wide range of backgrounds who do not all look just like them. I am not always thrilled with the academics. Philadelphia has fallen victim to high-stakes testing and directs too much of its curriculum to pursuing the holy grail of test scores. My children have had some great teachers along with a few not so great ones. But the social experience has been invaluable.

Brown did not desegregate the Philadelphia public schools. Indeed I would bet that they are more segregated now than they were in 1954. Certainly there is a higher percentage of children of color and a lower number of white kids in the public schools here these days than there was forty years ago. But *Brown* had an impact in expanding the horizons of children of color and making clear that all children are entitled to an education. My daughter's high school experience was ideal in bringing the *Brown* vision of inclusion to life. No ethnic group had a majority in her high school but all were there and were full participants in the life of a very challenging academic environment. She would not have been able to go to this school if not for *Brown*, at least indirectly.

The school excluded girls until 1983. Although the opinion that led to the admission of girls did not rely explicitly on *Brown*, it did rely on *Brown*'s vision of inclusion and equality.[1]

The neighborhood I live in, Mount Airy, is green, leafy, and full of old stone houses. It is historically liberal and historically committed to racial integration, though it is becoming less integrated economically. I love Mount Airy but I regret that the neighborhood schools do not reflect the entire community. They don't because too many white middle-class residents have chosen private schools instead. These same thoughtful, smart, caring people who would never accept or tolerate formal segregation and who genuinely value the message of *Brown* are not willing to help bring its message and vision of inclusion to life with their own children. The public schools of Mount Airy actually work quite well. But white people have to accept being in the minority and have to value the social capital generated by that experience.

Public education in Philadelphia is far from perfect. The school buildings are old. The libraries have outdated books and, often, no librarians. Foreign languages are not taught in elementary school. Music and art programs are always at risk. Too many schools are teaching only the children of the poor and are struggling to meet that challenge. I envy the private schools and the suburban systems their well-appointed facilities and small classes. But the solution to these problems and the disparity is funding equity, not abandonment of public education. We need to apply *Brown*'s vision to demand equal funding for all public schools. In the words of Justice Marshall:

> It is an inescapable fact that if one district has more funds available per pupil than another district, the former will have greater choice in educational planning than will the latter. In this regard, I believe the question of discrimination in educational quality must be deemed to be an objective one that looks to what the State provides its children, not to what the children are able to do with what they receive. That a child forced to attend an underfunded school with poorer physical facilities, less experienced teachers, larger classes and a narrower range of courses than a school with substantially more funds—and thus with greater choice in educational planning—may nevertheless excel is to the credit of the child, not the State. . . . Indeed, who can ever measure for such a child the opportunities lost and the talents wasted for want of a broader, more enriched education? Discrimination in the opportunity to learn that is afforded a child must be our standard.[2]

Unfortunately, the Supreme Court failed to see equity in funding as vital in *Rodriguez*, so the struggle for equality today is in the legislatures, not the courts. That battle is most likely to be won if the parents of children of privilege have a personal stake in the public schools. The more the children of privilege are educated with the children of the disenfranchised, the more likely it is that the parents with power will wield it to improve education for everyone.

I hope we can rise to the challenge and recognize the importance of public education to our entire community. *Brown* says we have a collective responsibility to educate all our children—rich and poor, charming and difficult. If we look out only for the kids we are related to, our entire society is going to suffer. We can build gated communities and prisons to keep the kids we failed at bay—but building and using good public school systems offers a lot more hope for all of us.

NOTES

1.   See *Newberg v. Bd. of Public Ed.*, 26 Pa. D. & C. 3d 682 (1983). Judge Gibbons explicitly referenced *Brown* in his dissent from an earlier challenge to the single-sex status of the school. He noted that he "was under the distinct impression . . . that 'separate but equal' analysis, especially in the field of public education, passed from the fourteenth amendment jurisprudential scene" after *Brown*. *Vorcheimer v. School District of Philadelphia*, 532 F. 2d 880, 888 (3d Cir. 1975) (Gibbons, J. dissenting).

2.   *San Antonio Independent School Dist. v. Rodriguez*, 411 U.S., 1, 83–84 (U.S. 1973) (Marshall, J. dissenting).

Susan L. DeJarnatt was born in 1953 in Sterling, Colorado, and attended elementary and secondary school from 1958–1970 in Longview, Washington. She is now an associate professor, Beasley School of Law of Temple University in Philadelphia, Pennsylvania.

40 Entering Another's Circle

Kathryn R. Urbonya

Although I grew up in Beloit, Wisconsin, far from the notoriously segregated South, I still experienced racial separation as I began first grade, five years after the United States Supreme Court's 1954 *Brown* decision. Despite having students from different racial backgrounds, many classrooms in Beloit did not reflect this diversity. Even as a child, I saw adults drawing circles delineating who could enter and who could not, separating whites from "others," males from females, and those who had a "correct" understanding of God from those who didn't.

About one-third of my schoolmates were black, but I rarely saw them. My elementary school separated children according to perceived academic ability. My class, comprised of those children thought to exhibit greater promise, included only white children. In junior high school, only my homeroom and gym classes included both black and white children. When I entered senior high school, I did have a black classmate in my band class. Tracy played trombone and said very little. My high school friends spoke of another black student named Karen Bolton. Karen wasn't in my classes, but she too was enrolled in the academic track. My friends described Karen as being "like a white person." Her mom, a black woman, provided career counseling to many students, including me. I never learned much about Mrs. Bolton or her background, but my life would ultimately take a different course in significant part because of her.

Mrs. Bolton, like several of my teachers, encouraged me to go to college. I did not know what college was, but I kept hearing that it was somewhere I needed to go. My father, the youngest child in a large immigrant family from Slovenia, had dropped out of school as a high school sophomore. My mother, another child of immigrant parents, had finished high school, but only because she fled the family farm at age thirteen, cleaning houses to support herself. Neither of them knew what college was, much less that it was something that their children should pursue.

My father worked as a machinist in a factory that provided a relatively steady check, one that eventually permitted my parents to buy a small house with an upstairs apartment rental. Despite our strained family finances, my father refused to allow my mother to work outside the home, even when the kids grew up. As "head of the household," his word was law. My mother stayed home caring for two boys and two girls. A fifth child, a girl, died in infancy while my mother was in a psychiatric hospital.

My father set the limits on our family's associations, and he drew a rather small circle. One day when I was a teenager, I heard my mother tell prospective tenants that she had already rented our upstairs apartment when in fact she had not. After shutting the door, she explained to me, with great frustration, that my father did not permit her to rent to "them"—Negroes. My father also barred his children from playing with black friends. I well remember the day my father sent home my sister's black girlfriend, Yvette Bolton. He told my sister not to play with Negroes. The smallness of his circle made no sense to me.

My father also decided that only my brothers would learn to drive the family car. My mother never learned to drive and my father refused to permit my sister and me to learn because girls did not need this skill. (I finally learned to drive in my twenties.) One of the males in my family would have to drive the females when we needed to go somewhere farther than we could walk. My father would sometimes drive us, but generally only in the morning because alcohol interceded thereafter. On Sunday mornings, my father would drive our family to the local Lutheran church. He stopped attending with us, though, because the Lutheran minister would excoriate Catholics, including my father, for their misguided theology. Meanwhile, the Catholic church would embrace neither of my parents because my father had not received an annulment following his divorce from his first wife.

When I was in grade school, my family experienced significant financial distress. My father lost his job and health insurance. My mother had a number of stays in a psychiatric hospital, imposing debts that we could not pay. Fortunately, the government provided us with free food. I fondly remember the large silver and blue plastic-wrapped chunks of American cheese, lots of real butter, and large cans of creamy peanut butter, jellied beef, and pork. (But I never did learn to like the powdered eggs.) I fretted about having so few clothes to wear to school. My mother assured me that my classmates would not tease me for having only two outfits to wear as long as they were clean and I kept myself well groomed. She taught me to bathe myself using the bathroom sink. I could take baths on occasion, provided that I did not use too much water.

Through the encouragement of my teachers, I began saving for this thing called "college," recognizing that there would be no family money to send me. I regularly cleaned a neighbor's house, babysat, taught music lessons, and worked in a department store as a checkout clerk. My little bank account began to grow. My mother, to her credit, insisted that I keep all my earnings for my college aspirations rather than use them to help support the family.

During the fall of my senior year of high school, Mrs. Bolton, the school counselor, called me to her office to discuss college. She encouraged me to apply to Beloit College for "early decision," a term I did not know. When Beloit College accepted me, it gave me generous financial aid and work-study opportunities. Mrs. Bolton reviewed the financial aid package and told me I could make it work if my parents could contribute the value of the tax deduction that they received for claiming me as a dependent. When my parents declined to pay anything toward my college expenses, Mrs. Bolton angrily told me to tell my parents that they could no longer declare me as a dependent if they made no contribution toward my living expenses. I never expected my parents to be able to help, so I didn't tell them what Mrs. Bolton had said. I ultimately made up the financial shortfall by working extra hours.

When I arrived at Beloit College, I met my roommate, Lindsey, who was from New York. Lindsey had already taken college classes as a high school student. She explained to me that I had to go to the college bookstore to buy my course books; I had thought that the teachers would give us our books as they did in high school. Lindsey also gave me her heavy blue wool coat to keep me warm during the winter. At the end of the first year, Lindsey invited me to go home with her to New York. I declined only because I did not know how to receive such generosity from another human being.

With an expanding group of teachers and classmates encouraging me, I graduated from Beloit College in 1975. Later, I earned a master's degree in English and a law degree, and I eventually began a career as a law professor. None of this would have happened had not several people, particularly Mrs. Bolton, encouraged me to pursue higher education. My parents did not know much about the value of college, but thankfully others in my life did. They showed me the path of education, one that has allowed me to live with financial stability, vocational fulfillment, and opportunities my parents could not have conceived of.

I have often wondered how my life would have unfolded had I been born black. Who would have been there to guide a poor black child from a family on welfare, one with alcohol abuse and significant mental illness? Maybe things would have worked out the same way, but I'm not so sure. For the most part, blacks and whites in Beloit in the 1950s and 1960s lived in separate worlds. Thankfully, there were a few exceptions like Mrs. Bolton, the black school counselor who embraced a poor white girl and encouraged her to dream of college.

In 1954, the U.S. Supreme Court struck a blow against separate racial circles, declaring that separate is not equal. It explained that separate spheres robbed children, especially black children, of the opportunities that lie inside the circles of those who live in privilege. I think the Court was right.

I will never forget a sermon I heard in 1997 by an Episcopal priest in Atlanta. He invited us to look at the circle of people in our lives and to consider whether our circles were too small. I realized that the circle of my life had come to include many people who did not seem, on the surface, to resemble me—friends with different racial and economic backgrounds, vastly divergent religious perspectives, and different expressions of their sexuality. As I delighted in the richness of my circle, I also felt sad for my deceased parents, who had not experienced this fullness of life, having been shaped by their culture and illnesses. I also thought of Mrs. Bolton. Mrs. Bolton wasn't in the accepted circle of my childhood. But she gave me the greatest gift of all.

Kathryn R. Urbonya was born in Beloit, Wisconsin, in January 1953 and attended elementary and secondary school in Beloit from 1958–1971. She is now professor of law at the William and Mary School of Law in Williamsburg, Virginia.

Appendix

The Survey

Richard J. Bonnie and Mildred Wigfall Robinson

Practically all law professors are listed along with their birth years in the *Directory of Law Teachers* published annually by Thomson West and Foundation Press, Inc. We sought to identify and contact everyone in the legal academy holding an academic title (assistant professor or above) with a birth year between 1936 and 1954. With assistance from the Association of American Law Schools and financial support from the University of Virginia School of Law, we wrote to approximately 4,750 of our colleagues. We received approximately 850 responses to this first mailing. Because of the relatively light response from law schools in the southeast, we resurveyed professors in that region. This second effort generated approximately 125 additional responses, giving us almost 1,000 respondents.

Demographic Characteristics

The one thousand law professors who chose to respond to our survey are a self-selected group; presumably, they were either intrigued by our project or wanted to use the survey as a way of stirring up their memories of this period. Notwithstanding their distinctive motivations, however, our respondents are demographically representative of the universe of all professors in the 1936–1954 birth cohort teaching at American law schools at the time of the survey (see Table 1). Almost 75 percent are male, about 90 percent are white, and they are distributed among the regions of the country in more or less the same proportion as the cohort of law professors from which they were drawn.

The respondents are also representative of the universe of teachers in the 1936–1954 birth cohort in terms of age at the time of *Brown*. About a fourth of the cohort, including the survey respondents, were not yet in school at the time of *Brown*; more than half were preteens in primary or middle schools; and the remainder (about one-fifth) were in high school. Interestingly, a larger percentage of the black respondents (about 40 percent) were preschoolers in 1954. This difference probably reflects a combination of self-selection and trends in law school hiring that have diversified the professoriate over the past three decades. (It should hardly come as a surprise that the percentage of mi-

Table 1. The *Brown* Generation Respondents: Demographics

	% of respondents	% of AALS pool
Gender		
Male	72.8	75.3
Female	27.2	24.7
Race/ethnicity		
White	89.3	89.1
Black	6.0	5.9
Other	4.7	5.0
Age at time of *Brown*		
<5	26.0	28.7
5–12	53.7	52.0
13–18	20.3	19.2

Note: Data totals may be off slightly because of rounding.

nority faculty now teaching in U.S. law schools is highest among the youngest age cohorts).

Region of Birth

As we expected, a substantial and somewhat disproportionate number of our respondents were born and spent their childhoods in the South and in other states with legally segregated public schools; about 31 percent were born in states with de jure segregation (see Table 2). Most of the other respondents were born in the Northeast (31 percent) or the Midwest (26 percent). Not surprisingly, 63 percent of our black respondents were born in states with de jure segregation.

Region of Schooling

Families of children born in the 1940s and early 1950s were not particularly mobile. About two-thirds of the respondents remained in the same school system throughout their post-*Brown* educational period. This reflects the fact that the families of 65 percent of the respondents remained in the same community throughout their childhoods. About 20 percent of the respondents' families moved once during their post-*Brown* schooling, and the remainder (16 percent) moved more than once. Even among those whose families moved during their schooling, they usually remained in the same state. (Interestingly, only about 10 percent of the black respondents moved at all during their schooling.) In light of the relatively low frequency of family relocation, it

Table 2. Race, Age, and Birth Region of Respondents

	% of black respondents	% of white respondents	% of all respondents
Age at time of *Brown*			
<5	40.4	24.3	26.0
5–12	46.2	54.7	53.7
13–18	13.5	21.0	20.3
Region of birth			
De jure states	63.2	29.1	31.4
Northeast	15.8	32.7	31.1
Midwest	19.3	27.3	26.2
West	1.8	9.8	9.4
Residence in 1954–1955			
De jure states	51.6	29.2	31.9
Northeast	22.6	28.9	27.8
Midwest	16.1	25.0	25.7
West	9.7	11.1	10.7

Note: Data totals may be off slightly because of rounding. In addition, data for "Region of birth" and "Residence in 1954–1955" may total to less than 100 percent because of missing data.

should come as little surprise that, among the respondents who were in school at the time of *Brown*, the regional distribution at the time of *Brown* is about the same as the regional distribution at time of birth (see Table 2). Because a disproportionately larger number of the black respondents were preschoolers in 1954, the percentage of blacks then living in states with de jure segregation is a bit lower (52 percent) than the proportion born in such states.

Schooling at the Time of Brown

We asked the respondents whether the schools in which they were enrolled in 1954–1955 were segregated. According to their recollections, almost half were attending segregated public schools; naturally, the proportion attending integrated schools varied from region to region, ranging from 9 percent in the de jure states (these were largely students in parochial schools) to 67 percent in the West. Among those who were in school at the time of *Brown*, only one-third attended *integrated* public schools throughout their schooling, a figure that was naturally very low in states with de jure segregation (9 percent) and considerably higher in the West (54 percent), Northeast (40 percent), and Midwest (35 percent).

Specific School Board Responses to *Brown*

Studies of the aftermath of *Brown* have routinely shown that there was little immediate change in the school experiences of most students, black or white, even in the states with de jure segregation. Our survey reinforces this finding. We asked all respondents whether they recalled specific measures being taken by school boards in the aftermath of *Brown*, either to desegregate the schools or to resist doing so. Table 3 reports the results.

We focus first on persons reporting that they attended segregated public schools in 1954–1955 (Table 3). Among this group, more than 80 percent reported no such efforts being undertaken throughout their schooling; only 15 percent recalled that specific steps were taken to integrate their own schools, while 3 percent recalled being either reassigned or bused to another school. Measures aiming toward desegregation were more likely to be reported by black respondents (36 percent) than white ones (16 percent), and by respondents attending school (at the time of *Brown*) in states with de jure segregation (31 percent) than those attending school in other regions of the country.

About one-fourth of the respondents were too young to be enrolled in school in 1954–1955. However, the pace of desegregation clearly accelerated over the course of their schooling. As shown in Table 4, among those who said their schools were segregated when they first enrolled (between 1955 and 1960), a significantly higher proportion of the respondents recall steps being taken to integrate their schools (40 percent) or to desegregate the school system (46 percent) than in the older cohort.

The survey also inquired about whether the respondents recall steps being taken to resist desegregation. This survey was stimulated in part by the fact that one of the authors (RJB) grew up in a part of Virginia that closed its schools during the period of "massive resistance" to the command of the Supreme Court in *Brown*. Eleven respondents (about 1 percent of the total, and 3 percent of the respondents in the de jure states) reported that their schools were closed to avoid desegregation. (One was black.) Another five white respondents reported that their parents placed them in private schools to avoid integrated public schools.

Table 3. Impact of *Brown* on Respondents Enrolled in Segregated Schools in 1954–1955 (N = 265)

	Steps taken to integrate respondent's school? (% who answered yes)	Steps taken to desegregate system? (% who answered yes)	Any impact on schooling? (% who answered yes)
Region			
De jure states	26.4	31.0	26.4
Northeast	5.0	5.0	3.3
Northwest	3.2	6.3	6.3
West	—	—	—
Age at time of *Brown*			
5–12	13.8	17.7	16.7
13–18	16.7	13.7	7.4
Race			
White	14.5	16.1	14.5
Black	7.1	35.7	28.6
All respondents	14.7	17.7	15.0

Table 4. Impact of *Brown* on Respondents in Segregated Schools in 1954–1955 or in First Year of School Recorded in Survey (N = 344)

	Steps taken to integrate respondent's school? (% who answered yes)	Steps taken to desegregate system? (% who answered yes)	Any impact on schooling? (% who answered yes)
Age at time of *Brown*			
<5	40.4	45.7	44.7
5–12	14.4	12.9	16.8
13–18	21.6	21.6	10.2
Race			
White	21.6	23.5	21.6
Black	22.2	40.7	48.1
All respondents	22.4	25.6	23.8

Desegregation in the Classroom

We asked our respondents whether the racial makeup of their schools changed—year by year—over the course of their schooling. However, because we did not tie these questions specifically to changes in the law or school board policy, the responses also reflect family relocations (which, of course, might be attributable to many variables). However, the responses to these questions

Table 5. Changes in Racial Character of Schools Attended by Respondents after *Brown* (% of Respondents)

No Change

	Segregated	Integrated	Private/ parochial school	Total
Race				
White	23.8	31.2	9.2	64.2
Black	21.4	33.3	2.0	56.7
Age at time of *Brown*				
<5	20.3	27.8	8.4	
5–12	21.8	25.6	7.4	
13–18	24.4	44.3	13.6	
All respondents	23.7	31.3	8.8	63.8

Some Change

	Segregated to integrated	Integrated to segregated	Other change	Total
Race				
White	27.6	8.2	—	35.8
Black	33.3	10.0	—	43.3
Age at time of *Brown*				
<5	29.5	7.0	7.0	
5–12	31.1	9.5	4.6	
13–18	10.8	4.0	2.9	
All respondents	27.9	8.3	—	36.2

reinforce the overall study finding that the educational experience of most of the respondents was unchanged in the aftermath of *Brown*.

As Table 5 shows, the racial make-up of the schools attended by about two-thirds of the respondents remained unchanged after *Brown*. Among all respondents, about one-third attended *integrated* public schools throughout their schooling, about one-fourth attended *segregated* schools throughout their schooling, and, about one-tenth attended private or parochial schools throughout their educations. The racial makeup of the school was more likely to change for respondents who were in preschool (43 percent) or primary school (45 percent) at the time of *Brown* than it was for those who were in secondary school (18 percent), and it was somewhat more likely to change for black respondents (43 percent) than for whites (36 percent). However, the changes did not move in one direction. In fact, only 28 percent of the respondents changed from segregated to integrated schools during their schooling, whereas about 8 percent moved from integrated to segregated schools. (Again, we emphasize that this pattern does not necessarily reflect race-conscious parental decision making.) As expected, the proportion of respondents who changed from segregated schools to integrated ones was considerably higher in the states with de jure segregation as the time of *Brown* (33 percent) than it was in the Northeast or Midwest (22 percent) or West (16 percent) (see Table 6).

Table 6. Desegregation after *Brown* by Region of Respondents' Schooling, 1954–1955 (% of Respondents)

	De jure states	North- east	Mid- west	West	All respondents (N = 621)
No change	49.7	66.8	68.9	71.7	62.8
Segregated	35.2	16.6	23.0	10.8	23.2
Integrated	9.3	40.1	34.8	54.1	30.4
Other	5.2	10.2	11.2	6.8	9.2
Change	50.3	33.2	31.1	28.3	37.3
Segregated to integrated	33.2	22.5	22.4	16.0	24.8
Integrated to segregated	8.3	5.9	6.8	12.3	8.1
Other	8.8	4.8	1.9	—	4.3

Note: Data totals may be off slightly because of rounding.

Judgments about the Overall Impact
of *Brown* on Schooling

Table 7 presents data regarding the respondents' assessment of the overall impact of the *Brown* decision on their education. Less than 20 percent reported that *Brown* had a discernible impact on their schooling, whether positive or negative. For those reporting some effect, about half reported that the impact was positive, and most of the others reported that the impact was neither positive nor negative.

As expected, however, the proportion reporting some impact of desegregation was highest (about one-third) for the respondents who were preschoolers at the time of *Brown* and lowest (less than 6 percent) for those who were then in secondary school. Also as expected, black respondents were substantially more likely to report some educational impact of desegregation than were whites. About 43 percent of blacks reported some effect, as compared with 17 percent of whites, and about half of each group assessed the impact on their schooling as a positive one; slightly more blacks described the impact as negative (one in six) than did whites (one in nine).

It is noteworthy (indeed, it would have been shocking otherwise) that the reported impact was significantly higher in states with de jure segregation than in other regions of the country—among respondents who were attending school in a state with de jure segregation at the time of *Brown*, 26 percent reported some effect on their schooling as compared with 6 percent or less in the other regions of the country. Again, only a small handful of respondents characterized this effect as a negative one (see Table 7).

Summary:
So Little Change

The immediate post-*Brown* period emphatically dispelled the myth of America as melting pot. The stories shared by our colleagues presently serving on faculties in law schools all over the country tell of a region (and much of a nation) divided not only by race but also by ethnicity, class, and—to some extent— religious beliefs.

These data reveal the same pattern shown by other studies of desegregation. Among this sample of people who were in school at the time of *Brown*, only one-third attended integrated public schools throughout their schooling, a figure that was naturally very low in the states with de jure segregation (9 percent) and considerably higher in the West (54 percent), Northeast (40 percent), and Midwest (35 percent).

Table 7. Perceived Impact of Desegregation (% of Respondents)

	No effect	Neutral	Negative	Positive
Age at time of *Brown*				
<5	63.6	13.2	4.4	18.9
5–12	84.7	6.3	1.8	7.2
13–18	94.1	2.7	1.1	2.2
Race				
White	82.7	7.3	1.9	8.1
Black	57.1	12.5	7.1	23.2
Region				
De jure states	73.2	12.1	2.5	12.1
Northeast	95.1	1.6	1.1	2.2
Midwest	93.8	3.7	.6	1.9
West	97.2	1.4	1.0	1.4
All respondents	81.3	7.3	2.3	9.1

Note: Data totals may be off slightly because of rounding.

Among those who were attending segregated schools in 1954–1955, there was little change in the racial character of their schooling: Less than 15 percent recall steps being taken to desegregate, and even in the de jure states, only a fourth reported that such steps were taken while they were in school or that these post-*Brown* developments had an impact on their educational experience—an impact that was described as positive except in a handful of cases.

The pace of desegregation accelerated for the respondents who were toddlers or preschoolers at the time of *Brown*—of whom more than 40 percent reported steps toward desegregation. Nonetheless, among all our respondents who began in segregated schools, about half reported attending segregated schools throughout their schooling. Steps toward desegregation and some educational impact were reported twice as often by black respondents (about 40 percent) as by whites (about 20 percent).